Women in British Cinema

Rethinking British Cinema

Series Editor: Pam Cook, Lecturer, University of Southampton

This series is dedicated to innovative approaches to British cinema. It expands the parameters of debate, shedding new light on areas such as gender and sexuality, audiences, ethnicity, stars, visual style, genre, music and sound. Moving beyond narrow definitions of national cinema, the series celebrates the richness and diversity of British film culture.

Published titles in the series:
The Beatles Movies, by Bob Neaverson
Dissolving Views, edited by Andrew Higson
Gainsborough Pictures, edited by Pam Cook
Searching for Stars, by Geoffrey Macnab

Women in British Cinema

Mad, Bad and Dangerous to Know

Sue Harper

CONTINUUM

London and New York

Continuum
Wellington House, 125 Strand, London WC2R 0BB
370 Lexington Avenue, New York, NY 10017–6503

First published 2000

British Library Cataloguing-in-Publication Data
A catalogue record for this book is available from the British Library.

ISBN 0–8264–4732–5 (hardback)
      0–8264–4733–3 (paperback)

Library of Congress Cataloging-in-Publication Data
Harper, Sue
     Women in British cinema: mad, bad and dangerous to know /
     Sue Harper.
          p.   cm.—(Rethinking British cinema)
     Includes bibliographical references and index.
     ISBN 0–8264–4732–5 (hb)—ISBN 0–8264–4733–3 (pb)
          1. Women in the motion picture industry—Great Britain.
          2. Women in motion pictures.
     I. Title. II. Series.

PN1995.9.W6 H28 2000
384'.8'0820941—dc21   99–086631
                                                                CIP

Typeset by York House Typographic, London
Printed and bound in Great Britain by TJ International, Padstow, Cornwall

Contents

Acknowledgements

I am very grateful to the British Academy, which funded this research with travel money and with a grant from the Research Leave Scheme. I should also like to thank the History Research Centre at the University of Portsmouth, which generously provided me with funds for teaching relief and travel. Fergus Carr, the head of the School of Social and Historical Studies at Portsmouth, has been supportive of my research throughout.

Staff have been most helpful at a range of libraries: the Frewin Library at the University of Portsmouth, the Public Record Office and the British Library. I am particularly indebted to staff at the British Film Institute Library, who have been patient with my often importunate demands. Special thanks to Janet Moat and Saffron Parker at the BFI's Special Collections, and to staff at the National Film Archive.

I should like to thank Manchester University Press for permission to reuse some material from an article I wrote in Gledhill and Swanson's *Nationalising Cinema: Culture, Sexuality and British Cinema in the Second World War*. Stills were provided by the BFI Stills Department and my own collection, and acknowledgements are due to Canal + Image, Carlton International and Hammer Film Productions for permission to use them.

I am grateful to Jonathan Balcon for giving me permission to consult the Aileen and Michael Balcon Collection at the BFI. Thanks too to the custodians of the BECTU Archive (housed at the BFI), who have allowed me access to the interviews I needed. I am grateful to Wendy Toye and the late Jill Craigie for talking to me; it was a real privilege.

One of Dr Johnson's best apophthegms was, 'Sir, a man should keep his friendships in good repair.' I have been very fortunate in my friends and colleagues, and it seems to me that they have kept me in good repair (rather than vice versa) during the writing of this book. All the people named below have given me information, or painstakingly read over drafts. I should like to thank Tony Aldgate, Russell Baldwin, Tim Bergfelder, Sue Bruley, James Chapman, Pam Cook, Rajinder Kumar

Dudrah, Laurie Ede, Alan Everatt, Mark Glancy, Robbie Gray, Adrian Hill ('Sammy – could it be Wedding Bells?'), Searle Kochberg, Verena Wright Lovett, Madeleine Mason, John Moore, Robert Murphy, Lucy Noakes, Betty Owen, Ray Pettitt, Jeffrey Richards, Brigitte Rollet, Jason Smith, Andrew Spicer, Elizabeth Tuson and Linda Wood. Marilynne Hunt reminded me at a crucial juncture whose book it really was: 'However high a bird may soar, it must sooner or later perch on a tree top, to enjoy quiet.'

Sometimes writing this book has felt like going over Niagara in a barrel. I want to mention two friends who have kept me afloat, though there can be no adequate thanks for all they have done. Viv Chadder, who takes many intellectual risks herself, has listened to my daily telephone wails of despair over the project. While sharing with me some of her own Millennial Anxieties, she has been unfailingly supportive. Vincent Porter has been incredibly helpful. He read through the whole project, tightened it up, stimulated fresh ideas and helped with factual errors.

Finally I want to thank my family for putting up with the domestic maelstrom occasioned by this book. My mother Josephine Harper knows (none better) why it had to be written. My husband Walter Ditmar was heroically tolerant, and helped in more ways than I can say.

The book is dedicated to the memory of my grandmother, Florence Amy Rockley (1900–95). She loved 'the Pictures'.

It is common to end acknowledgements with a kind of benediction. Instead, I should like to end mine with an imprecation – a 'curse from the mouth of womanhood', as Elizabeth Barrett Browning puts it. May all those wither who have imperilled the creativity of others. May the Froth Be With Them.

There be four things that are little upon the earth, but they are
exceeding wise:
The ants are a people not strong, yet they prepare their meat in the
summer;
The conies are but a feeble folk, yet they make their houses in the
rocks;
The locusts have no king, yet go they forth all of them by bands;
The spider taketh hold by her hands, and is in kings' palaces.

(Proverbs 30:24–28)

Introduction

This book is both modest and ambitious. It refers exclusively to British cinema, and to the 'woman question' within it. In one sense, therefore, its focus is narrow. Hopefully there are infinite riches to be found in a little room, since my aim is to chart substantial transformations: the ebb and flow of mainstream representations of women from 1930 to 1990, and also the contribution made by women to British films. Such a large undertaking might seem foolhardy, and probably is so. But nothing venture, nothing gain.

Of course, much work on women in British cinema has already been done, and I hope to build on that, giving due cognizance to other people's work. However, I shall not waste much time on critical *frottage* – that engagement in so-called controversies which adds nothing to the sum of historical knowledge, but only to citation indexes. That is just a sort of academic 'feeding frenzy'. The time is ripe for a fresh look at the big issues – at the way in which the raw material of women's bodies and experiences can be variously shaped by the film industry, and at the relative strengths and weaknesses of women as players in the cultural game. We have scarcely begun to write a history which will chart the broad sweep of the representation of women in British cinema, and offer an explanation for its richness and variety. Nor has there been a detailed comparison of male and female cinematic creativity in this field. Shulamith Firestone valuably noted that

> an exploration of the strictly female reality is a necessary step to correct the warp in a sexually biased culture. It is only after we have integrated the dark side of the moon into our world view that we can begin to talk seriously of universal culture. (Firestone, 1971, p. 189)

These are radical words, but they are salutary. This book aims to make the 'dark side of the moon' visible, and to ensure that, in the history of British cinema, woman is no longer the Dark Continent.

With such a broad remit, some organizing principles need to be made explicit. I choose to concentrate on feature films and fictional shorts, rather than documentaries, since the latter have a different history and social meaning. Since this is a 'grand narrative', a balance will have to be struck between interpretations and historical facts. The latter can never be neutral, since they have always been selected with a particular problem in mind. This book has been researched using revisionist methods – that is to say, using official documents, manuscript materials, interviews, studio publicity handouts and so on. But a satisfying account needs to combine such methods with textual analysis, and to be unafraid of making judgements about aesthetic quality. Moreover, just because the material is scholarly, there is no need for it to be dry. It is appropriate in a work of this kind to develop a 'buxom' style – a sinuous, moist, fruity manner which is capable of irreverence and humour.

Such a broad canvas must perforce make omissions, though some of them are deliberate. Not every key text or film-maker has had proper attention; with world enough and time, I suppose it might have been possible. It would have been nice, too, to draw a map of female film taste, and I have begun the task elsewhere.[1] But in the end I decided that a proper review of female audience response would unbalance the book, whose chief preoccupation is female creativity. In pursuit of my own creativity, I decided to abandon the notion of symmetry, and to be led by the richness of the evidence. Chapters are therefore of unequal length, according to the amount of new material I have found to excavate. But anyway, it is pointless to insist that all sections of a work can be equally weighted. Many an intellectual enterprise has been scuppered through a zeal for symmetry. And many an academic one too.

I shall avoid the comforts offered by orthodox theories. It would be convenient if the varieties in narrative forms could be completely accounted for by explanatory paradigms such as the Carnivalesque, the Monstrous-Feminine or the Unruly Woman. Such models are seductive because they impose order onto otherwise intractable material, but they do not help us to distinguish between the complexities of different texts, genres or periods.

This book rests on two convictions: first, that film is an industrial as well as a cultural product, in which the film text is the result of struggles that took place before and during its production. And second, it rests on a belief in the absolute nature of sexual difference, which is the condition for entry into the symbolic order, the universe of meaning. The dynamic relationship between these two convictions is what informs both parts of the book, and sets the whole thing in motion. I want to be eclectic and pragmatic in my method. Part I of the book is entitled 'Mainstream Representations' and is divided up by decade. This can be a problem, since cultural history does not necessarily occur in neat ten-year cycles. I shall buttress my analysis by reference to the economic and legislative constraints of the industry in each period, and will categorize film production in terms of what I see as the prevailing *agency* of the period. That is to say, in the 1930s and 1940s the production company operated as the ultimate determinant of the ways in which women functioned in film texts. In the 1950s, it was the distribution company; in the 1960s, the director. In the 1970s and 1980s, it became an unpredictable mélange of different types of agency.

Of course, film culture never reflects social reality. It responds in a selective way and according to its own inner laws, which change radically over quite short periods of time. Cinematic representations of women (or any other social group) are simply the traces left by the struggles for dominance during the production process – by the contest for creative control. We should not, therefore, judge films according to the extent that they replicate 'real life'. Rather, we should judge them by the coherence of their world-view, and the competence of the artistic discourses embedded within them. This may sometimes lead us to uncomfortable conclusions. For example, films expressing traditional gender values can often be stunningly beautiful: consider the seaside scene in *The Edge of the World* (1937), as the women sing and the child lies in its mother's arms. In addition, films which are artistically unexceptional can often be morally loathsome – the unspeakable in pursuit of the uneatable (the 1960 *Peeping Tom*, for example). Some films can operate like a Maori *haka* – they are intended to intimidate the opposition before the contest or viewing begins. There is a category of 'masculinist texts' whose business is the keel-hauling of recalcitrant females, and the historian must decide what proportion of the overall output of a period can be characterized in this way. Then the colour, shape and pattern of the sexual politics of a particular film culture can be established.

Part II of the book concentrates on Women's Work, exploring the intervention women made in the production process, and the way in which female creativity generated different sorts of settlement with the industry. Parts I and II are set in dialectical relationship to each other: one is structured diachronically, the other synchronically. The reader can come to conclusions about the meaning of the relationship between them, which may be different from my own.

Part II is divided into different professions – women scriptwriters, costume designers, directors and so on – but I have only selected those which I could fashion into a coherent linear narrative. There were hundreds of women involved in film production whose history is impossible to write. Secretaries, for example, have at all times been the grease which oiled the studio machine, yet there is very little surviving evidence about their labour and its complexities. The secretary of one 1930s Gainsborough producer had to learn

> the art of buying, for it was left to me to choose gifts for the stars, and in one week to find a house for an Austrian film director, help furnish it, to make a heart of primroses to put on his little girl's pillow the first night of her arrival from Vienna, and to produce for his nursemaid an abortionist as quickly as possible.[2]

But the importance of secretaries was so minimal that few people thought to document them. The same goes for women's work in continuity. This area was regarded as a female prerogative, with all its attendant lack of status. Martha Robinson, one of the most experienced continuity girls, noted in 1937 that the job

> is extremely important, but deals with the kind of details that appear insignificant. This apparent insignificance is made the most of by the men. In a typically good-humoured way they keep the Continuity Girl 'in her place'. Her various duties are regarded with tolerant scorn. She is subjected to leg-pulling even at her most harassed moments. Difficulties are wickedly put in her way, and information is withheld with an air of bland innocence.[3]

In addition, the British film industry contained exceptional, powerful women who ploughed their own furrow but did not set up a professional dynasty. Jenia Reisser was casting director for Romulus. Olive Dodds became head of the Contract Artists' Department at Rank, and Molly Terraine ran the Rank Charm School with such a firm hand that she customized all the accents. She was

> a very formidable lady. She would insist on this plummy accent

4

whatever their natural accent was. They came in all shapes and sizes but they all had to be ironed into this flat tone. I don't know whether it was what the producers and directors wanted, but it was what they got.[4]

Such women left clear tracks of their work, but they were eccentric individuals and we cannot imbricate them into a coherent professional narrative.

In an interview with me, the great director Wendy Toye suggested that if there were lacunae in the patterns of women's employment in the industry, it was simply that no women had thought those jobs important enough to struggle for; if women wanted to enter any particular cinematic profession, then they could. While I have the utmost respect for Miss Toye, I do wonder about this. We have to account for the absence of women as sound engineers or camera operators or lighting cameramen, until they performed these tasks in their own films in the 1970s. Doubtless union intransigence had something to do with it. But we also have to consider whether habits of production and management militated against certain kinds of female creativity. Freddie Young suggested that the British system worked by having 'star' cameramen who brought their chosen team of personnel with them, some of whom would be trained up in due course (Young and Petzold, 1972, pp. 23–39). Such a system was virtually impervious to outsiders, especially when they were of the awkward gender. Some areas in British cinema were run as a virtual closed shop until the late 1960s: the composition of musical scores, for example. The only woman to do any musical work in cinema until recently was Elizabeth Lutyens, who had scored documentaries from 1944. Lutyens had a healthy pragmatism about her craft: 'It's a form of musical journalism which can be excellent of its sort, like an enormously good and interesting article in a paper. In contrast, lyric poetry is written with a trust in a long future.'[5] She came into her own in the 1960s, specializing in composing for horror films such as *Paranoiac* (1962) and *Dr Terror's House of Horrors* (1964). Lutyens's work for such low-budget projects is adventurous, self-reflexive and often works contrapuntally to the script.

I decided not to have a discrete section on actresses, since it seems to me that, although they were called upon to play a broad range of stereotypes, the degree of autonomy they had in most periods was too limited to allow performance style to be elevated into a separate category. Hence I have studied actresses' work in Part I rather than in Part II. Every period contains recognizable social stereotypes (the flapper, the bluestocking, the sex kitten) which are the result of historically specific constraints, and which are determined by shifting definitions of class identity and respectability. Cultural forms do not reflect these stereotypes; rather, they engage with them, sometimes critically, sometimes tangentially. Just as there is an ebb and flow of social stereotypes, so codes and patterns of representation shift too. In British, as in other national cinemas, there are discrete 'clusters' of gender types, which develop and dissolve over quite short periods of time, and vary according to their topicality and intensity. Some have deeper cultural roots than others. I have tried to sketch the ways in which different female types were invented in the industry, and the degrees of rigour with which it enforced them.

Let us begin, then, to sew the quilt, placing the red female cloth judiciously in the pattern – sometimes at the edge, sometimes at the centre, and sometimes not there at all.

Notes

1. Harper (1994); Harper and Porter (1996, 1999); Porter and Harper (1998). Another field ready to be tilled is a history of British women film critics – not just the big figures like Dilys Powell and C. A. Lejeune, but lesser-known ones like E. Arnot Robinson, Freda Bruce Lockhart and Catherine de la Roche.
2. Unpublished autobiography of Grace Slater, in the possession of the author. Miss Slater refused to procure the abortionist. Quoted by permission of her family.
3. See Robinson (1937), pp. 34–5, and the BECTU interviews with Doris Martin and Betty Bigsworth in the BFI Library.
4. BECTU interview with Sheila Collins, production co-ordinator in the 1950s.
5. Interview with Lutyens in *Sight and Sound*, Autumn 1974.

PART I
MAINSTREAM REPRESENTATIONS

The 1930s: Chaos and Opportunity

It has been fashionable to characterize British society in the 1930s as fragmented, riven by contradictory notions about class and national identity. However, the 1930s can be interpreted as a period in the painful process of establishing a consensus about the significance of World War I and about (small) changes in class composition. Certainly, the cultural and social forms of the 1930s are a great deal more homogeneous than is commonly thought. The economic difficulties of the period – the failure of protectionist measures, the difficulties of internationalist interventions, the deteriorating business situation – preoccupied opinion leaders far more than constructing debates about women.

British film-makers of the period were much more interested in profiting from the volatile economic situation than in constructing a coherent response to any cultural, social or sexual change. The 'Klondike era' of British film production was characterized by flexibility, informality and financial crisis. Studios were acutely prone to market fluctuation, and they depended on the instincts (and often personal collateral) of their producers. Entrepreneurialism was the *raison d'être* of the industry, and expedience drove some film-makers to sharp practice. In order to avoid paying royalties or performing rights, they were prepared to invent tunes on the spot (Carstairs, 1942, p. 17). To evade paying union rates to actors, smaller companies would cast electricians or clapper-boys in quite important speaking roles (Hurst, n.d., p. 95). Some producers would shift props in their own cars to save removal fees (Grantley, 1954, p. 163). A few studios were notoriously informal in their payment arrangements, and would regularly fail to pay their salaried staff. Books or ideas could be bought, transformed and resold at lightning speed; actors and actresses could be hired, fired or exported. Companies flowered and faded, genres were unstable and star popularity was evanescent. Patterns of female representation and female creativity were volatile too.

There did exist official checks and balances which were intended to impose order onto the mass-culture industry. It was one of the tasks of the British Board of Film Censors (BBFC) to nuance the industry's representations of women, sexuality and family life. The Board displayed a puritanism (or prurience) about such matters. The Readers' Reports would not permit any reference to prostitution, of course, but female desire was taboo as well: in *The Water Gypsies* (1932), 'Jane's desire for Bryan would have to be very carefully handled and not overstressed'.[1] The list of prohibitions is endless: bridesmaids in their undies, fat ladies on vibrating machines, women engineers, a woman's despairing cry of 'Liverpool! What a place to commit adultery!'[2] Needless to say, the censors did not like Lady Chatterley: 'I cannot find any excuse for Constance. Her liaison with Mellors is just plain animal passion.'[3]

The government had intervened more directly in production with the 1927 Cinematograph Films Act, which was a protectionist measure designed to boost the native industry. It obliged renters and exhibitors to show an increasing proportion of British films. This meant that many more British films had to be made if foreign films were to be imported. The number of films could be made up by native British companies; it could also be swelled by 'British' companies financed by Hollywood, but with three-quarters of the salaries paid to British employees. The scenario or scriptwriter had to be British. This had profound implications for the representation and employment of women. More films were made, more risks could be taken, and more women were employed in the industry, especially in scripting.

The industry produced few films addressing female audiences or dealing with women's issues. Tony Aldgate (1998) has suggested that, due to changes in BBFC personnel and flux in the industry, there was a short period between 1930 and 1932 during which films displayed a greater emotionality and some attention was paid to women's issues. But this phenomenon was short-lived. The plots of some later 1930s films toy with the themes of sexual equality, but closer examination reveals that they were deeply conservative. *Girls Will Be Boys* (1934) converts the potent theme of cross-dressing into an anodyne comedy. *The Dominant Sex* (1937) deals with a woman's struggle to keep her independence after marriage, but it was marketed with a very particular spin:

Now comes the decisive battle between husband and wife. Dick has a chance to buy back the family farm and go and live in the country. Angela hates the idea and tries to dissuade Dick. But he insists, though it may mean the end of his marriage. What will Angela do? Will she refuse to go and live with her husband in the country, living a life she does not like? In the end, she submits, like a true wife.[4]

Clothes and the Woman (1937) also defuses a potentially explosive sexual theme. It deals with the way women use clothes to appear powerful, and yet again the studio's publicity material neutralizes the radical impact of the tale: 'clothes which are extravagant are a disadvantage in impressing men . . . what a woman wears and what she does go hand in hand ever since grandmama's day'.

Financial crises, various government demands and a volatile political situation meant that the studio system was under pressure throughout the decade. Nonetheless, it was capable of functioning as a system of authorship. The representation of women was an area where different powers in the film-making process struggled for dominance. The producer, or the executive producer, was the figure who held the most cards in his hand.

Alexander Korda's approach to film culture was liberal and eclectic. He combined an absolute respect for the mass audience with a high premium on artistic value.[5] His films evoked a high degree of audience creativity: he relied on the viewers' cultural knowledge without ever condescending to them. His costume films encapsulated a radical conservative view of history. He believed in its therapeutic powers, and thought that representations of the past gave mass audiences access to an aristocracy of style which could transform their own perceptions. His modern-dress films often deployed aristocratic motifs, and they insisted on the desirability of risk and surprise.

Korda's radicalism in social and cultural matters did not extend to the sexual sphere, however. The women in his films are statuesque figures who stimulate the social market to greater emotional and capital outlay. Although there is a sophisticated urbanity in the films' sexual politics – they are never puritanical – women are the providers rather than the receivers of pleasure. In Korda's costume films, the women are marginal to aristocratic style. In *The Private Life of Henry VIII* (1933), they are whores, termagants or gorgons; the only good Queen is dead before the film begins. The solacing of female desire is the theme of *The Private Life of Don Juan* (1934), but only the desire of young girls: the hero's 'favourite dish is a middle-aged woman's tongue, cut out by the roots, chopped very small, and eaten raw'. In *The Scarlet Pimpernel* (1935) and *The Return of the Scarlet Pimpernel* (1937), the women are peripheral to the main theme of masculine resourcefulness. *Rembrandt* (1936) contains a trenchant analysis of the artist's role in society. An essentially bohemian film, it argues that the conventional regulation of sexuality is not conducive to artistic creativity. The catch in this system is that women have to be passive. Rembrandt apotheosizes them in a set piece of remarkable intensity. It was written by American screenwriter June Head, who was specially bought in. The artist, declares Charles Laughton as Rembrandt:

> had a vision once. A creature, half-child, half-woman, half-lover ... he knew that when one woman gives herself to you, you possess all women – women of every age and race and kind, and more than the moon and the stars, all miracles and legends. The brown-skinned girls who inflame your senses with their play, cool yellow-haired women who entice you, the gentle ones who serve you, the slender ones who torment you. The mother who bore and suckled you, all women whom God created out of the teeming fullness of the earth, but you love one ... lay your tousled head on her breasts, she is a Delilah waiting for you. Take her garments from her, strip the last veil from her, she is a chaste Susanna, covering her nakedness ... never call her yours, for her secrets are inexhaustible. Call her by one name only. I call her Saskia.

The only Korda costume film which does not conform to this pattern of inspiration and titillation is *Catherine the Great* (1934), which had a more radical female scriptwriter, the playwright Clemence Dane.

Korda's modern-dress films adopt a similar view of women. In *Wedding Rehearsal* (1932), the twin aristocratic girls marry beneath them, thus opening up a debate about cross-class desire. One twin loves kittens, the other puppies, and the visual style concentrates on their similarity to their furry friends. *The Divorce of Lady X* (1938) extends the theme of female 'doubleness', but this time duplicity is centred in one character, Lady Steele (Merle Oberon). Although grossly manipulative and seemingly promiscuous, she is in fact virginal, and this contradiction impels the hero-barrister (Laurence Olivier) to contrast two female types. In court he rails against the modern woman, who

> has disowned womanhood but refuses man's obligations. She demands freedom but will not accept responsibility. She demands time to develop her personality, cogitating which part of her body to paint next ... modern woman is unprincipled, relentless, and exacting. The sooner man takes out his whip again, the better for sanity and progress.

The traditional type of female is 'a tender, delicate organism put into this rough world to make life a little brighter, a little happier, by her beauty and her tenderness and her purity'. The film argues that both types can coexist within the same body. The same theme, and the same railing by Olivier against the female species, occurs in *Q-Planes* (1939). *Twenty-one Days* (made in 1937 but not released until 1940) contains the same vulnerable but duplicitous female role.

Forget-Me-Not (1936) is atypical. It was conceived by Korda as a 'woman's picture', for which he imported the great Italian singer Gigli. Both verbally and visually, the film privileges women's extraordinary arousal by the tenor voice. Although Gigli is short, fat and naïve, the erotic charge of his voice for the women in the film is indubitable. It is tempting to classify this film as a Tenor Romance. *Forget-Me-Not* has much in common with Richard Tauber musicals: BIP's *Blossom Time* (1934) and *Heart's Desire* (1935), Capitol's *Land without Music* (1936), Trafalgar's *Pagliacci* (1936). In all these films, the sublime effeminacy of the tenor voice transports the female listeners into such an intense state of ecstasy that it must be construed as orgasmic; but ratified, of course, by the status of high art.

The other major executive producer of the period was Michael Balcon, who led two studios. Gainsborough was located in Islington and Gaumont-British, the 'mother' company owned by the Ostrers, was in Shepherd's Bush. Although their production policies were intimately related, the studios had separate staff and different styles. Gainsborough was mainly dedicated to low-status fare, while Gaumont produced quality films with a tendency to high seriousness. Since the combined operation was so large, Balcon found it very difficult to put his personal stamp on the films it produced.

During the 1930s, Balcon concentrated on comedies and musical productions at the Gainsborough studios. They were mainly frothy in tone, and dealt with gender relations in a conventional way. The performances expected from the female starlets were not demanding. The 'Gainsborough Girls' of the early 1930s were a means of marketing the studio, but they proved an irritant to directors: 'one forgets her powder, the other wants to telephone, a third has a date at the hairdresser's – no thanks, just one or two at a time is all I can handle'.[6] The Will Hay comedies were all produced at Gainsborough, both before and after Balcon's resignation in December 1936. The films had a stable production team, and most of them were scripted by Hay and Marriott Edgar, who had written the wonderful monologues performed by Stanley Holloway (such as 'The Lion and Albert'). The Hay films contain powerful females who set the narrative in motion: Lady Dawkins in *Boys Will Be Boys* (1935), Emma Harbottle in *Windbag the Sailor* (1936), Mrs Trimbletow in *Oh Mr Porter!* (1937). These women are all large and resentful, and once they impel the Hay character into action are of no further narrative significance. When Hay visits the old father in bed in *Ask a Policeman* (1939), the son enquires, 'Don't you want to see the old lady?' Hay recoils in horror, commenting, 'I've seen Adam, I don't want to see Eve.'

Society in the Hay films is irreparably ramshackle, and its members have no interests in common. Members of the same class are inevitably at odds with each other, and the enormous chasm between men and women can never be bridged. The films work on the premise that the central myths of the culture necessarily exclude women. However, there was another group of comedies made at both Gainsborough and Gaumont whose sexual politics provide a strong contrast to the Hay films. These were the Ben Travers farces, which originally played at the Aldwych Theatre. Balcon objected to the autonomy given to Travers, and conducted a long-standing feud with the director/lead actor Tom Walls. Nonetheless, the Aldwych films did very well at the box-office, and their star, Ralph Lynn, was then the highest-paid actor in the British film industry. The Travers farces were more sexually liberal than the Hay films, and their debates about class were thoroughly integrated into a coherent position on gender.

The Aldwych films were structured around the notion of equality in sexual pleasure. Men could adopt a buccaneering technique with impunity; but women could pursue their own pleasures as well, and would only turn nasty if deprived of consummation. Unruly females abound in these films, which also contain seeming ingénues with an eye to the sexual main chance, fierce landladies in pursuit of their dues, large wives with a taste for humiliating their husbands, and older women too sophisticated to be churlish about a slice from a cut loaf. Two little scenes typify the films. In *Cuckoo in the Nest* (1933), the inebriated old husband (Tom Walls) tries to fondle the elderly landlady (Mary Brough): 'You're just the kind of woman I like!' His dalliance is met by a tornado of rage, and the final close-up of the film is of the triumphant Brough blowing a police whistle to summon the forces of law and order. In *A Cup of Kindness* (1934) the frustrated bridegroom (Ralph Lynn) dreams about courtship practices in the Stone Age, and imagines simple rituals of clubbing and abduction. When he awakes, he ruefully accepts modern problems such as female prevarication.

The Aldwych farces are the result of a unique combination of established scripts, strong direction and powerful stars. It was an intractable combination for Balcon, and the liberal sexual politics of the films cannot be ascribed to him. His other company, Gaumont-British, did not specialize in comedy but in high-quality entertainment with expensive art direction and a serious edge. The roles which women play in Gaumont films are qualitatively different from Gainsborough. In a range of films which require women to play the Eternal-Feminine role, their narratives punish those who are neither noble nor inspiring. *Little Friend* (1934) and *The Iron Duke* (1935) fall into this category, as does *Jew Süss* (1934). This film, which is a liberal pro-Jewish apologia, insists that the audience discriminate between the bad woman, who is rapacious and experienced ('choose an Englishman, they're as discreet as they're clean'), and the good woman, who is a despoiled virgin. For good measure, there are two of the latter in the film: the hero's beloved and his daughter. The motivation of the whole narrative depends on Süss becoming the *pater dolorosus*, mourning and avenging the lost girl.

The second function of females in Gaumont films is that of the decorative irritant. In *Rome Express* (1932), *King of the Damned* (1936), *Rhodes of Africa* (1936) and *King Solomon's Mines* (1937), the female protagonist is a piece of grit in the machine of the tale: she inhibits its smooth development, but is present in order to provide surface interest. The audience is encouraged to admire the woman's beauty, but also to censure her for delaying the dénouement. There remains *The Passing of the Third Floor Back* (1934), which is the only Gaumont film to deal with female ambiguity – the possibility that fallibility and goodness might be mixed. It was directed by the German Berthold Viertel, who was a Marxist of sorts, a friend of Murnau and had worked at the Vienna Volksbühne. The film is based upon a play by Jerome K. Jerome, which the script (partly by Alma Reville) improves. It deals with the entry into a suburban guesthouse of a saintly stranger, who transforms everyone's lives. In Viertel's film, the lead role is played by Conrad Veidt, and the female characters are given much more prominence than in the original play, outnumbering and outshadowing the men. Displaying great subtlety, *The Passing of the Third Floor Back* deals with the pains of modernity. It considers the traduced servant girl, the daughter sold into a loveless marriage, the embittered spinster and the venal landlady, and shows them poised between autonomy and exploitation.

Gaumont-British's internationalist projects displayed more liberal sexual politics, and Michael Balcon's authorial control was intermittent. He left Gainsborough and Gaumont-British in December 1936, and the companies were then headed by the Ostrer brothers and Ted Black, who had quite different policies and cultural capital. More populist than Balcon, and less concerned with quality, their films were more directly attuned to the mass audience, and they were disinclined to take expensive risks. The Crazy Gang's 1930s comedies – *Okay for Sound* (1938), *Alf's Button Afloat* (1938), *The Frozen Limits* (1939) – were right up to date in their system of references. However, prewar Gainsborough could not manage contemporary references in the melodrama mode. *Bank Holiday* (1938) dealt with topics such as extra-marital sex and unrequited love, but gave them such a narrow spread that the film appeared limited and provincial. It would require the spin of wartime exigencies for Gainsborough to deal with contemporary issues in a vital and engaged way.

There were other large outfits too. BIP was owned by John Maxwell and run at Elstree by Walter Mycroft. In the early part of the decade, it specialized in comedies. After 1934, Mycroft shifted the studio towards more ambitious films, which looked expensive but were not. BIP production under Mycroft fell into three categories. The first was the Continental or Ruritanian romance. In such films as *Blossom Time*, *Invitation to the Waltz* (1935), *Heart's Desire* and *I Give My Heart* (1935), the women are there in order to make or cause mistakes. Their function is also to respond to the seductive power of the tenor voice. The second category is the boisterous comedy with a working-class background, such as *The Outcast* (1934) and *Those Were the Days* (1934), in which the women do not initiate mayhem, but resolve it. The third BIP category is the up-market historical vehicle, such as *The Old Curiosity Shop* (1934), *Royal Cavalcade* (1935) and *Drake of England* (1935), in which women are the most decorative (and least intelligent) part of the national heritage. From 1937 the company was renamed as the Associated British Picture Corporation (ABPC) and, with Maxwell and Mycroft still at the helm, produced mainly stage adaptations and comedies in which women had little narrative significance.

Herbert Wilcox, as a smaller independent producer, was able to take control of his product, and can certainly be accorded authorship status. He was authoritarian in his management of visual style, narrative structure and acting interpretation. Wilcox favoured verisimilitude, insisting during an egg-eating scene that the actor consume it shell and all (Carstairs, 1942, pp. 12–13). He headed British and Dominions in the early 1930s, where he specialized in comedy. Wilcox's output became more focused after 1932 when he became involved with Anna Neagle, and his films accommodated his changing view of her image. *The Little Damozel* (1933), *Bitter Sweet* (1933) and *The Queen's Affair* (1934) all starred her in anodyne singing/dancing roles. With *Nell Gwyn* (1934), Wilcox radically revamped Neagle. As Charles II's mistress, Neagle's body language was transformed into a parody of erotic readiness: elbows akimbo, pelvis presented, pectoral muscles flexed. Neagle was instructed to play Nell with a hoydenish sexuality. Her erotic mark-up was extended with *Peg of Old Drury* (1935), in which she played the eighteenth-century actress Peg Woffington as a wayward harlot. Wilcox then established his own company, significantly named Imperator, and proceeded yet again to recast Neagle's persona. In *Victoria the Great* (1937), traditional femininity is re-established with vigour. In one marital tiff, Albert locks Victoria out of the bedroom. She knocks imperiously: 'Albert, it is the Queen', and receives no reply. Then, 'Albert, it is Victoria', which meets with the same response. Finally, 'It is your wife, Albert' (uttered cooingly) causes the door to open. The lesson which is enjoined is that only female submission will result in pleasure, and that goes for queens as well as for lesser mortals. With *Sixty Glorious Years* (1938), the case is made with greater emphasis. This is a revamp of the first Victoria film, but with one important difference: the more domestic perspective (it is supposed to be based on the Queen's private diaries) presents the monarch as even less autonomous. *Sixty Glorious Years* is a powerful threnody on patriarchal marriage: 'When you are alone with me,' says the commoner to the Queen, 'you are nothing but my wife.' Nothing indeed.

Smaller studios had less coherent policies. Julius Hagen, who owned Twickenham Studios, believed in expedience rather than aesthetic coherence, and none of his films linked debates about society with considerations of gender. Max Schach's Capitol Film Productions only offered leaden roles to actresses in such films as *When Knights Were Bold* (1936). Basil Dean was motivated by his crusading attitude to high culture, and by his desire for a folkloric representation of society, but he had major financial problems with his company ATP, and only a spasmodic understanding of the box-office. Dean's major female star was Gracie Fields, but he was unsure how to make best cinematic use of her. He employed J. B. Priestley to script *Sing as We Go* (1934), possibly in an attempt to enhance Fields's status. The film locates her solidly in Lancashire working-class culture, but the imaginary locale of *Queen of Hearts* (1936) is unfocused. Fields's last film for Dean, *The Show Must Go On* (1937), is ill-proportioned and inconsistent. When Michael Balcon became head of production at ATP, he tried to revive the 'populist' aspect of a Fieldian character by using the young Betty Driver in musical comedies such as *Let's Be Famous* (1939). However, the times were out of joint for her informal feistiness, and the film sank without trace.

If a company was very small, it could afford to take intellectual risks. Mayflower Pictures did just that. Formed by Charles Laughton and Erich Pommer in 1937, it made three films, all of which were unusual in their treatment of the battle between the sexes. *Vessel of Wrath* (1938) deals with the subjugation of an over-assertive missionary wife. *St Martin's Lane* (1938), which was written by Clemence Dane, deals with a young artiste (Vivien Leigh) who becomes a star, abandoning the busker who loves her (Charles Laughton). The film portrays the heroine's naked hunger for fame, which is forcefully connected with her desire for sexual equality. She is accorded complex motivation, and the old guard of Laughton and his friends ruefully accept her as part of an emergent order: 'the hansoms have gone and the horses have gone and now soon we'll have to go'. The tone of the film is marvellously elegiac, and it works by making a connection between the new woman and the old ways. *Jamaica*

Inn (1939) has the same attitude. The lively heroine (Maureen O'Hara) carries all before her, and the squire (Laughton) dies quoting Burke's sublime evocation of the *ancien régime*: 'the age of chivalry is gone'.

The creative freedom in the 'quota quickies' was very variable. They were knocked out quickly, with minimal attention to 'finish', but they did function as a meal ticket or training ground for needy British technicians. Lawrence Napper has argued that the 1927 Act gave British film production a much-needed boost, and that the quickies appealed to those parts of the audience who were uneasy with American social and production values (Napper, 1997, p. 43). If we take the example of George King, who made 50 quota films for a variety of American companies, we can see that the aesthetic as well as social system embedded in his films is deeply residual and conservative. King's *Sweeney Todd, the Demon Barber of Fleet Street* (1936) is predicated on rigid gender roles. The cross-dressing motif only serves to intensify the separation between male and female behaviour. In all King's films, the body language refers to music-hall melodrama, and depends on its stereotypes of bad squire and outraged virgin. His *Ticket of Leave Man* (1937) is structured around the Maria Marten syndrome too. However, some quota films present gender issues in a less traditional or more aggressive manner. The early films of Michael Powell can be interpreted as a rehearsal for his complex later position on women. For example, *The Love Test* (1934) is about a women chemist, whom the other (male) scientists in the laboratory persecute and use as a butt for their wagers. Her vulnerability and unpredictable passion are symbolized by repeated shots of a blonde celluloid doll bursting into flames: the company tries to render it fireproof, in spite of its essential volatility.

If we now turn to the range of roles which women were required to play, we can see that the 'clusters' extant in 1930s cinema were remarkable for their range and quantity. As I suggested in the Introduction, all clusters feed important social hungers, and address specific parts of the audience. The conditions of production in the period meant that competition was fierce, and actresses would sometimes go to outrageous lengths to secure a part (Roye, 1955, pp. 65–6). The financial rewards were mixed. Potential starlets were given small retainers and then paid on a daily basis if they were chosen to appear (Bouchier, 1995, p. 67). Bigger companies would pay £20 a week on a five-year contract. Sometimes actresses were only paid per foot of completed film, and in order to survive, they 'doubled up' by filming during the day and appearing on stage at night.[7] However, once they achieved star status, significant sums could be made. Evelyn Laye, for example, commanded £5000 per picture (Laye, 1958, p. 93). Jessie Matthews earned much more, and Gracie Fields made £40,000 per film in a four-picture deal struck in 1933 (Fields, 1960, p. 90).

For young actresses with no clout, physical conditions were gruelling. Old equipment and poor ventilation meant that some studios were intolerably hot, and dresses sometimes had to be taken off and dried between every take.[8] Young actresses were the cheapest unit of exchange. When Alexander Korda had money problems during *The Private Life of Henry VIII*, Binnie Barnes recalled that

> he lent me out to BIP which was right next door. It was for a film called *An Old Spanish Custom*, so I played a Spanish woman in the morning and Catherine Howard for Alex in the evening. I got sprayed with a bucket of water at BIP and then I had to run across the street and be glamorous.[9]

There was considerable transnational traffic in film personnel in 1930s Britain, and this extended to actresses as well as to actors, directors and designers. Continental women were invited to bring a sense of sophistication to the bill of fare – Elisabeth Bergner, for example. The French actress Renée St-Cyr completely transformed Gainsborough's 1938 *Strange Boarders*. Her performance as the wife is remarkable for its sophistication. Europeans could be given lines expressing a world-weary cynicism which would be polluting if spoken by British females. The French comedienne Yvonne Arnaud appeared in a range of films in which her plump persona administered correctives to bourgeois respectability. She was aware of the difficulties which her urbanity and age posed for producers: 'I am not what you would call a sweet young ingénue – no? That is what they really wanted.'[10] She thought that only Ben Travers and Tom Walls were capable of making good use of her talents. Their *Cuckoo in the Nest* is an example of her best work. Arnaud plays an MP's wife who is wrongly accused of adultery with an old flame. Her performance is marvellously knowing. With a po-faced expression, she displays her supposed lover to her husband with a shrug: 'Go on! Look at him!' Her manner suggests that she has avoided adultery not because it is wrong, but because the co-respondent is too silly. No British actress would have been cast in such a role.

Many 'exotics' were marketed in studio press books as the leaven which would raise the dough of ordinary films. Nina Mae McKinney, for example, was brought over from America to star in *Sanders of the River* (1935).[11] But her role is so thoroughly integrated into the debate about responsible Empire leadership that there is no space for any acting manoeuvres. Instead, McKinney's function is to be decorative throughout, and to endorse Western definitions of the family: 'one paper, one wife', as Sanders instructs her and Bosambo after their marriage. The narrative of *Sanders* is structured around McKinney's physical vulnerability, but she is important only for what events she can set in train; she is not important in herself.

The same can be said of the Chinese actress Anna May Wong, who, after a successful career in German silent cinema, made four films in Britain: *Piccadilly* (1929), *Tiger Bay* (1933), *Java Head* (1934) and *Chu Chin Chow* (1934). In the first three, her racial 'otherness' is signalled as a source of moral danger (Bergfelder, 1998). In *Chu Chin Chow*, Erno Metzner's florid sets are as heavily laden as Sternberg's, and Wong is their chief piece of dressing – decorated, ambiguous and sinister. She symbolizes a love object which is profane because it is heavily inflected. Sacred love objects, by implication, are single-faceted.

Tamara Desni was used for different purposes. Russian-born, her heavily fractured accent and ethereal appearance were always used as an index of vulnerability. In *Fire over England* (1937), Desni plays Spanish Elena, who falls in love with the English hero (Laurence Olivier). It is necessary for the patriotic resolution of the narrative that he reject her. In *The Squeaker* (1937), Desni plays a nightclub singer, and her performance throughout is like someone walking under water. Her voice has a thrilling vibrato, and she sings in the manner of Dietrich, while walking backwards and wearing a transparent dress. The signs of excess weigh too heavily in the scales against the signs of reason, and accordingly Desni's power is overcome by the cool righteousness of the character played by Ann Todd. This pattern is replicated in Desni's other films: her Tamara in *By-pass to Happiness* (1934), Conchita in *Jack Ahoy!* (1934) and Tanya in *Love in Exile* (1936).

Other companies too were ambitious for the status which Continental stars could confer. The German star Camilla Horn was brought over for

Matinee Idol (1933), *The Love Nest* (1933) and *The Luck of a Sailor* (1934). As these turned out to be low-budget items, Horn felt insulted as well as miscast, and concluded that British producers tarred all foreign actresses with the same exotic brush (Horn, 1985, pp. 169, 177). The German actress Lilian Harvey was signed for a three-picture deal with BIP, but only completed one (*Invitation to the Waltz*), because she felt her roles were predictable soubrettes with no emotional breadth (Habichon, 1990, p. 49).

When American-owned companies imported exotic women into their British films, they over-egged the pudding. Fox's 1937 *Wings of the Morning* was structured around the French actress Annabella.[12] First of all she is a gypsy, then she is disguised as a boy, and lastly she is the aristocratic heir to a great estate. The film almost collapses under the overload of motifs, and the range of symbolic functions borne by the heroine makes her role preposterous.

Marlene Dietrich was the biggest international actress to be imported. Alexander Korda brought her over to star with Robert Donat in *Knight without Armour* (1937). Dietrich's reputation was based on films in which her ambiguity intrigued the viewer. *Knight without Armour*, however, which dealt with the rescue of a countess from the marauding hordes of the Russian revolution, required Dietrich to function in a more one-dimensional way. Artistically, the film is a wonderful achievement, but the designs by Lazare Meerson, which present Dietrich as the chief ornament of the *mise en scène*, concentrate on the light rather than the dark aspects of her persona. She is there in order to be saved, but she cannot be understood.

The case of Merle Oberon provides us with interesting problems. She was of Indian/Eurasian descent, but took great pains to conceal this. Korda discovered her in 1932 and married her in 1939. Oberon starred in a range of London films in the 1930s, such as *The Private Life of Henry VIII*, *The Private Life of Don Juan*, *The Return of the Scarlet Pimpernel* and *The Divorce of Lady X*. Her performances in these films suggest that she was split between the desire to exploit her exotic charisma and the need to conceal her racial origins by assuming an extreme refinement and impassivity.[13] She also had to operate as the central female symbol for Korda's philosophical system. These conflicting demands account for the acute inconsistency of Oberon's persona and performative styles.

One home-grown British actress, Chili Bouchier, was used as an exotic, but the typecasting inhibited her career. When producer/director Herbert Wilcox discovered her 'Latin looks', he put her under contract, and set about constructing her as a star with non-English allure. According to Bouchier, her spirited rejection of Wilcox's amorous advances caused him to take revenge by loaning her out for lacklustre films (Bouchier, 1996, p. 73). When Anna Neagle replaced Bouchier in his affections, the débâcle was complete. With Wilcox's final words ringing in her ears ('you are going to find it very difficult'), Bouchier noted that hers was 'a cautionary little tale which demonstrated what happens to little actresses when they refuse to reward their mentors'.[14] The 'foreign' persona Bouchier had acquired in Wilcox's films proved hard to shed, and all she could get were Romany roles. In *Gypsy* (1936), she was presented as 'a wild half-naked creature with fuzzy-wuzzy hair who fought like a wild-cat'.[15] Bouchier's career declined steadily, and an actress of great beauty and versatility was lost to the cinema.

So an exotic persona was a disadvantage in the British film industry, but only if you were female. Male stars with such qualities were presented in a different way. Sabu always appeared as fresh, eager and inventive, while Conrad Veidt's dark, saturnine qualities were used to positive effect by British producers (Harper, 1998).

There was a group of 'ladylike' actresses whose entry into films was often via C. B. Cochran's revues (Cochran, 1941, pp. 124–36). Evelyn Laye was one, and she appeared in a range of Ruritanian musical comedies such as *Princess Charming* (1934), in which her role is to raise the tone of events. Sarah Churchill was another Cochran graduate who brought a quality gloss to a range of films (Churchill, 1981). So too was Florence Desmond, an interesting figure who allowed film and revue to cross-pollinate in her work. She 'quoted' the furniture-touching scene from *Queen Christina* in her revue *Why Not Tonight?*, and implicitly referred to her Cochran act in many of her films (Desmond, 1953, pp. 72–3). Gertrude Lawrence also used her revue connections to give status to her film persona. Her role in *Rembrandt* is of particular interest. She uses the housekeeper role to suggest a combination of sexual hunger with a desire for social revenge. Her performance as Desdemona/the wife in *Men Are Not Gods* (1936) is similar in the way her manner saturates the central issues (jealousy, duplicity and control) with upper-middle-class resonance. Interestingly, Lawrence was marketed as a star with particular appeal to women (Lawrence, 1954, pp. 194–5).

There were other ladylike actresses who functioned in a similar way: Kathleen Nesbitt in *The Passing of the Third Floor Back*, for example. Binnie Barnes invested her role in *The Private Life of Henry VIII* with such a degree of controlled calculation that she undermined some of the intentions of the script.[16] Benita Hume did the same in *Jew Süss*.[17] The 'ladylike' characters always raised the tone of events. Their textual function is to operate as a brake on the narrative, and to encourage the viewer to recall a period when definitions of class and culture were comfortably stable.

Another cluster of younger actresses emerged who counterbalanced the residual effect of the 'ladies'. Nova Pilbeam, Wendy Barrie, Renée Ray, Googie Withers, Madeleine Carroll, Margaret Lockwood and Ann Todd were all Wholesome Sensible Girls who projected an air of competence and energy, and had the forthright manner of a socially emergent group. Equipped with a brisk verbal delivery, their gaze was direct and unambiguous. Their textual effect is bracing, and they are clearly intended to evoke confidence in a new social order. The dense population and the intensity of the Wholesome Girls group were designed to give the audience confidence in modernity – to let them see that women could be spirited and pure at the same time.

There was a smaller cluster of Mannish Women – females who were not conventionally beautiful and who engaged in quasi-masculine activities. These women could feasibly struggle for power and status, since they wasted little textual time in the pursuit of romance. They were given narrative space in order to rehearse questions about sexual identity and social power. All these Mannish Women are regretful about their position as men by proxy, and the narrative structures ultimately consign them to the position of female eunuchs.

Flora Robson possessed a remarkable spiritual beauty and technical virtuosity. During the 1930s, she made several films in which she played powerful women who suffer because they are extraordinary. In 1934 Robson played the Empress in Korda's *Catherine the Great*. The screenplay (by Marjorie Deans) required her to express some feminist sentiments. Robson turned in a performance of great subtlety, in which her face and demeanour bore witness to the loneliness of power and promiscuity. In 1937 Robson played Elizabeth I in Korda's *Fire over England*. The screenplay by Clemence Dane presents the monarch as someone torn apart by internal conflict. Elizabeth wishes to symbolize victory over the flesh, but also to enjoy being that flesh. Robson's most intense scenes are when she is riven by desire to be both young like her ladies-in-waiting and old in wisdom like the monarchy itself. This conflict makes her unreasonable and interesting. Her delivery throughout suggests that it is feasible to be both a monarch and a citizen, to be both alive and dead and to be both male and female. Robson knew she had turned in an unusual performance:

> Elizabeth was essentially a woman of action, and that is just the kind of woman I like best to portray. Whether they are characters of actual history, or just folklore, or of pure fiction, such women – women whose lives and works were far more important than their loves – are much more in tune with our modern idea and tempo of life than many of the sexy sirens who have figured as heroines of sexy and sentimental films in the past.[18]

This extract comes from an essay entitled 'My film future', but unfortunately there were few empresses left for Robson to play. All she would be offered was a depressing parade of spinsters.

Another Mannish Woman was Cicely Courtneidge, who specialized as a male impersonator in music hall and revue, and whose role model was Vesta Tilley (Courtneidge, 1953, p. 77). She and her husband Jack Hulbert were close friends of Michael Balcon, and they both appeared in a range of Gaumont-British comedies. In *Soldiers of the King* (1932) she doffs and assumes the appearance of manliness with aplomb, and makes that seem an artificial disguise. Her transgressive brio is even more evident in *Me and Marlborough* (1935). The scenario, partly written by Marjorie Gaffney, required Courtneidge to masquerade as a soldier in order to rescue her press-ganged husband. Even in female dress Courtneidge is a better man than most: legs akimbo, she halloos loud, and bewails her unconsummated marriage.[19] Yet her character operates as the mouthpiece of authority: in a prolonged dissolve at the end of the film, she appears superimposed over images of the army and weaponry.

Courtneidge was very popular, coming second only to Gracie Fields as the favourite British film star in the Bernstein Poll of 1933. But her popularity was short-lived, and by 1937 she had slipped to 31st place. Fields had a much longer pedigree in the popularity charts, and she was a far more significant star. We might tentatively assign Fields to the Mannish group, not because she aspired to power in any literal way in her films, but because her film persona was so resolutely desexualized. Fields could only attain broad symbolic status because she lacked glamour, which would have located her in an internationalist and de-classed context. She is always cast as a woman who is defined by what she does rather than by whom she loves or what she wears.

Mannish Women in the film texts of the 1930s throw positive light onto traditional feminine roles, which are presented as more appropriate for the production of happiness. A more combative cluster is one we can call the Madcap Girls. This was an ensemble of small, feisty females who are social parvenues. Their role is to bring about a minor perturbation, and then to encourage the audience to turn from the textual maelstrom to still waters. Evelyn Dall, for example, was an American vaudeville star who appeared in a range of musicals. Her persona was extremely abrasive, and her diminutive height was used to good effect (Levy, 1948, pp. 158–9). Mary Morris was a Madcap too. Openly lesbian in her private life and in her acting style, Morris played a reform school inmate in *Prison without Bars* (1938) and the Nazi chauffeuse in *The Spy in Black* (1939). In these and later roles, Morris gave the impression of a tiny whirlwind, liable to destroy at will (Bourne, 1996, pp. 48–51).

The most important Madcap was Jessie Matthews. She had been successful in Cochran's stage revues, but became a much bigger star with her film roles. Of humble origins, which she disguised with an elocutionary zeal, Matthews's accent now seems dated, but it was clearly part of an attempt to float free and to impel herself into a classless demimonde.[20] Insecurity underpins all Matthews's performances, and fuels their energies and ambiguities. Physically, she was extraordinarily talented: lissom, sinuous and uncannily alert, her style of movement could accommodate extremes, from incredible high kicks to a sashaying, shimmering glide. Matthews owed much to the lessons and choreography of the great black dancer Buddy Bradley. She exhibits a wilful persona, acutely at issue with duty; it works by alluding to important anxieties and then resolving them. The optimism of Matthews's performance encourages audiences to feel that the social and sexual system is flexible enough for any eventuality. In *Evergreen* (1934), for example, Matthews has to masquerade as her mother and pretend that her boyfriend is her son. *First a Girl* (1935) also deals in masquerade, this time between the sexes rather than generations. Matthews has to take over the part of a drag artist (Sonnie Hale), and is a women playing a man playing a woman. In one scene, her beloved (Griffith Jones) rescues her from drowning, and he still thinks she is a man. Lying supine on the sand in a clinging swimsuit, Matthews's expression changes utterly. It burns and glows with erotic power, and there can no longer be any doubt as to what gender she is. The scene is clearly shot in this way to reassure viewers that beneath wild tomboy façades, 'real women' reside.

But there are social masquerades as well. In *It's Love Again* (1936), Matthews plays the ideal woman, who can be virginal and loose, huntress and hunted. Her persona was classless, and this holds good for all the Madcaps, who have a destabilizing effect on the narratives of their films. Other female stereotypes were more class- and genre-specific. Larger, older and more combative women had quite a different textual function. There was a range of older, Difficult Dowager roles, played by actresses such as Grace Edwin, Marie Lohr, Mary Brough and Norma Varden. These dowagers are unruly women who have transgressed the boundaries of respectability, and are freed from the time-consuming pursuit of sexual desire. Significantly, their textual spread is not confined to one class, but to the genre of comedy. These ladies of misrule usher in a short Saturnalia, in which anarchy and bad behaviour are the just rewards for a long life of conformity.

Varden was the most important of the dowagers. She was trained as a Shakespearean actress, but found her comic form when she appeared in the Ben Travers farces at the Aldwych Theatre. Varden turned in some superlative performances in two Travers films (Ernestine Stoatt in the 1933 *Turkey Time*; Mrs Hornett in the 1935 *Foreign Affairs*) and in a couple of Will Hay films (Lady Dorking in *Boys Will Be Boys*; Olivia Potter-Porter in *Windbag the Sailor*).[21] In all these roles Varden deployed her majestic size to full effect. Tall, deep-breasted and moving like an ocean liner, she delivered withering ripostes to hapless males. Her phrasing and pattern of gaze were very precisely orchestrated. She was always assertive and domineering, and her roles were middle class. There were other 'difficult' and combative females who played working-class characters. Mary Brough, for example, played comic landladies who were meant to look like 'a paper bag, blown up and ready to burst'.[22]

We cannot discuss older, unruly females without dealing with the films of Old Mother Riley. The first of the cycle was *Old Mother Riley* in 1937, and the series continued until the early 1950s. In all the Old Mother Riley films, the heroine outrages the canons of good taste and is uninhibited in her pursuit of self-expression. But Mother is played by a man, Arthur Lucan, and 'her' daughter Kitty is played by Lucan's wife, Kitty Mac-Shane. (In one sense, of course, the whole act can be construed as a loud bellow of marital pain.) The Old Mother Riley films had their roots deep in vaudeville, where the tradition of drag and pantomime dames was well assimilated. Cross-dressing encourages the audience to play a kind of sexual hide-and-seek. But what you think might be there is not; and what *is* there is not what you expect. This game is played with vigour in the Old Mother Riley films. An interesting index of Lucan's original style is a filmed extract from his act in an early 1936 revue, *Stars on Parade*. Mother waits up for the erring daughter. Her body language is jerky: her arms flail, her head bobs, her legs swivel. Like a comic character from Dickens, her body has lost coherence and rebels against itself. Mother disrobes for bed, and in a grotesque parody of the dance of the seven veils, seven petticoats are removed, four vests and a corset. Finally, the awful truth is revealed: the flat chest, the scrawny arms, the desexualizing effects of age. It is suggested to the audience that what gives Mother her insane energy is that time has made her like a man. The fact that 'she' *is* a man deliberately muddies the issue.

The Difficult Dowager roles were clearly intended to alert audiences to the big issues: desire, decay, death and revenge. Their playful assumption of masculine behaviour is transgressive, but its edge is blunted by the comedy, and it serves to return the audience to a sense of comfort in the status quo. All the female stereotypes in 1930s cinema question stable gender definitions, and invest them with debates about generation and class; they then return the audience reinvigorated to the mental landscape of the status quo.

Notes

1. BBFC Scenario Notes 16 August 1931, in BFI Library.
2. *Ibid.*, 2 November 1931; 20 April 1932; 30 April 1934; 29 June 1931.
3. *Ibid.*, 14 June 1935.
4. Publicity material for *The Dominant Sex*, in BFI Library.
5. *Film Weekly*, 7 November 1936.
6. *Film Pictorial*, 26 August 1933. The director was anonymous.
7. Nesbitt (1975). Gertrude Lawrence worked on stage while filming *Rembrandt*: see Lawrence (1954), p. 197. Binnie Barnes was moonlighting as well: see interview with Barnes in *Films in Review*, May 1990.
8. Nesbitt (1975), p. 169. See also McCallum (1979), p. 78 for an account of hectic acting schedules.

9. Barnes interview, *Films in Review*.

10. Interview with Arnaud in *Film Weekly*, 8 March 1933, p. 11. See also *Picturegoer*, 20 April 1945, p. 10, and Malet (1961). For her obituary, see *The Times*, 22 September 1958.

11. For a full bio-filmography, see *Films in Review*, January/February 1991.

12. For material on Annabella, see *Classic Images*, November 1996. For a 1936 interview with Annabella, see *Picturegoer*, 25 July 1936; for a 1983 interview, see *Films and Filming*, October 1983.

13. She went to great pains to remove Indian traces from her accent (Higham and Moseley, 1983, p. 27), and introduced her own mother as her maid (p. 28).

14. Bouchier (1995), p. 84. See also Bouchier's interview in the BECTU archive for a more measured account.

15. *Evening Standard*, 7 October 1936.

16. For interesting early interviews with Barnes, see *Picturegoer*, 3 June and 2 December 1933.

17. See *Film Weekly*, 23 March 1934.

18. *Film Weekly*, 2 January 1937.

19. See interview with Courtneidge in *Film Weekly*, 11 January 1935.

20. Matthews and Burgess (1974), p. 5. See also Michael Thornton (1975). This suggests that Matthews's class insecurities were the reason behind her many nervous and physical breakdowns.

21. See *Film Fan Monthly*, March 1975.

22. See an interesting interview with Brough in *Film Pictorial*, 14 October 1933. Brough's role model was Marie Dressler.

World War II: Control and Evasion

The outbreak of war in 1939 meant that the fabric of everyday life was transformed; nothing could be taken for granted, especially personal or family survival. Two major transformations affected women's lives during World War II: they could be conscripted, and there were more opportunities for sexual freedom. The film industry dealt with these changes in an extremely nervous and selective way. For the first time, films were made which foregrounded female employment: *Millions Like Us* and *The Lamp Still Burns* were released in 1943. The sea-change in women's sexual behaviour was examined in an indirect form in melodramas about female desire, such as *Madonna of the Seven Moons* (1944) and *The Seventh Veil* (1945). *The Wicked Lady* falls into that category too, even though it was released just before Christmas in 1945. Its script had been submitted to the BBFC in late 1943, and the planning and filming took place during the war. The same was true for *Brief Encounter*, which was released in the same month. It was made during black-out conditions in late 1944 (Huntley, 1993, p. 15). Both films deal with issues of gender which are specific to the war. I shall therefore categorize any film released before the end of 1945 as a war film.

During the 1930s, production patterns had revealed a cultural free-for-all: companies flowered and faded with astonishing speed, and the power of the free market (protectionist measures aside) meant that producers could do virtually what they liked, as long as they complied with the BBFC and were not actually caught with their hands in the till. Once war broke out, the freedoms of producers and exhibitors were severely curtailed, and they had to submit to the behests of the Ministry of Information (MoI), which had firm policies about gender representation. In a classic swings-and-roundabouts situation, producers lost one set of controls, but gained another. The BBFC was subject to the MoI, and its range of operations was severely limited after 1939. Its Scenario Reports favoured projects supported by the MoI.[1] The BBFC continued its prewar attempt to purify film output. It took a dim view of the sexual content of *The Wicked Lady*, and requested the removal of some explicit erotic action.[2] But to no effect: the producers could afford to ignore the Board's wartime strictures, because the MoI was more interested in boosting morale than in debating questions of decency.

The MoI was in a very powerful position *vis-à-vis* the feature film industry. It opted for a carrot-and-stick approach, exerting influence on film producers by releasing stars and key technicians from military service; it also subsidized compliant producers by giving them administrative and practical support. The Ministry established an 'Ideas Committee', which organized informal discussions between its own personnel and handpicked members of the Screenwriters' Association. The Ideas Committee, all of whom were male, discussed topics aligned to government propaganda policy.

How did the MoI nuance its film policies on the gender issue? Early in the war, Ministry personnel were attracted by the findings of the International Propaganda and Broadcasting Enquiry; this argued that propaganda bodies should 'in a stratified society, persuade the dominant group'.[3] From the outset, therefore, the Ministry was not inclined to give subordinate groups like women any privileged address in its feature films policy. Moreover, it rejected other propaganda expertise. The British Psychological Association was roundly rebuffed.[4] The influential Professor Frederick Bartlett (1940) also offered help. His work on propaganda would have been useful, since it considered symbolism, subliminal messages and sexual difference. But the MoI preferred the ideas of Dr Edward Glover, largely because he dismissed 'the more morbid aspects of the science of psychoanalysis'.[5] Glover had mechanistic views on propaganda, insisting that subjectivity and gender were unworthy of attention. By favouring Glover's ideas, and by recommending them as official policy, the Ministry effectively banished subjectivity, gender and the tools of psychoanalysis from its repertoire.

The Films Division of the MoI formulated a number of directives on feature film which, although seemingly bland, were in fact élitist and misogynist. Early in 1940, the Policy Committee had argued that they should promulgate films glorifying 'histories of national heroes'.[6] This suggestion was made without reference to the instincts of commercial producers or the tastes of their customers; Ministry personnel expressed contempt for the industry, and saw its protestations of patriotism as 'little more than the timely use of an unusual opportunity of getting something for nothing'.[7]

Until mid-1941, the Films Division prioritized history as a tool in its propaganda war, but it was opposed to sensational histories. The MoI wanted history to sell Britain's heritage to the Americans.[8] Otherwise, films should teach the lesson that 'in human history Britain has the special contribution of fair play'.[9] After mid-1941, MoI film policy altered drastically: film-makers were encouraged to concentrate on purely contemporary issues. In 1942, *Kinematograph Weekly* noted that the MoI now only wanted films 'which were not nostalgic about the old ways and old days ... but realistic films of everyday life'. It warned that if the Ministry had its way, the changing recreational needs of the mass audience would not be met.[10] As the war progressed, the MoI vetoed support for any non-realist films.[11] It insisted that the best films for propaganda purposes were 'simple, direct, and man to man'.[12] The Films Division developed a coercive policy towards the mass audience and its pleasures. Jack Holmes, the MoI documentarist, expressed irritation with those parts of the audience (probably female) which persisted in a preference for fantasy, and thought that 'most people can easily be made interested in contemporary life'.[13]

So, although the Films Division did not produce its own feature films after 1940, it did attempt to skew production. The MoI was predominantly composed of middle-class and male personnel, and its files contain overwhelming evidence that, while the idea of socialism was tolerated, feminism was anathema. Helen de Moulpied was virtually the only woman in the middle echelons, and in memo after memo her recommendations were ignored. The Ministry was loath to address gender as an issue in its propaganda policy on feature film. This was not the case for its documentaries. The MoI's documentary arm was the Crown Film Unit, and many of its short films were addressed to women, often by a male voice-over who instructed them about such matters as the correct recipe for a pie. Short 'message' films and documentary films on domestic or security matters did engage with gender difference. Besides the Crown Film Unit itself, there were a number of small independent companies that worked for the MoI. Their shorts on 'female' topics, although conforming to the main propaganda framework, were more carefully nuanced in their gender address.[14]

The feature films which the MoI actively supported ranged across different genres and companies. Early in the war, the MoI actually funded Powell and Pressburger's *The 49th Parallel* (1941). Powell suggests that he was encouraged in the early stages of the project by Kenneth Clark and Duff Cooper, heads of the Films Division and the MoI respectively, to the tune of £60,000 (Powell, 1986, pp. 345–8). The film is a patriotic thriller, and plays against a backdrop of rugged Canadian scenery. All the communities visited by the Nazi interlopers are hierarchical. The backwoods retreat of the anthropologist (Leslie Howard) is exclusively masculine: there are men who do the rough work, and Howard, 'the Boss', who studies Indian culture and the European avant-garde. Females are an irrelevance to both forms of labour. In the German Hutterite community, which is clearly meant to function as a utopia, the gender roles are rigidly stereotyped. The women are biddable and winsome; they are represented by Anna (Glynis Johns), who is content with traditional feminine tasks. Women played quite a different symbolic role in the films Powell and Pressburger made outside the aegis of the MoI. *The 49th Parallel*'s emphasis on the ideal female type as asexual and malleable should be attributed to MoI 'authorship', rather than to Powell and Pressburger.

Production companies responded to MoI initiatives in different ways. Two Cities, under the tutelage of Filippo del Giudice, was dedicated to the production of 'quality' films which would enhance the audience's range of cultural reference. This company policy came to full fruition with the 1945 *Henry V*, but earlier in the war Del Giudice made a range of films fully consonant with MoI propaganda behests. Women were centrally positioned in all these films, and they validated the notions of social reform and control. Their reward in the texts was to be cleansed of undignified emotional mess.

In 1943, Two Cities released three propaganda films addressing female topics. *The Gentle Sex* was made partially as a recruitment film for the ATS, and was produced and directed by Leslie Howard, aided by Maurice Elvey. Howard's presentation of events is a soft target – to criticize it is like shooting fish in a barrel. The film opens with a high-angle shot, over which his voice encourages the audience to 'swoop down for a couple of armfuls' of the female protagonists, and it concludes with the rueful 'let's give in at last and admit that we're rather proud of you, you strange, incalculable, wonderful creatures'. If that were all, the film would be tedious indeed, but the narrative argues more impressively that female solidarity can provide compensations for sacrifices. Aimée Stuart contributed to the script, but her input was limited by Howard. The film certainly eschews reference to the vigorous sexual activity undertaken by many women in uniform – what one called 'the great man-chase' (Moore, 1943, p. 47). Overall, *The Gentle Sex* argues that what women must sacrifice in wartime is love, expressivity and sensual gratification.

The Demi-Paradise was also released in 1943, and it had considerable government backing. Its director Antony Asquith was on the MoI Ideas Committee with the producer Anatole de Grunwald, and both were experienced in propaganda work. The main purpose of the film was to express the official line on the Anglo-Russian alliance; but it also held a position on sexual alliances. Anne (Penelope Dudley Ward) falls in love with the Russian engineer Ivan (Laurence Olivier), and confesses her feelings. But all she gets for her pains are well-kissed knuckles from mumbling Ivan, and he deploys her passion as a source of inspiration for industrial designs. The pageant scene clarifies the role allotted to females, when a village woman, in classical attire and teetering on a column, is used to symbolize liberty. Neutral, heroic and uncomfortable, she is an icon whose personal feelings are expendable.

The Lamp Still Burns was the third of the 1943 trio, and deals with the career of a female architect (Rosamund John) who decides to train as a nurse. The film was based on Monica Dickens's *One Pair of Feet*, which contains some trenchant criticism of bureaucracy. But Leslie Howard turned the novel round, and instructed scenarist Elizabeth Baron and director Maurice Elvey to make the heroine submit to the rules of the hospital, even though some of them are clearly mindless and pettifogging (Wood, 1987, pp. 27–9). *The Lamp Still Burns* is about obedience, sacrifice and reform – obedience to the authorities, sacrifice of a woman's will and a reformed social order stripped bare of desire.

The propaganda aims of Two Cities's *The Way Ahead* (1945) were also firmly welded to MoI directives. Due to a mixture of official tardiness and hamfistedness, the film missed the propaganda boat, and was released too late to fulfil its war aims (Porter and Litewski, 1981). The function allotted to females had a family resemblance to the other Two Cities films. In *The Way Ahead*, women exist in order to be left behind; they provide a secure backcloth for the real action. *The Way to the Stars* (1945) displays the same sexual politics, but the argument is more fully developed. The female protagonists, plucky and lively though they are, are born to suffer and sacrifice. Their behaviour under stress is modelled on a middle-class ethic of impassivity. *The Way to the Stars* mounts an argument in favour of such repression. The film's aims are twofold: to sing an elegy for the lost young men of the RAF, and to forge stronger links between Britain and the USA. The female characters are comprehensively absorbed into both schemes.

Two Cities used a range of directors and scriptwriters but managed to weld women into a place in their framework, and to produce a range of feature films which did the government's propaganda job. Ealing is directly comparable. Michael Balcon was its head of production, and as it was a more modest outfit than the Gaumont/Gainsborough combine he had led in the 1930s, he was able to intervene more directly in the production process. Ealing had a smallish group of directors, producers and scriptwriters, who were called 'Mr Balcon's young gentlemen'. The films they made were sympathetic to MoI aims. *The Next of Kin* (1942) was originally commissioned by the War Office as a training film, and as the project took shape, its aim became consonant with the 'Careless Talk Costs Lives' campaign being mounted by the MoI. The enemy within, as constructed by *The Next of Kin*, is woman. The original sin of indiscretion is committed by a nightclub dancer – a performing female whose displays are scrutinized by men. She is first seen on stage dwarfed by a gigantic grotesque silhouette of a woman. She is both Pandora and Circe, and leaves her illicit messages of national betrayal written in lipstick on a mirror. Female duplicity and vanity are ineluctably linked to a sense of national risk.

Ealing's 1942 *Went the Day Well?* was a quasi-official film which carried the MoI stamp of approval (Aldgate and Richards, 1986, pp. 115–37). Its notion of national identity is represented by older women. The lady of the manor, the vicar's daughter and the postmistress all display heroism and the propensity for self-sacrifice; but they are all women 'of a certain age' whose maturity makes them reliable. There were other Ealing wartime films about which there is no hard evidence of government intervention, but which are thoroughly consonant with MoI policies on gender and realism. *The Foreman Went to France* (1942), for example, deals with an expedition to bring vital machinery into Britain. The hero is aided by a bright American (Constance Cummings), who is decorative but bears little moral weight. That is all carried by an old Frenchwoman. At the very cusp of the tale, she persuades her compatriots to sacrifice their belongings for the sake of the machines. The camera tracks in on her –

white-haired, wrinkled, shawled – as she urges, 'Allons, mes braves, c'est pour la patrie.' It is inconceivable in the Ealing scheme of things that such words could be uttered by any female who was not old, not ugly, and not past inspiring troublesome desire.

Other Ealing films, even those without war subjects, interpret women's social function in the same way. *Pink String and Sealing Wax* (1945), the studio's only full-blown wartime attempt at costume drama, is fuelled by distaste for the beautiful and amoral heroine. *Dead of Night* (1945) is particularly interesting. It is a portmanteau film, with stories by different directors, yet the overall colour of its gender politics is consistent. 'Christmas Party', directed by Cavalcanti, is about a young girl who runs from the sexual attentions of her male playmate and finds a secret room where the cruelties of the past can be discovered. Only a sexually innocent girl can gain access to such insights. In 'The Haunted Mirror', directed by Robert Hamer, it is the fiancée who purchases the fateful mirror; when it makes its frightful demands – 'give me blood' – *after* the marriage, the beleaguered husband tries to murder the wife, the importer of greed and lust. 'The Ventriloquist's Dummy', also directed by Cavalcanti, can be read as a sustained meditation on sexuality and its discontents. The dummy is a combination of woman and child; its size is small, its voice high-pitched, and it aspires to control its keeper (Michael Redgrave). In one scene, the dummy's wet mouth is shown in close-up, and its sharp teeth literally bite the hand that feeds it. The story can be read as a powerful fable about procreation, blood and the loss of power.

Most wartime Ealing films manifest a fearful and punitive response to female excess, and they mount a coherent case for its repression under conditions of national emergency. In some, MoI precepts are followed directly; in others, they are carried to extremes. Ealing was a British company, but American companies could sometimes be persuaded to part with money for MoI-approved projects. *Thunder Rock* (1942) was financed by MGM, but made by the Boulting brothers, who insisted that it was made at the direct behest of the MoI.[15] The visual style which the film deploys – the set was built at an angle of 12 degrees and called 'Boulting's Folly' – is avant-garde. The narrative structure is modernist as well. The film deals with an alienated intellectual living in a Canadian lighthouse who has peopled it with his imaginative reconstruction of the victims of an ancient shipwreck. One of the victims is an early feminist (Barbara Mullen), who suffers humiliation and imprisonment for her ideas. Her history is

more detailed and more pessimistic than the other tales; the whole narrative
is proportioned so as to discomfort those espousing radical sexual views.
Thunder Rock's aim was to inspire *déraciné* intellectuals, but it also
validated biological determinism.

All the films discussed so far were aimed at general audiences, and
attempted to raise the level of debate about the conduct of the war. *Millions
Like Us*, which was released by Gainsborough in 1943, was a different
case. It was commissioned by the government to address a female problem:
the low levels of recruitment and poor morale of women in factory work.
Frank Launder, who was honorary secretary of the Screenwriters' Association and a member of the Ideas Committee, liaised with the MoI when it
wished to contract the Association as a voluntary intellectual workforce.
The first project was *Millions Like Us*. It was shot in real factories and used
serving soldiers as extras, but the combination of documentary and fictional modes is inconsistently managed. The film also elides the discourses
of patriarchy, class and culture. Traditional working-class life is shown to
be dominated by the father: the new postwar life is structured by the dour
will of the new patriarch (Eric Portman). The ideal female behaviour is a
sweet vacuousness. The heroine Celia (Patricia Roc) is diffident, and her
body language, with its lowered gaze and closed posture, expresses a
demure primness. *Millions Like Us* suggests that female happiness can only
be assured within the normalizing rituals of society. The film was originally
intended to alleviate female anxieties about industrial labour; in the event,
it repositions those anxieties in the context of familial experience, where
they can be straightforwardly resolved.

Some commercial producers were unconvinced by the policies of the
MoI. Walter Mycroft disliked its 'intellectuals who have attached themselves like limpets in decorative clusters to film production'.[16] John Baxter
thought the Ministry was mistaken in its insistence on contemporary
realism, and he insisted that the Old Mother Riley films were better morale-
raisers than official propaganda. Gabriel Pascal argued that wartime
conditions intensified audience needs for non-realist films. Even Rank was
chary of the MoI's puritanism, and he emphasized the necessity of 'entertainment of integrity that will bring happiness'.[17] Maurice Ostrer too had
no time for the MoI, noting 'costume melodramas pack the box-office. I
suggest that this is an escape from the drabness of the present-day world of
clothes coupons and austerity.'[18]

The British Film Producers' Association (BFPA) was uncooperative towards the MoI. There was tension between its president Michael Balcon and the other members. The producers were prepared to band together to lobby the Ministry and to operate restrictive practices. For example, in 1941 the government wished to release 400 film technicians for active service, and to replace them with fully trained female workers, who would of course be paid less. The Association vetoed the suggestion. It was only interested in women as consumers, and in the type of visual pleasure for which they were prepared to pay.

As the war progressed, the BFPA became increasingly deaf to Ministry demands. The producers loudly ignored Jack Beddington's suggestion that a film be made about the changes in women's social roles.[19] The BFPA forced its president to deliver a stinging critique of the Ministry, and to suggest that the public 'was asking for films which took their minds off the tragedy now taking place'.[20] It responded very negatively to an MoI memo which warned that 'special support would be given to films dealing in a realistic way with everyday life'.[21]

During the war many producers took exception to government meddling in the free market, objecting to MoI desires to reform popular culture. The producers had developed a sophisticated sense of the changes in audience taste, and they wished to operate unhindered. They wanted to provide pleasure for the female audience, because that would have an automatic effect on profits. But producers (and directors) rarely angled their films specifically for women. Gainsborough was an exception, advising cinema managers about 'curiosity, that great feminine characteristic. Trade on this!'[22] Only Leslie Arliss, director of *The Man in Grey* (1943) and *The Wicked Lady*, welcomed the appellation of 'a women's director': 'I am not afraid of sentiment, and am working to overcome this shyness and to put unashamed feelings on the screen, rather than to depend on speed of action.'[23] Some career advantages would certainly accrue to those who produced images of women which were commensurate with government propaganda policy. Other producers were simply motivated by profit, or by the urge to make their voice heard in the prevailing babble of cultural forms.

If we now turn to the independent producer/directors, we can see that they changed in wartime too. I suggested in the previous chapter that, when he had control over the script as well as production and direction, Alexander Korda preferred to portray women as pleasure-giving yet duplicitous. His wartime career was complex, since he intercalated a period in Hollywood from 1941 to 1942; he also made a range of films for London Films, and one co-production with MGM, *Perfect Strangers* (1945), which is particularly interesting. These films vary in their style of representation according to their production context. Korda made the first part of *The Thief of Bagdad* (1940) in Britain. He directed the love scenes with June Duprez, and determined her function in the film (Kulik, 1975, pp. 224, 231). Duprez is an innocent houri: astonishingly beautiful, diaphanously clad, kittenishly playful. In the Paradise Garden, the script organizes the female questions and male responses thus:

> Who are you?/ Your slave.
> Where did you come from?/ From the other side of time.
> How long have you been searching?/ Since time began.
> Now that you've found me, how long will you stay?/ Till the end of time.

The exchange ends with a declaration by the male lover (John Justin): 'For me, there can be no more beauty in the world but yours.' To which Duprez replies: 'For me, there can be no more pleasure in the world than to please you.' It is a sublimely romantic scene, which is saturated with Korda's ideal of chivalric love and the absolute separation of male and female spheres.

Korda then went to Hollywood, where he shot *Lady Hamilton* (1941) and other films. While not technically a British film, it was made at the behest of the British government. However, it was not the MoI which promulgated the film, but the Foreign Office. The FO had a long history of involvement in the film industry that went back to the 1930s, when it showed a catholic and permissive tendency. This continued into the war period, and provided a strong contrast with the shrill moralism of the MoI. All that need be said here is that Lord Lothian, Britain's ambassador to Washington, castigated MoI films. He thought that there were other British film-makers who could persuade American audiences of the evils of neutrality. Lord Vansittart, the permanent head of the FO, replied that what was needed was a 'big film' which would 'get at the emotions'. He recommended Korda for the job, and that it be made in Hollywood by personnel who would 'be delighted to make films which would work our way'.[24] *Lady Hamilton* was this 'big film'.

Korda had remarked that 'propaganda ... can be bitter medicine. It needs sugar coating – and *Lady Hamilton* is a very thick coating of sugar indeed' (Olivier, 1982, p. 91). The propaganda message was cloaked in a disguise of female desire, romantic love and visual pleasure. The *mise en scène* foregrounded the erotic aspects of the tale, and Korda insisted that the sets should be richly evocative. *Lady Hamilton* suggests that women are not besmirched by sexual exchange. The argument about erotic love is augmented by one about class. It is Emma (Vivien Leigh) who can negotiate her way through any class dialect, and who can teach Nelson (Laurence Olivier) to inhabit the opera and the public house with equal ease. In the balcony scene on Nelson's return, the only reciprocal gaze is between Emma and the crowd; she circumvents the middle class. The 'glue' holding this complex transaction together is female desire. Exhibitors were encouraged to aim exclusively at the female audience, suggesting tie-ups with local beauty shops. It is of the greatest significance that this arrangement of class and gender obtained under the leadership of the FO. It could never have occurred under the MoI, in whose propaganda films women were rigidly clamped into a middle-class ethic of respectability, routine and impassivity.

Korda returned to Britain to make *Perfect Strangers* in affiliation with MGM. Shot under difficult conditions, but with considerable support from the Admiralty,[25] *Perfect Strangers* deals with the revolutionary effect the war has on the marriage of a lower-middle-class couple, Kathy and Robert (Deborah Kerr and Robert Donat). They are both transformed: she from an adenoidal homebody to a confident Wren; he from a shuffling valetudinarian to a sprightly officer. The script stresses, with an explicitness which is rare in modern-dress wartime films, the way that everyday domesticity impinges unequally on the woman. It hints at the absurdity of marital duty – of feeling obliged to curry or grant sexual favours.

And indeed the script is the rub. Korda directed *Perfect Strangers*, but the script and the original story were written by the feminist Clemence Dane, for which she received an Academy Award.[26] We shall return in Part II to the work of female scriptwriters during the war, but we can safely assume that *Perfect Strangers* is unlike the rest of Korda's canon because Dane was preoccupied by very different questions. Not for her the charms of the kitten-princess. Dane's film is about the demolition of the 'wall' of old-style marriage, and the wide blue expanse that opens up beyond.

Korda needed to control the script and be able to combine elements of production and direction in order to put his stamp on a film's gender politics. Since he was unable to achieve this in all his wartime films, his desired themes – of aristocratic style and courtly love – failed to develop in a consistent way. That was not the case with Michael Powell and Emeric Pressburger (The Archers). Due to Rank's munificence, they were able to combine production, directing and scriptwriting roles, and developed a position on women and culture which is thoroughly coherent. They too are preoccupied by aristocratic style, but nuance it more carefully than Korda. Their wartime films celebrate the fertility of the gentry topos, and females are both its inspiration and its apotheosis. *The Life and Death of Colonel Blimp* (1943) is an elegiac paean to a vanished officer class which could once have unified Europe. The three females attached to this group (all played by Deborah Kerr, in an audacious evocation of the Eternal-Feminine) challenge traditional roles: Edith by engaging in political action and marrying a foreigner; Barbara by marrying out of her generation; and 'Johnny' by her generally aggressive behaviour. The connection with the gentry also leads to self-realization for the heroine of *A Canterbury Tale* (1944). Through her acquaintance with the Squire / 'Glue Man', the landgirl Alison (Sheila Sim) comes into real contact with history. The Squire is a conduit via which a sense of the land can flow, and through him she gains real blessings, regardless of the absurdities of his misogyny. The clearest exegesis of the gentry theme is *I Know Where I'm Going!* (1945), in which wilful Joan Webster (Wendy Hiller) decides to marry sensibly for money. But she falls in love with Torquil, the virile, impecunious, charismatic Laird of the Isle. His mystical, aristocratic attraction encourages her to transcend the limitations of common sense – to hear the silkies and the eagles, and to believe in what she cannot see.

A Matter of Life and Death (1946) was first mooted in 1944 by Jack Beddington of the MoI, who wanted Powell and Pressburger to make a 'big film' which would build on improved Anglo-American relations and prepare audiences for the postwar international situation. It is a visual and intellectual extravaganza which celebrates the complexity of subjectivity. Within individual consciousness, history lies coiled like a snake; everyone can call up the resources of past culture. *A Matter of Life and Death* insists, with an intensity which is rare in wartime cinema, that the old social system is perfectly competent for the social job in hand. Rather like Matthew Arnold's 'aliens', who are a group of autonomous intellectuals, the film's enlightened individuals can come from any class. The Archers' system is essentially a courtly one, in which the woman is primarily an inspiration. At the symbolic apex of the social triangle, she is frozen in space and time, and her tear is caught at the heart of a rose. The disposition and balance of creativities in Powell and Pressburger's wartime films were such that they could construct a body of work in which women were accorded erotic power. Powell claimed that as his own victory, calling Pressburger 'the anti-feminist' (Powell, 1986, p. 411).

The aristocratic motif also proved useful for other independent producers. It was a very fertile topos in British cultural life, and one whose roots go back to the early nineteenth century. Since the Regency period, aristocratic style has been used as a way of accruing confidence and status by any group experiencing anxiety, and the aristocrat has acted as a potent symbol of marginality and energy. This trajectory clearly extends to World War II film culture. A whole range of 'wilful women' appear in films in a firm alliance with the aristocratic motif. This motif worked as an enabling device, permitting the appearance of women who were autonomous, resourceful and demanding, women who took as well as gave.

In the late 1930s, Herbert Wilcox, with his unerring sense of cultural exigencies, had produced images of the British aristocracy which had made it more bourgeois and domestic. During the war Wilcox sensed that more aggressive female stereotyping was in order, and, like Korda, The Archers and Gainsborough, he deployed the aristocracy as a useful symbol. In his *Yellow Canary* (1943), the heroine (Anna Neagle) actively engages her own destiny. She is allied to the aristocracy and has absorbed its style, thus ensuring her own survival. As an aristocratic socialite, she assumes the disguise of a quisling, and exposes traitors. In *I Live in Grosvenor Square* (1945), Neagle plays a Duke's daughter who wilfully plights her troth to a sergeant from the aptly named Flagstaff, Arizona. In both films, the bouncy female protagonist is empowered, by her aristocratic connections, to make surprising alliances which derail the predictable train of events. It is worth contrasting these with Wilcox's postwar *Piccadilly Incident* (1946). This deals with a Wren, supposed drowned, who returns from a desert island to find her aristocratic husband remarried. She has no aristocratic position of her own, and (it is no coincidence) displays a propensity for self-sacrifice which is absent from the other two heroines. The film ends on a very uncompromising note, with the judge (the husband's father) asserting the dominance of the law over human desire.

Gainsborough made three types of film during the war – costume pictures, modern-dress melodramas and comedies. Only the first deployed the aristocratic motif. However, the costume melodramas were a major innovation, and had a profound effect on the representation of women. They were very popular with female audiences, but received stingingly bad reviews from critics, because of their lack of realism and quality gloss. Gainsborough was organized in a classically 'Taylorist' manner, in which the creative decisions were made by the management and filtered down to the workforce below. Producers R. J. Minney, Ted Black and Maurice Ostrer chose the original projects, had a special relationship with the scriptwriters and kept the different sections of the workforce separate from one another. The Gainsborough melodramas were visually lush, and they contained outrageously wilful females who commit various sorts of hubris. They eventually come to grief, but have a wonderful time en route to their destruction. Within the Gainsborough film texts, there were contradictions between the different languages of script, décor and costume, but this in no way inhibited the audience's enjoyment.

The Gainsborough films containing the most 'wilful' women are also those that display the strongest use of the aristocratic motif. In *Fanny by Gaslight* (1944), *The Man in Grey* and *The Wicked Lady*, the aristocracy is deployed as a symbol of a dark, unspeakable sexuality which provides inspiration and sustenance for the heroines. Each of them goes on to make links with the social residuum – with public house society in *Fanny by Gaslight*, with the stage in *The Man in Grey* and with the highwayman in *The Wicked Lady*. The heroines are empowered to make these connections by the confidence they have gained from the symbolic exchange with aristocratic culture.

The Man in Grey begins with a flashback from the present war to the Regency period. It contains two heroines: one good aristocrat (Phyllis Calvert) and one bad bourgeoise (Margaret Lockwood). There are also two heroes: one good bourgeois (Stewart Granger) and one bad aristocrat (James Mason). The good woman first mates with the bad man, and the bad woman with the good man; then they all change over, and both the women are destroyed. The Lockwood character is fuelled by a powerful social and sexual hunger: she lies, cheats, steals and kills her friend. She gets a gruesome comeuppance, but gains sensual pleasure and social advancement en route to her doom. *The Wicked Lady*, which displays a similar cynicism towards monogamy and social power, was an immediate runaway success. It deals with Lady Barbara Skelton who, bored with her polite husband, amuses herself by keeping company with a highwayman, wearing trousers and killing her servants. What is remarkable about Barbara is her intense identification with her mother: in one prolonged scene she cradles her mother's ruby in the palm of her hand, and embarks on a life of crime to win it back. Of course, she dies in the end, but quickly; the intense sexual and sartorial pleasures she has experienced dominate most of the film's narrative.

The Wicked Lady privileges visual language. The set work of art director Maurice Carter suggests that history is a sensual cornucopia to which viewers can gain easy access. The costume designs of Elizabeth Haffenden, as I shall show in Part II, celebrate the opulence of the female body in a way hitherto absent from British film culture. *The Wicked Lady* provided pleasure for its audiences by its powerful evocation of *ease* – of the possibility that revenge could be straightforward, that desire could be slaked without effort and that there was such a thing as sexual luck.

There remains the amazing *Madonna of the Seven Moons*, which we must classify as a costume melodrama despite its contemporary setting. It deals with Maddalena, the schizoid wife of a wealthy Italian merchant. In her hidden self, she is Rosanna, the passionate and murderous doxy of a Florentine gangster. A childhood rape splits her psyche, and she wavers between her sacred and profane personae. The film proceeds, via costume, music and Roman Catholic ritual, to usher the audience into the country where they can, in their imagination, have what goods they want, eat whatever they wish and make love to whomever they desire. And without guilt, because the psyche in its wisdom has willed it so.

Madonna of the Seven Moons is preoccupied by the issue of women and free will. A range of females choose their own manner and dress: the gypsy mother (Nancy Price) makes a marvellous entrance, spitting with excellent aim and hefting a dead rat onto the dinner table. She insists on absolute equality in sexual fidelity: 'Fair's fair, my son. You had other women.' The daughter Angela (Patricia Roc), the servant Vittoria (Jean Kent), the older Mrs Fiske (Hilda Bayley) and even old Tessa (Amy Veness) behave how they like. But they are all single: the married women show damage when they attempt to combine wilfulness with monogamy.

Nesta Logan (Dulcie Gray) exhibits speech disturbance and stammers when her husband touches her, and Maddalena is destroyed when she tries to be both mother and lover. The symbols of the two states, the cross and the rose, can only lie together on her breast after she is dead.

With the second tranche of Gainsborough's wartime productions, the contemporary melodramas, the aristocratic motif is absent. Ted Black and Maurice Ostrer chose not to locate their tales of modern women in a class context. Instead, the films propose an essential femininity, which is predicated on sexual desire and which excludes female comradeship. *2000 Women* (1944) is set in a women's internment camp, and opens with a vicious war of words between two inmates. The two most extreme female types, the nun (Patricia Roc) and the floozie (Jean Kent), both fall for airmen and transform their lives: Roc decides not to take the veil, and Kent dies to save her lover. The film suggests, with some frankness, that when the commodity of the male body is in short supply, the laws of the sexual market will prevail. When that happens, class matters are of secondary importance. That also obtains in *Love Story* (1944). This film deals with pianist Lissa (Margaret Lockwood), who has a fatal heart condition, and airman Kit (Stewart Granger), who is going blind. Faced with respective futures of the morgue and St Dunstan's, they embark on an affair based on the premise of the song of the Miller of Dee: 'I care for nobody, no, not I / And nobody cares for me'. What gives *Love Story* its power (and doubtless accounts for its high place in the popularity charts) is that cynicism in love is shown to be corrosive. Kit and Lissa eventually enter into that world of mutual obsession which makes all other creatures shadowy. Kit's friend Judy (Patricia Roc) is also in love with him. She is combative, and she and Lissa fight over Kit like terriers over a bone. *Love Story* insists that female friendship, like the Miller-of-Dee philosophy, is not something which women can afford under conditions of sexual emergency.

This philosophy motivates *They Were Sisters* (1945), which was also very popular. This deals with three sisters, Lucy, Vera and Charlotte, played by Phyllis Calvert, Anne Crawford and Dulcie Gray. Charlotte is maltreated by vile husband Geoffrey (James Mason) and dies. The flighty Vera runs off to the Veldt with her lover, and 'good' sister Lucy, who is childless, acquires all her sisters' children. What might on the face of it seem to be a tale about sisterly affection is in fact a story about the ruthlessness of desire. Charlotte forbids the sisters to criticize her beloved

Geoffrey, and this leads indirectly to her downfall. Lucy wants children and pets above all: she gets them in exchange for her two tiresome siblings. *They Were Sisters* is extremely cynical about the family and its romances. An inspired piece of casting gives Geoffrey an unhealthy love for his own daughter, played by Mason's then wife Pamela Kellino.

The modern Gainsborough melodramas do not need to use aristocratic symbolism as a way of disguising or ratifying female desire. Indeed, they argue that any class issue is irrelevant to modern women competing for diminishing erotic returns. The third tranche of its wartime product, comedy, also avoids an explicit class theme. There were four groups of wartime comedies at Gainsborough: the films of Will Hay, the Crazy Gang, Tommy Handley and Arthur Askey. Women play a minor role in the first three groups, but they are a major component of the Askey films, which are less permissive in their social attitudes. Askey films such as *Ghost Train* (1941) and *I Thank You* (1941) endorse social consensus. *King Arthur Was a Gentleman* (1942) and *Miss London Ltd* (1943) evince extreme anxiety about women, and both narratives are structured around a quality contrast between the petite heroine (Evelyn Dall) and her buxom friend (Anne Shelton). *Bees in Paradise* (1944) is particularly important. It is set on an island ruled by women, where men are required to commit suicide three months after the wedding, a fact that makes them understandably reluctant to marry. The island contains female brick-layers, potters and rugby players; it evokes a dystopian Britain where the law of the father has given way to what one native calls 'the law of the beehive, which is that woman is paramount in all things'. To Askey's horror, the women behave like men: they comment that one of his friends 'has an A1 body and an F4 mind'. Askey is forcibly married to the Queen (Ann Shelton), who is twice his size. Wearing women's clothes, he scuttles off when she breaks down the bedroom door.

Ealing had avoided the use of aristocratic symbolism in its representa-tion of women, concentrating instead on the anxieties of the middle class. Cineguild was the only other company to do this in wartime. Founded as part of Rank's Independent Producers Ltd, its chief personnel were David Lean, Anthony Havelock-Allen and Ronald Neame (with Noël Coward informally attached). Cineguild made *This Happy Breed* (1944) and *Blithe Spirit* (1945), which were joint Two Cities/Cineguild productions, and *Brief Encounter*.

Cineguild's attitude to filming was uncompromisingly self-indulgent, as the pragmatic Betty Box recalled:

> You can bet your bottom dollar that Cineguild never did anything under twenty weeks ... Cineguild were always the clever boys of the organisation. I have seen David Lean sit on the set the whole day and not shoot anything and say 'Oh God! Give me inspiration!' It's all very well, isn't it! Why didn't he get the inspiration before he started shooting? (Macnab, 1993, p. 95)

Cineguild's high-art perspective was combined with a rigorously class-specific approach. All the films made by the group attempted to define particular middle-class fractions, to delineate their language and above all to *defend* them. But they are particularly conservative on women who are imbricated into middle-class ethics. *This Happy Breed* places women centrally in the lower-middle-class home; but they have no meaning outside. This is the morality which lies behind *Brief Encounter*.

This film provoked wide-ranging responses. The preview audiences in Rochester were boisterous: 'isn't 'e ever going to 'ave it orf with 'er?' (Hoare, 1995, p. 361). French critics were bewildered by some aspects of the film: one headline argued 'Laura A Eu Tort'. Even the star, Trevor Howard, could not understand: 'Why doesn't he fuck her? All this talk about the wood being damp' (Brownlow, 1997, p. 199). But what is clear is that one of Laura's tasks is to defend middle-class style: the right hat, the right present, the right timbre of voice. And she has to defend its culture too: hence the laughter at the lowbrow *Flames of Passion*. Laura's judgement of other women is severe. The middle-aged woman earning a crust by playing the cello and the cinema organ elicits the most savage mirth, presumably because she is playing instruments more properly reserved for males.

The turning-point in Laura's affair is the return of her lover's friend, Stephen (Valentine Dyall). Laura has decided to act on her desires and has returned to the borrowed flat. Dyall returns virtually at the moment of consummation, and she escapes down the tradesman's entrance(!) In the only scene in the film not witnessed by Laura, Stephen sneeringly berates his friend, and his tirade is a combination of bombast, jealousy and hypocrisy. His voice is unopposed.

So far we have seen that some commercial producers used aristocratic motifs as an enabling device for the representation of wilful women. Other companies wanted to purge women's images of moral taint, and they used the discourse of middle-class reticence and restraint to do so. However, some companies used working-class registers and body language as a covert means of describing unruly women. The Gert and Daisy films were made by Butcher's, and did excellent business despite having absolutely minimal status. The duo (who were Jack Warner's sisters) had done music hall and made popular lowbrow radio programmes, and their films – *Gert and Daisy's Weekend* (1941), *Gert and Daisy Clean Up* (1942), *It's in the Bag* (1943) – give us unique access to a working-class culture no longer in existence. Gert and Daisy display a portly nonchalance in the face of polite society. They are exceptionally rude, and the height of their ambition is to speak their minds, to be rid of men and to have clean 'pinners' of a Friday. Their first two films, which were scripted by Kathleen Butler, are firmly anchored in contemporary events. *It's in the Bag* is their most interesting film, since it is full of sexual innuendo. It is about an old dress belonging to Gert and Daisy's grandmother. She is thought to have hidden a fortune in the bustle, and the film is a sustained double entendre about the riches (real or imagined) hidden in the mounds and recesses of the female form.

We saw in the previous chapter that the 1930s was characterized by a rich variety of 'clusters' of female stereotypes inhabiting specific genres – exotics, wholesome girls, ladylike ladies and so on. The structure of the industry encouraged actresses to remain within one stereotype, once it had been established as profitable. In the war period, everything changed. The range of female stereotypes became much more narrow, there was less variety within each category, and the clusters of females were much less class-specific. However, actresses had more leeway to shift between categories and were less typecast. Phyllis Calvert, for example, usually played 'good' characters but was also able to play the schizoid heroine in *Madonna of the Seven Moons*. Changes in the star system and contractual arrangements within the Rank empire were partially responsible.

In the 1930s, major cultural and economic capital had been made from the exotic or foreign actresses who were imported. This group was almost entirely absent from British film culture in wartime. There were a few foreign character actresses – Françoise Rosay, Lilli Palmer, Mai Zetterling – who were offered roles as solid, respectable Europeans. But it was not part of the repertoire of British cinema in wartime to require exotic alien females.

The roles created for women in the MoI films had a very clear 'family resemblance'. Across a range of studios and genres, Ministry attitudes to women were perceptible in the speech patterns and body language of the actresses paid to play their roles. The actresses' function was to remind audiences, on behalf of the government, of the supposed advantages accruing to patriarchal structures, and the ills likely to befall those who challenged them. What should be stressed is how much is *missing* from the ratified women in MoI films. They do not laugh; they do not move with any sensual grace; they do not enjoy their own bodies or anyone else's. They are respectable, and never reckless in love. Half of their identity has been sliced away, in the interests of the state.

Another group which represents an extension of the 1930s Wholesome Sensible Girls are the strong yet feminine women – roles which require females to be impassive, and to show grace under pressure without sacrificing their surface beauty. Actresses who play such roles include Valerie Hobson, Deborah Kerr, Wendy Hiller and Penelope Dudley Ward. They are not ingénues, since they are characters capable of duplicity and determination. Their gaze and body language are direct and, although they are attractive, their sexuality is in abeyance – held in reserve for later.

There is a small group of 'split' heroines in wartime films, who are riven by contradictory desires which they cannot resolve. The heroines of *Brief Encounter* and *Madonna of the Seven Moons* are fatally split: Laura Jesson has to rid herself of her profane self, and Maddalena dies because she cannot exist in a state of internal war. In both these films, the heroines are directed so as to deploy the upper registers of the voice, which attests to a sense of strain and anxiety. More importantly, both heroines are hypersensitive to music, and use it as a way of gaining access to the forbidden world outside common sense. Laura uses Rachmaninov, Maddalena employs popular music. The split between Maddalena's frigid bourgeois side and her wild gypsy self surfaces for the first time while she is playing the piano. Initially, with her whole body held in rigid tension, she plays a classical piece. Then the tune changes to a popular ditty, and the impassioned self emerges, full of confidence, desire and expressivity. The whole narrative takes off from that moment, and the music leads her to her doom.

The Wicked Lady roles are a small but intense and innovatory group. These females have unstable psychic identities, and can come from any class. They are the only group to experience the pleasures of consummation outside the law. Most of Margaret Lockwood's wartime roles, Patricia Roc's character in *Love Story*, Jean Kent's and Anne Crawford's roles – all these represented women who were physically confident, with fast, balanced movements and a poised, symmetrical carriage. Their gaze pattern is firm and still, and is often focused on the middle distance rather than on their male partners.

We can conclude that the war period gave rise to some major innovations in the roles women had to play in films. In contrast to the volatile 1930s, the war was a period of unparalleled control for the film industry – control by the MoI over certain types of feature production, and control by the newly confident producer/director teams over their patterns of production. The fertility of the aristocratic topos was much in evidence during the war, as a means of firming up certain sexual themes or smuggling in otherwise unacceptable debates about gender and class. On one level, the aristocratic theme operated as a protective device cloaking the most threatening group of all – women who wanted to lead their own lives. Such a group could not issue forth naked into the world of art.

Notes

1. BBFC Scenario Notes, 4 July 1941, report on *Thunder Rock*, in BFI Library.
2. *Ibid.*, 29 December 1943.
3. PRO (Public Record Office, Kew) INF 1/724, 1 June 1939, recommendations 28, 29, 31.
4. PRO INF 1/318.
5. *Ibid.*, unsigned handwritten MoI memo dated 1 May 1940. On the Bartlett issue, see an exchange of letters between the Parliamentary Secretary and the Director-General, November 1940.
6. PRO INF 1/867, Policy Committee document, undated, but from internal evidence, January 1940.
7. PRO INF 1/196, undated MoI memo, which from internal evidence must be from early 1940.
8. *Ibid.*, MoI memo, 18 April 1941.
9. PRO INF 1/251, MoI memo, 27 May 1941.
10. *Kinematograph Weekly*, 30 July 1942 and 6 July 1943.
11. PRO INF 1/867, Feature Films Policy, March 1943.
12. PRO BW 4/21, MoI memo, July 1942.
13. PRO BW 4/40, Holmes to Bundy, 18 August 1944.
14. See Mass-Observation File Report no. 458, *MoI Shorts*. For a full survey of official films, see Thorpe and Pronay (1980). Of particular interest here is *They*

Also Serve (1940), which was directed by Ruby Grierson for her brother's company Realist Films. It was dedicated to 'the housewives of Britain'. The copy in the Imperial War Museum gives the credit as 'R. Grierson'.

15. Bernard Lewis, *Always and Everywhere*, unpublished manuscript in BFI Library, p. 171. For other evidence on official support for the film, see PRO LAB 26/35 and PRO BW 4/18.
16. *Kinematograph Weekly*, 14 January 1939.
17. *Ibid.*, 16 August 1945.
18. *Ibid.*, 20 December 1945.
19. Minutes of the BFPA Executive Council, 7 May 1942. See also 19 March 1942, where they scotch Beddington's suggestion that a film be made about Mary Kingsley and her life on the Gold Coast.
20. *Ibid.*, 25 June 1942.
21. *Ibid.*, 13 July 1942.
22. Publicity material for *Madonna of the Seven Moons*, in BFI Library.
23. *Picturegoer*, 3 April 1943.
24. PRO FO 371/22839, memo from Vansittart, 21 October 1939.
25. British Council Programme note, microfiche of *Perfect Strangers*, BFI Library.
26. For useful material on Dane, see Morgan (1994), pp. 61–6.

3

The Postwar Period: Settlement and Retrenchment

The British film industry was in economic crisis from 1947, due to the Treasury's mishandling of its relationship with Hollywood. The BFPA was unfocused in its policies, and industry personnel were in turmoil as servicemen returned from the war. The industry also had to digest wartime social changes, and represent them in palatable ways. These factors had profound effects on the representation of women in films.

The postwar settlement in Britain was premised on a return to traditional family values. The war had provided a watershed in many women's sexual and work experience, but many of the old class antagonisms remained unaddressed. There is ample evidence (from Mass-Observation, surveys and journalism) to suggest that in the postwar period the population desired a return to an improved domestic sphere, and was resistant to state enterprises such as British restaurants and community laundries. These may have been expedient in wartime, but were widely felt to provide facilities inferior to the privacy of home. Indeed, after 1948 the postwar Labour government did not significantly extend the incursions of the state into domestic life. For many, wartime social changes were neither permanent nor deep-rooted. The wartime liberalization in sexual behaviour did not generate a new radicalism in sexual politics. In general, film culture responded conservatively to changes in women's roles. Films from several production companies suggested that female excess in sexual or consumer matters should be rigorously punished; concentration on deviant females reached a peak in 1948/9.

First of all, we need to consider the attitude of the government to film producers. During the war, the MoI had influenced every level of feature film production, and its policies had been unevenly assimilated. After the war, the Central Office of Information took over the MoI's job, but its staff were not in accord with the new government's policies.[1] The COI was as cynical about the competence of the mass audience as the MoI had been. The Board of Trade was even less helpful, since it thought that 'most of the people engaged in the industry are rogues of one kind or another'.[2] It was riven by conflicting schools of thought. One championed Del Giudice and his brand of quality film, arguing that Britain should continue to specialize in films like *Henry V*.[3] Another influential caucus petitioned for Alexander Korda, arguing that he was a better businessman than the other producers.[4] Sir Stafford Cripps favoured J. Arthur Rank.[5]

For the Board of Trade, women were merely potential consumers, as evidenced by its support for Herbert Wilcox's fashion epic, *Maytime in Mayfair*.[6] Generally, the Board held views about national identity and the cinema which were at odds with commercial instincts. Stafford Cripps argued that film should be a combination of education, tourism and national self-promotion:

> The vast majority of our citizens never have the chance to move outside the narrow field of our own locality, and the films provide them with a window through which they can glimpse the greater world that lies beyond their own limited view … films should become the demonstration of British culture and tradition to the people of other countries. It is not propaganda that we want in our films, but a national interpretation of what is good and interesting, amusing and hopeful in our cultural and historical heritage.[7]

The BFPA had a tense relationship with the government, particularly with the Board of Trade.[8] Film producers in the postwar period were disinclined to favour socialism, and the BFPA's Executive Council wasted energy in acrimonious exchanges with the government, instead of formulating a coherent policy. The producers were in combative mood with the BBFC too. Their wartime relationship had been fairly emollient: under conditions of national emergency the censorship behests of government had been respected by almost everyone. The BBFC's postwar Scenario Reports are very conservative on social matters, and they scorned any scripts which celebrated mass culture.[9] It is possible that their political bile was exacerbated by the 1945 election results. But the BBFC's readers were very conservative on sexual matters too. They saw themselves as gatekeepers of public morality, turning back the tide of permissiveness which had been in flood during the war. They objected to *Caravan*'s torrid love scenes, naked bathing and prostitutes; they wanted to excise the duel with whips in *Idol of Paris*; they would tolerate no love affairs in *The Bad Lord Byron* (1948).[10] The producers felt confident enough to flout BBFC strictures, and project after project bore no sign of them.

So the postwar film industry developed a hostile relationship with a number of government bodies. Official policy on film met with no coherent response from the industry. Economic crises and producers' alienation from bureaucratic institutions meant that competition shook loose a wide variety of approaches, which fall into broad patterns according to their director, screenwriter or production company.

If we turn first to those director/producers who had taken such coherent positions in the 1930s and the war, we can see evidence of a clear sea-change. Herbert Wilcox, for example, had possessed an outstanding sense of the anxieties produced by social change. In the 1930s, he shifted the image of his wife Anna Neagle from romping hoyden to stately icon. During the war, other film-makers were finding aristocratic motifs profitable, so Wilcox attached Neagle to that theme. In the postwar period, he changed tack again. He made three outstandingly popular 'London' films – *The Courtneys of Curzon Street* (1947), *Spring in Park Lane* (1948) and *Maytime in Mayfair* (1948) – in which Michael Wilding starred opposite Neagle, who was then in her mid-forties. Wilcox was ubiquitous during production, maintaining a solicitous regard for Neagle and organizing all shots to favour her (Kochberg, 1990). By now, he had established a loyal ensemble of technicians who were paid between films and he exerted total control over the filming process: 'Herbert decided where the cut would come … he knew exactly what he wanted … he stood behind the cameraman, to decide on camera positioning.'[11]

The London films are escapist romances: Neagle called them 'pleasant films about pleasant people'.[12] Their glossy appearance is partly because they were filmed at the technically superior MGM studios. They are unusually self-referential: one character comments that the heroine 'reminds me a bit of Anna Neagle', and another thinks that the hero 'looks like Michael Wilding'. The dance sequences in *Maytime in Mayfair* quote Astaire and Rogers numbers, and the mistaken-identity motifs are nuanced like Hollywood comedies of the 1930s. The films were targeted at the female audience, and Wilcox fine-tuned them: 'you must know that the goods you are turning out are aimed at the market for which you are designing them'.[13]

The Courtneys of Curzon Street, which was the biggest box-office success of its year, dealt with the marriage of an Irish maidservant (Anna Neagle) to an aristocrat (Michael Wilding). Throughout the narrative's 45 years, Neagle functions as a kind of ideological bulldozer. Everything is crushed in its wake: the Irish accent, the class system, 1920s hairstyles. Neagle's appearance transmogrifies through decades of fashion, but the essence remains the same: a femininity outside class, time and desire. *Spring in Park Lane* was also the *Kineweekly* Top Moneymaker of its year. It purported to be about cross-class marriage, but was in fact about the difficulties of the postwar settlement. Wilding plays an aristocrat disguised as a footman who falls in love with Neagle, the niece of a diamond magnate. Initially, it is the hero who is winsome and sub-servient: his repertoire of facial expressions is feminine, and depends on an averted gaze and unruly mouth. In one scene, Neagle plays the grand piano while Wilding polishes the floor beneath. He gradually wriggles nearer to her, until he is simultaneously kissing her foot and looking up her skirt. The whole narrative turns round from that point: Neagle falls in love and becomes less assertive, whereas Wilding becomes more so. He sheds his disguise and comes into his inheritance, both of gender and class. The old order is reasserted with extra vigour, because comedy has temporarily suspended it.

Maytime in Mayfair, a heady brew of high fashion, camp sensibility and menopausal desire, was also an enormous hit. The plot deals with a fashion house run by Eileen Grahame (Neagle) which is inherited by Michael Gore-Brown (Wilding). Wilding falls in love with Neagle and nearly ruins the firm. En route we see some fashion ensembles by Molyneux and others. Harold Wilson, then president of the Board of Trade, was often on set to see how British couture was being sold (Kochberg, 1990). The script contains some nice double entendres. One of the camper designers sings to his customers, and Neagle knowingly warns that 'we must not overwork that glorious organ of yours'. Gore-Brown and his cousin are afraid that the rag trade will impugn their heterosexuality ('is my slip showing?') and they react in horror to the gay Darcy Davenport (Peter Graves), who tells women what they want to hear. The lines of sexual difference are drawn in a conservative way. Eileen Grahame may be a mature career woman, but she is not happy until the final wedding scene.

Maytime in Mayfair is a sustained meditation on the New Look.

Audiences are shown what it means when a skirt is cut on the bias and when ruching is added, and they are told about boned bodices and how it feels to wear one. But all the major fashion and romantic sequences take place in the fantasy mode, and are signalled as such by slow motion, dissolves or mist. The audience is subliminally instructed that romance and high fashion are of the other, and not the real, world. Wilcox's postwar films are unique for the intensity of regard which they give to older women. They evoke a world of residual class and gender values, and suggest that middle-class insecurity could be assuaged by making a minor settlement with the new ways.

Alexander Korda, like Wilcox, had a successful prewar and wartime career, but in the postwar period, he lost his way. Korda was a favourite at the Treasury and at the Board of Trade,[14] but not with audiences; the times were out of joint for films which combined gentry motifs with kittenish females. London Films was the production company behind some important films, such as *Mine Own Executioner* (1947) and *Gone to Earth* (1950), but Korda took no part in their production and cannot be construed as their author.

In all the postwar films in which he had a hand, Korda presented women as beautiful static victims. In *Anna Karenina* (1948), he took executive decisions on the script, and, in order to throw greater weight onto the Anna/Vronsky relationship, omitted most of the Levin story from the original novel (Tabori, 1959, p. 262). The script suggested that Anna experienced sexual pleasure, whereas Tolstoy's heroine did not. Yet the disposition of the camerawork and the *mise en scène* dominate her, and she is presented as someone whose chief function in life is to be looked at, rather than to feel. In consequence, her actions seem merely the result of feminine whim.

In the postwar period, Korda was using his female actresses as a touchstone for assertions about the desirability of emotional control. At the same time, he wanted them to be assimilated into the *mise en scène*, and to contribute to seamless films for the international market. *An Ideal Husband* (1948) has sumptuous décor and costumes, but the female protagonists are even more mannered and artificial than in the original Wilde play. The film is visually impressive but emotionally null. Korda returned to real historical events with *Bonnie Prince Charlie* (1948), but the film founders artistically because there is an imbalance between its political and emotional levels of operation. Clemence Dane, who had worked for Korda before, had a contract for the script, and parts of it display the verve and style we have come to expect of her. For example, Flora MacDonald (Margaret Leighton) tells the Prince (David Niven):

> A week ago I had my life snug and warm about me like a furred cloak with nought in it but kind memories and clear, firm hopes. Then you came like a high wind and blew my cloak away. Where is my past? Emptied out of my mind. Where is my future? Blown away to nowhere. . . . If you fail, still your life is filled, if only with eternal grief. But my life stays empty. I am no question mark on the page of history. I am just the one whose cloak was blown away.

Melodramatic it may be, but it has a degree of radicalism, both social and sexual. However, Dane did not write the whole script; bad managerial timing meant that other writers were brought in, and there was never a coherent screenplay (Niven, 1973, pp. 258–9). Consequently, *Bonnie Prince Charlie* is lumpy, albeit with sublime moments. Korda's last film of the decade, *The Elusive Pimpernel* (1950), is inferior to his 1930s *Pimpernel* films. The authorship of the film is a moot point, and it could be argued that it is really Powell and Pressburger's film. Sir Percy (David Niven) negotiates his way through various class discourses, but the female leads are less complex than in the earlier Pimpernel films, and the vitality of the Regency theme is vitiated. Korda's postwar films are inert, because the discourses about sexual and class power never coincide.

Michael Balcon's postwar arrangements at Ealing were identical to those he had developed during the war: a small creative élite and a large administrative staff which followed his intellectual leadership, with little autonomy being granted to separate studio units. Diana Morgan was the only woman screenwriter, and she had problems because much of the intellectual life of the studio revolved around the French Club, a drinking côterie frequented by film intellectuals (Drazin, 1998, pp. 235–44). Morgan never attended, 'because I had a husband and a child, so I went home'. Balcon himself became increasingly conservative on gender matters, and Morgan noted that 'Ealing was a very male studio . . . they didn't like actresses at all. So many of their films are male-dominated' (MacFarlane, 1997, p. 420).

Ealing's postwar films have the same preoccupations as the war years: with creating a taxonomy of the middle class, and with censuring profane females. *The Loves of Joanna Godden* (1947) made significant alterations to the novel by Sheila Kaye-Smith. The story of a woman farmer who decided not to marry the father of her child, it ended with a celebration of female independence. But the Ealing script insists that the heroine (Googie Withers) is 'a mare who ain't never been properly broke in, and she wants a strong man to do it'. She cannot gain acceptance in the male domain of farming, and is lonely in her single state. Joanna remains virtuous, and the sexuality is parcelled off onto her wanton sister (Jean Kent), who is dispatched to the outer moral darkness amidst images of pestilence and incinerated animal corpses.

Frieda (1947) has a similar agenda. The German heroine is the victim of her husband, brother and British class society. The role was given to the Swedish Mai Zetterling, who suggested that Ealing was too prejudiced to cast a German actress (Zetterling, 1985, p. 67). Frieda represents a specific type of womanliness (timid, blonde, self-sacrificing) which the narrative ultimately celebrates. She is favourably juxtaposed to the career woman (Flora Robson), who is unflatteringly lit and dressed throughout, and who is presented as consumed by sexual frustration and Vansittartism. The heroines of *It Always Rains on Sundays* (1947) and *Saraband for Dead Lovers* (1948) are fatally split. In *It Always Rains on Sundays*, Rose has a past blonde self who experiences sexual pleasure with wide boy John McCallum. Her present brunette self is a bored but dutiful wife whose first utterance is 'Any murders?' Once the blonde self erupts into the life of the brunette self, disaster ensues. *Saraband for Dead Lovers* contains two heroines, who are both paralysed by the split between their appearance and essence. Sophia Dorothea (Joan Greenwood) has a chaste exterior but raging sexuality within. Countess Platen (Flora Robson) is presented as an ageing harridan who feels inappropriate desire. She confesses to her young lover that 'I love you, but I shan't be a woman for much longer.'

In the Ealing comedies of the period, women are a minor component of the overall project. The comedies make challenges and adjustments to the social system, and they rely on a set of stable assumptions about gender. In *Hue and Cry* (1947) and *Whisky Galore* (1949), the women's role is to fit in decoratively. In *Kind Hearts and Coronets* (1949), the only d'Ascoyne female is a suffragette, whose balloon is fatally pierced by the hero's arrow. The two female leads are rigorously differentiated: the glacial Edith (Valerie Hobson) and the lascivious Sibella (Joan Greenwood). The ending is constructed around the impossibility of possessing both: 'How easy 'twould be to love either / Were t'other dear charmer away.' *Passport to Pimlico* (1949) contains the eccentric Professor Hatton-Jones (Margaret Rutherford), whose intellectual fervour is vitiated by battiness. The director Henry Cornelius had originally wanted Alistair Sim, but he was unavailable. In a revealing aside, the film's scriptwriter argued that the translation would be simple, since 'the professor's change of sex necessitated the changing of just one single word' (Clarke, 1974, p. 161). It is the very blandness of the remark which is interesting. The gender change makes a vital difference, but it was politic to hush it up.

In Ealing films, the only ratified female conditions were virginity or respectable conjugality. Any departure from these norms met with severe punishment, and this held good for Ealing films by a range of directors, set in a variety of historical periods, and dealing with all classes. The most extreme example is *Scott of the Antarctic* (1948), which was a Royal Command Performance film. *Scott* should be interpreted as a paean to male bonding, and it evinces the utmost unease about women. One of the heroes can see 'the place where the letter's going to, I mean, where she is; but her face is always misty'. And the female body is presented as a source of anxiety. In a key scene, Ponting (Clive Norton) delivers a long rhyming monologue. The one he selects is about the difficulties of wriggling into his fur sleeping bag and ends, 'so the fur side is the outside and the skin side is the inside'. This could be read as a covert metaphor for female genitalia. They are the site of danger and distaste, if the manner of the verse's delivery and of the explorers' sniggering response is taken into account.

There were other patterns of gender representation elsewhere. Independent Producers Ltd was set up by J. Arthur Rank at Pinewood. Each group had artistic autonomy, while Rank provided an administrative 'umbrella' which relieved directors and producers of financial and distribution worries. As we have seen, Michael Powell and Emeric Pressburger (The Archers) produced films during the war which assimilated women into an argument about élite cultures and eroticism. The postwar films refined the position. All the protagonists are on the edge, either literally or metaphorically, and the emotional temperature of the films is volatile.

Black Narcissus (1947) should be interpreted as an intense meditation upon female sexuality. It argues that female desire is robust, and will surface in inimical conditions. Two little scenes instance this. An early shot juxtaposes Mr Dean (David Farrar) and Angu Ayah (May Hallatt) against a mural in the erstwhile harem. This is a faded erotic fresco, and Ayah exchanges a marvellously complicitous glance with Dean: old as she is, she remembers enough to facilitate others' pleasure. A second telling scene shows Kanchi (Jean Simmons), before the arrival of the Young General (Sabu), dancing alone: self-appeasing, self-delighting, the curves of her body complement the architecture. *Black Narcissus* is unusual in the priority it gives to female desire. But it flattens out the difference between individuals, arguing that although there *appear* to be two kinds of women – those who use the talisman of a lipstick and those who use a prayerbook – the women are the same beneath their dress or habit. The film suggests that all females require a Mr Dean: priapic, rude, domineering and with legs to die for.

The final scene of *Black Narcissus* was originally a cathartic confrontation between Sister Clodagh (Deborah Kerr) and Mother Superior (Nancy Roberts), when the younger woman breaks down and confesses the erotic longings prompted by the House of Women. This would have balanced the red hysteria scene of Sister Ruth, especially as its dominant colour was black. However, Powell decided to end the film with Jack Cardiff's shot of rainwater on a gunnera leaf (Cardiff, 1996, p. 91). This meant that the tensions were unresolved and the film shimmers on without a resolution.

The Archers' postwar films do recognize women as erotic beings; but that is all they are. The problems occur when the female protagonists want something besides love. *The Red Shoes* (1948) deals with ballerina Vicky (Moira Shearer) who wants to honour her own artistic creativity. To the question 'Why do you want to dance?' she retorts, 'Why do you want to live?' It is as unconscious and as necessary as breathing. Vicky's suicide is frequently attributed to her inability to choose between art and biological destiny. But great care is required in interpreting the final scenes. Vicky is not forbidden by her husband Julian (Marius Goring) to dance. Indeed, he says she may dance anywhere in the world; she simply must not dance for Lermotov (Anton Walbrook), because Lermotov has slighted Julian. Vicky is sacrificed not on the altar of domesticity but of male rivalry. The two men have the same love-object, and it is torn to bits in the competition.

Pressburger had been involved in a *Red Shoes* project since 1939. He kept it in his mind until 1946, finally writing the script unaided (Mac-Donald, 1994, pp. 274–80). It must not be forgotten that all Pressburger's intellectual instincts were bohemian. He was interested in art's autonomy, and thought that domesticity was inimical to any creative drive. In *The Red Shoes* it is bourgeois family life, with its suffocatingly mean horizons, which rings the death-knell of creativity. To Pressburger, art was everything, for male and female artists alike. Even Powell concurred that this was the film's main theme: 'We had all been told for ten years to go out and die for freedom and democracy, and now that the war was over, *The Red Shoes* told us to go out and die for art' (Powell, 1986, p. 653).

Powell and Pressburger then left Rank and made *The Small Back Room* (1949) for Korda. Powell was enthusiastic about Nigel Balchin's novel, and it is easy to see why: in a study of male insecurity and self-loathing, the protagonist Sammy constantly seeks greater risks (both physical and emotional) in order to distract himself from pain. Pressburger cared little for the project and, unusually for him, conceded passively to the BBFC's demand that the couple not live together 'in sin'. Kathleen Byron, who played the heroine Sue, suggested that censorship demands be overcome by having the lovers live in adjoining flats (Mac-Donald, 1994, p. 300). This was an inspired idea, since it permitted the construction of neutral emotional territory. When their relationship is operational, the telltale signs in Sammy's flat are Sue's photograph, her white cat and a saucer of milk. When the affair is on the rocks, these signs are absent. Impassivity characterizes Sue's behaviour. Sammy should not drink whisky; she sympathetically asks if he wants some. He is paranoid about being abandoned; she is repeatedly late for dates. He wants to be loved; she is laconic. The film suggests that she is as much the source of his pain as his original injury. She is his psychic Tin Foot.

Cineguild, too, operated under Independent Producers Ltd, and had been formed by Anthony Havelock-Allen, David Lean and Ronald Neame in 1944. Havelock-Allen thought that 'films which were artistically and culturally of the highest importance were made by producers not conditioned by the needs and notions of the front office of a major company'.[15] David Lean was in broad agreement with his cultural politics. Ronald Neame had considerable intellectual ambition, and applied to the cinema Bevin's remark about Britain's artisanal excellence:

We have never been able to compete with Americans in mass-producing articles. But when it comes to hand-made articles, everyone turns to Britain . . . let our films also be good hand-made articles, each individual and special in its own way.[16]

Cineguild exemplified an art for art's sake position, which insisted on the *ambiguity* of the handmade artefact. Its meaning was infinite because the conditions of its production contradicted the procedures of industrial capital.

But for Lean and his colleagues, the complex cluster of aesthetic feelings about the art-object was displaced onto the female psyche. All the female leads in Cineguild films are characterized by ambiguity, either in their motives or morality. Like a great painting, they are mysterious and endlessly significant. *Great Expectations* (1946) is masterly in its reinterpretation of Victorian realism. Lean and Neame loathed the first script by Clemence Dane, and they scripted the Dickens novel themselves by 'headlining' key scenes, filling in the visual detail and reconstructing the characters (Brownlow, 1997, pp. 207–8). The three female leads differ significantly from the book. The older Estella (Valerie Hobson) has a frigid composure which was the result of Lean's direction. Hobson reported that he was 'cold' to her: 'whatever talents I may have had, he nullified'. Her demeanour was, Lean said, 'exactly what's needed, someone without any heart or feeling at all. Splendid' (*ibid.*, p. 219). Miss Havisham (Martita Hunt) was encouraged to build up a private world between herself, the sets and art director John Bryan, and turned in a performance of astonishing self-sufficiency. Lean directed the young Estella (Jean Simmons) so as to obscure her motivation; her character is never fully displayed or comprehended.

This pattern was repeated in *Blanche Fury* (1948), which was directed by Marc Allegret. The film had scripting problems, and the successive versions indicate that it was the concealment, rather than the display, of the heroine's motives which was intended. The film encourages the audience to identify with its unfathomable protagonist (Valerie Hobson) by using distorted point-of-view shots and privileged flashbacks. But these are undercut by the script and the manner of its delivery, so that the final effect is a kind of moral bafflement towards the heroine.

The Passionate Friends (1949) contains Cineguild's most sustained treatment of female instability. It deals with worldly Mary (Ann Todd) who has three separate affairs with lecturer Steven (Trevor Howard) yet remains married to her banker husband (Claude Rains). It could be interpreted as a reprise of *Brief Encounter*, although the wood is certainly no longer damp. However, *The Passionate Friends* is really about one woman's rejection of the claustrophobia of romantic love, and her preference for a companionate marriage. In an exchange between Mary and her lover, he asserts that 'two people in love should belong to each other', to which she replies, 'I want to belong to myself'. This enrages Steven, who retorts, 'then your life will be a failure ... do you always want to belong to yourself?' She does, and wants 'a love without all this clutching'. The script, which was written jointly by Lean, Bryan, Eric Ambler and Stanley Haynes, lambasts Mary's lack of commitment, and structurally undercuts her by giving her a number of flashbacks in which she is shown to be downright silly.

A complicating factor was that Lean fell in love with Todd during shooting, and organized lighting to favour her: 'everybody complained that he kept the camera on me because he loved me so much' (Brownlow, 1997, pp. 261–2). So the finished film is a conflict between a script which belabours the heroine's moral ambiguity and visual procedures which celebrate her beauty. The same pattern obtains in *Madeleine* (1950), in which Todd also starred. This deals with a woman tried for poisoning her lover. Madeleine is never seen to commit the act (or not to commit it) and the final shot of her face has a male voice-over ask her again if she is guilty or not. Her only reply is a smile which can be interpreted in any number of ways.

Two Cities was also part of Independent Producers Ltd. It was headed until late 1947 by Del Giudice. He thought that popular films under-estimated the audience's intelligence, and films which pleased women were rigorously excluded from his canon: 'The masses are unfortunately more inclined to enjoy a *Wicked Lady* than one of our pieces of art.'[17] Del Giudice wanted an élite film art with its own distribution arrangements, and there were some in government who were prepared to take him on his own terms.[18] But his notions could not withstand the rigours of the postwar period.

Two Cities began to experience managerial problems after the war. Del Giudice was unable to reconcile his grandiose theories about quality film with the personnel at his disposal. *Hamlet* (1948) was the only postwar Two Cities film to accord with his cultural policies. Otherwise, the company's output was almost exclusively melodrama. This was probably because Del Giudice needed to make money, and the melodrama genre was seemingly a sure bet. However, melodrama needed to be specially nuanced to be successful at the British box-office in the 1940s. It had to relate different discursive languages to each other in a careful way, reject irony in emotional matters, and respect the female audience. Del Giudice's melodramas succeeded in none of these, and consequently they are all hamfisted farragos.

Beware of Pity (1946), for example, deals with a crippled girl who falls unhappily in love, and the position offered to the female audience is one of helpless misery. *Carnival* (1946) is carelessly scripted, and the melodrama idiom coarsely overdone, with an undisciplined register and body language. *Hungry Hill* (1947) was presented as Two Cities's respectable alternative to Gainsborough bodice-rippers. Margaret Lockwood was described in the publicity material 'not as a Wicked Lady, but as girl, wife and mother'. The studio boasted about the film's historical verisimilitude, while forgetting that melodrama and realism were mutually contradictory modes.

From the evidence of *The Mark of Cain* (1948), Two Cities staff neither understood nor liked the genre. The film deals with a woman who marries the 'wrong' brother, regrets it and then realizes she loves her husband after all. By this time it is too late, since he has been murdered by the 'right' brother and she gets the blame. *The Mark of Cain* has some common components of 1940s melodrama – murder trial, family romance, nuns – but they are misarranged. No care has been taken with narrative or textural coherence, so motivation is obscure. Normally competent actors such as Eric Portman deploy the Grand Guignol manner, but unevenly.

Del Giudice's attempt to inject high cultural values into cinema had a high cost. He produced films in which females were dangerous without being interesting, which may have been the result of trusting wilful and inexperienced personnel. Two Cities was also responsible for *Odd Man Out* (1947) and *Fame Is the Spur* (1947). But Del Giudice could not control these films, because Carol Reed was the producer as well as director of the first, as the Boulting brothers were of the second. Interestingly, both these films contained female protagonists with some autonomy and psychological complexity.

Joseph Somlo took over Two Cities after Del Giudice left for Pilgrim

Pictures (Drazin, 1998, p. 51). Somlo nuanced melodrama in a new way. *The Perfect Woman* (1949) is about an inventor (Miles Malleson) who makes a robot in the likeness of his niece (Patricia Roc). In his excessive rationality, he thinks that female function is all, and is mortified when the pretty facsimile runs amok and gets stuck in some unedifying postures. *Trottie True* (1949) deals with a chorus girl who has a taste for independence, and who is not subject to script moralizing.[19] *Madness of the Heart* (1949) is an extraordinary film, in which Margaret Lockwood portrays a businesswoman. She falls in love with a French aristocrat, goes blind, becomes a nun, leaves the convent, marries the Frenchman, nearly kills a child with her knitting, is sabotaged by her husband's former girlfriend, leaves her husband, has a dangerous operation, regains her sight, pretends to be blind, dispatches her rival and returns to her husband. It is a very busy film. What is remarkable is its utter conviction, and the fact that the heroine triumphs over adversities that would have felled any decent woman. Although Rank decided not to accord *Madness of the Heart* a London première, Lockwood's fans flocked to its first night in Blackpool, and it was a bigger box-office success than any of Two Cities's other films of that period (Timms, 1989, p. 157). Somlo clearly understood something about melodrama and its customers.

Smaller companies produced significant films under Rank's aegis. Wessex Films, headed by Ian Dalrymple, produced *Esther Waters* in 1948, which explored the privations of an unmarried mother. It was an innovative attempt to create a visual correlative of 1880s literary naturalism, but the problem was that this movement was an avant-garde phenomenon that had never been fully assimilated into British cultural life. Parts of *Esther Waters* have a documentary feel, which was predictable considering Dalrymple's former career as head of the Crown Film Unit. But such an approach was now old-fashioned, and anyway *Esther Waters*'s extreme determinism made the film a depressing experience. So although it contained a feminist interpretation of family life, *Esther Waters* was limited by its miserabilism and the naturalist aroma of its style.

If we now turn to postwar Gainsborough before the Boxes took over, we see continuities with its former style. It had slanted its wartime output towards women, and cared little for the critical opprobrium which attended its efforts. Until late 1946, the studio was run by Maurice Ostrer, Ted Black and R. J. Minney. They continued to make 'women's films' at Gainsborough until they left, and their films, like the wartime product, were visually flamboyant and contained autonomous women. However, a degree of sexual conservatism gradually crept into the narratives.

Caravan (1946) contains two heroines, the gypsy dancer Rosal (Jean Kent) and the English aristocrat Oriana (Anne Crawford). Both are in love with novelist Richard (Stewart Granger). The structure of the narrative favours Oriana. Rosal swims naked in a stream, expresses her erotic feelings in dance, and takes her wounded man 'to my cave near Granada'. Nonetheless she is shot shielding Richard, and the vapid Oriana wins the prize. *Caravan* focuses on the exotic and marginal, following the lead of the film's novelist, Lady E. F. Smith. The gypsy wedding scene is a celebration of the Dionysian instinct. But the orgiastic and untamed element gives way to the sober and cultured. The same pattern underpins *The Magic Bow* (1946), which charts the adventures of Paganini (Stewart Granger). Again there are two heroines: the impure (Jean Kent) and the pure (Phyllis Calvert). The pure heroine rejects Paganini for the sake of honour and begs him to play his violin as she leaves. Paganini's fingering is sublime, but the heroine temporarily abandons her dextrous lover nonetheless.

The later Ostrer films were increasingly conservative about female choice. *The Root of All Evil* (1947), the last of the cycle, has a heroine Jeckie Farnish (Phyllis Calvert) who has endured disappointment in love. She decides to follow her head rather than her heart; her wilfulness comes, says her father, directly from her grandmother. Jeckie develops a vengeful streak, becomes rich, and simultaneously envies and despises her sister (Hazel Court) who is happily domesticated. Jeckie's phallic oilwell is spectacularly destroyed, and the conflagration is a retribution for her unwomanly hubris. She returns to lick her wounds in the arms of a strong man.

The Root of all Evil, like the other postwar Black/Ostrer films, offers a powerful form of identification to the female viewers. The films invite them into a country in which males are constructed as the object of female desire, and in which hitherto forbidden modes of wilfulness are permitted. The catch is that, emotionally speaking, there is no such thing as a free lunch. The heroines have to pay for their pleasures, which are shorter and less intense than those of the wartime Gainsborough melodramas.

The Ostrer / Black collaboration eventually ran out of steam, and production ground to a virtual halt. When Rank appointed Sydney Box as head of Gainsborough in late 1946, everything changed. Box gave prominent roles to his sister Betty and his wife Muriel, whose work will be discussed in Part II. Sydney Box had become convinced that realist films were more appropriate for the postwar period. For Box, realism meant a congruence between the different languages of a film: script, décor, costume, music. In all Box's later films this congruence obtained. Films such as *A Boy, a Girl and a Bike* (1949) are stylistically coherent and socially narrow. When Box deployed the melodrama mode, its components were handled without finesse. The final court scene of *Jassy* (1947) is as overblown as anything in British cinema, and it resembles Tod Slaughter at his finest. Jassy (Margaret Lockwood) stands accused of the murder of her vile husband. The mute Belinda (Esma Cannon) has been made dumb by her own father and is in love with Jassy. She has committed the murderous deed with rat bane, and, in order to save Jassy, miraculously regains her speech, confesses and drops dead in the witness box.

The smaller independent producers had varied profiles on gender issues. Anatole de Grunwald ideally aspired to make films like *Queen of Spades* (1949), but was forced to undertake more workaday projects, such as *Bond Street* (1948) and *Portrait of Clare* (1950). Both films are unambitious vehicles which define women as an emotional underclass. British National, headed by Louis H. Jackson, had a different profile. All its films contained a female who caused nothing but trouble and ran the gamut from petulance to villainy.[20] *No Room at the Inn* (1948) is the most extreme example. It deals with Mrs Voray (Freda Jackson), who steals candy from babies and takes money from evacuee children to spend on gin; louche and cavernous, she crackles with ill intent.

Only one film from a small company achieved any popularity (it was shown as a 'cruise film' on both the *Queen Mary* and the *Queen Elizabeth*): *The Glass Mountain*, released in 1949 by Victoria. John Sutro was involved in the film, and he had connections with the larger Renown company at the time. The film was scripted jointly by the director Henry Cass and the producer Joseph Janni, and describes the triangle of composer Richard (Michael Denison), his wife (Dulcie Gray) and his Italian beloved (Valentina Cortese). Richard writes *The Glass Mountain*, an opera based on a legend from the Dolomites where he was hidden during the war. During the first performance, the wife is injured in a plane crash over the real Glass Mountain, and the mythical and modern levels of the tale coincide. The Italian beloved is rejected and the hero descends unscathed with his family.

The opera deals symbolically with profane love, with an echo which only rebounds when love is sincere, and with a wraith who leads her faithless lover to his doom over a precipice on the Glass Mountain. It is thoroughly satisfying on a subliminal and musical level. The lead is sung by Tito Gobbi (in absolutely top vocal form), in his only British film (Gobbi, 1979, pp. 87, 99). The arousing music is underpinned by a script of romantic conservatism. Richard discusses his ideal inspiration: 'really she's the eternal woman to whom all men return, no matter who they've loved in between. She's Helen of Troy, Cleopatra, Isolde, Lilith.' The words he chooses for one of his arias are 'And though you stop your ears / To my insistent voice / I shall not rest, my love / Or sleep until you come.' Gobbi, of course, is a baritone, and the masculine power and drive of his voice have quite different effects from that of Gigli and Tauber in the tenor romances which female audiences had enjoyed in the 1930s. This voice is vigorous and insistent, and the music instructs the listener to surrender to its power.

In general, small outfits needed the financial support of larger companies if they wanted to take risks with their subject matter. Examples are *A Man about the House*, which was produced by British Lion in 1947, and *Mine Own Executioner*, which was made by London/Harefield in the same year. The first was produced by old Gainsborough hand Ted Black, and directed by Leslie Arliss, and was a box-office success, probably because of the frank way it dealt with what the publicity material called 'the kindling of the fire of love in the sex-starved Agnes'. *Mine Own Executioner* was also radical, but too much so for profitability. It deals with a therapist unsuccessfully treating a psychopath, and reaches some remarkable conclusions about the complicity of psychoanalysis in the repression of females, which were ahead of their time.

Very rarely, a British director used American money in an attempt to duplicate his former success. *The Idol of Paris* (1948) was made for Warner Bros by the Gainsborough team of R. J. Minney, Leslie Arliss and Maurice Ostrer, and deals with the colourful life of a ragman's daughter (Christine Norden), who becomes a famous courtesan and fights a duel with whips against her rival for the favours of Napoleon III. But the whip fights and the inconsistencies of the heroine's persona were too much even for the aficionados of bad-girl melodrama.

What is remarkable about the postwar representation of women is its variety. During World War II, films had exhibited what we can call a 'can-do' mentality: they expressed an optimism about subordinate groups such as women. Some films had implicitly argued that women could rise to the occasion of war, gaining confidence by assimilating the discourses of other marginal groups. After 1945, all that changed. The postwar film industry was essentially a seller's market. Its interests were commercial, and producers nuanced their representations of women according to their own instincts about what would sell. Because of the acute nature of the cultural and social resettlement, postwar producers were in the grip of conflicting currents of feeling. On the one hand, they felt joyfully liberated from the controls of the MoI; on the other hand, they were unsure about what kind of gender representations were most appropriate. They simply tried anything on, to see if it would fit.

The postwar film industry was far more rigorous in the way it con-trolled female roles, and film actresses had less professional freedom than before. After 1946, the Rank Organization employed longer contracts, and narrowed the range of roles offered to its female stars.[21] Each studio had its own favoured pattern of female stereotyping, and the system was mature enough to enforce it. Also the style of cutting and composition changed in the postwar period. There were far fewer medium shots than there had been in the 1930s, and a corresponding increase in close-ups, especially for melodrama.[22] But this did not lead to increased inter-pretative freedom, as actresses were 'imprisoned' by the tight framing of the camera.

The range of stereotypes in postwar film differed substantially from earlier periods. Film culture was no longer preoccupied by Wholesome Sensible Girls. Some stereotypes faded out altogether. There is no female version of 'the standing-offer man' – the person 'devotedly waiting, ready to help, and undeterred by [the] failure to respond' (Wolfenstein and Leites, 1950, p. 45). The period is notable for the amount of screen time given to female villainy, and the care taken to discriminate between its different types and degrees. Although first inaugurated at Gainsborough, female deviants quickly spread from costume to modern melodrama and to other generic forms.

The Wicked Ladies comprised a school of villainy that included Margaret Lockwood, Greta Gynt, Christine Norden and Jean Kent. These actresses deploy similar techniques: wide-open eyes, a slow shift from one facial expression to another, and a majestic style of movement. All have opulent figures, and portray sexual hunger: their size and promiscuity are connected in the roles they play. All these actresses were well apprised of the value of the publicity stunts they were forced to perform. Lockwood hated the brouhaha, but Gynt revelled in it, appearing at one première 'like a fairy on the Christmas tree gone wrong – but of course it made all the papers next day'.[23] Wicked Ladies have a short pedigree in British film history; there are none before 1943 or after 1950. Producers were probably using the stereotype as a way of clarifying and alleviating audiences' anxieties about wartime changes in women's roles.

The stylish Difficult Dowagers of the 1930s had transmogrified into Old Slappers by 1945. A range of roles were invented for older women which made them decayed harridans of the scratch-and-sniff school of dress, who are on the far side of Old Mother Riley. Freda Jackson, Hermione Baddeley and Nancy Price belong to this group. They all specialize in characters with dubious morality and verbal incontinence. Such characters are an index of the drastic downward slide of older women in British film culture. They now represented a threat to national probity.

A new formation in postwar cinema are the Ice Maidens. This group comprises Deborah Kerr, Valerie Hobson and others. They play cerebral women who inspire fierce passion in others, but who are themselves frigid and confused. Ann Todd is the most skilled at this combination of repression and display: 'In myself I sense a kind of dividing line – a wall, I can't get to the other side of it'.[24] Ice Maidens were directed so as to exhibit extreme muscular tension, particularly of the shoulders, neck and jaw. Their roles do not encourage audiences to identify with them; they have assumed the male prerogatives of control and impassivity.

There is another new sub-group of Hysterics, women unhappily consumed by their own past. Its unresolved elements haunt them, so that they cannot behave coherently. The past is repressed yet invades the present through neurotic symptoms. Kathleen Byron, Dulcie Gray, Esma Cannon and others inhabit this category, and its conception clearly owes something to popular Freudianism. Class determinants are 'whitened out' in Hysterics, which is not the case with male neurotics. Film culture used

Hysterics as a means of neutralizing those extremes of feeling experienced in wartime – the violent swings occasioned by the proximity of love and death. They are a resolution, at the symbolic level, of the death drive. Another small group of Pragmatic Helpmeets contains Glynis Johns, Phyllis Calvert and Googie Withers. Usually, the characters they play are sexually active, but the potential danger of their desire is balanced by their practical nature. They are competent, hardworking companions more liable to approach sex as a contact sport than a life-changing cataclysm.

The cluster of Ingénues is insufficiently complex to neutralize the powerful effects of its enemies, the Wicked Ladies. Madcaps and Sensible Girls in 1930s films were saucy. In the postwar period, their successors are vapid, and their virginity is a matter of accident. The roles acted by Sally Gray, Susan Shaw, Sally Ann Howes, Patricia Roc and Petula Clarke do not make goodness interesting, because they are not encouraged to show it as a struggle.

In general, then, the postwar industry is characterized by its variety in gender representation, and by the rigour of its control. The female stereotypes invented by the cinema are a cautious response to a volatile domestic/sexual situation, and they are on the whole conservative in the awful warnings they present to audiences. All that changed in the 1950s, when new distribution arrangements had some surprising effects.

Notes

1. PRO INF 12/564, memo from Denis Forman, 1947. See also PRO INF 12/562, COI memo, 25 January 1947.
2. PRO BT 64/2366, undated memo, probably to Wilson from one of his aides, if we take into account its place in the file.
3. PRO BT 64/2366, Board of Trade memo, 4 May 1948.
4. PRO BT 64/4139, Board of Trade memo, 24 March 1946.
5. PRO BT 64/4139, memo from the president, 19 November 1945.
6. See Hansard, vol. 476, 1950; *Daily Graphic*, 21 February 1949; and an interview with the actor Peter Graves, in Kochberg (1990).
7. Stafford Cripps, after-dinner speech to the J. Arthur Rank Association on 19 January 1947, Muriel and Sydney Box Papers, Item 14, BFI Library.
8. Minutes of the BFPA Export Committee, 16 July 1946.
9. BBFC Scenario Notes, April 1945 and August 1947, in BFI Library.
10. *Ibid.*, 18 April 1945; 20 June 1947; 22 October 1947.
11. Interview with choreographer Philip Buchel by Searle Kochberg in 1989.
12. *Films in Review*, March 1967.
13. *Kinematograph Weekly*, 18 December 1947.

14. PRO BT 64/2366, memo from Eady to Somervell, 19 April 1949.

15. PRO BT 64/2366, letter from Havelock-Allen to the Board of Trade, 28 February 1948.

16. *Kinematograph Weekly*, 18 December 1947.

17. Letter from Del Giudice to Bernard Miles, 12 November 1947, in the Bernard Miles Papers, BFI Library.

18. PRO BT 64/2366, memo from Nicholas to Wilson, 10 June 1948, marked 'Private'.

19. This was perhaps because some of the original, more radical script material by Caryl Brahms stayed in, although she was replaced by another screenwriter: see Sherrin and Sherrin (1986), p. 175.

20. For example, *The Laughing Lady* (1946), *Woman to Woman* (1946) and *Green Fingers* (1947).

21. Lockwood (1948), pp. 71–2; Phyllis Calvert in Aspinall and Murphy (1983), p. 61.

22. Googie Withers, 'Acting for stage and screen', *Penguin Film Review*, 1947.

23. *Films and Filming*, October 1973. See also *Picturegoer*, 5 July 1947.

24. *Films and Filming*, October 1973.

The 1950s: Conformity and Deviance

The 1950s saw the emergence of a new form of consumer society. The watersheds which re-routed social life are commonly accepted as the Festival of Britain, the Coronation, Suez, the coming of commercial television and the publishing of the Wolfenden Report. Of course, a real understanding of the period must also be based on an awareness of the economic shifts which underpinned changes in consciousness. All we need to remember for the time being is that domestic consumption flourished as Britain's international role declined, and that the older, consensual definitions of duty, as well as familial and class hierarchy, were increasingly under question as the decade progressed. Consumerism itself, as well as 'Americanization', gave concern to commentators from both right and left.

Film culture responded selectively to changes in the social process, and was particularly preoccupied by new female aspirations and behaviour. The British film industry underwent major transformations in the 1950s, which radically affected patterns of gender representation. Changes in censorship and the new X certificate revolutionized production patterns (Aldgate, 1995). The government backed a small new outfit called Group Three (Popple, 1996). Economic structures changed too. While the postwar Labour government was still in office, Harold Wilson had persuaded the Treasury to invest £5 million in the National Film Finance Corporation (NFFC); this had a knock-on effect on film culture. There were also major changes in the industry's structure. Gainsborough and Two Cities had closed, and Independent Producers ceased operation. Ealing came increasingly under the everyday control of Rank. There was a proliferation of one-picture companies, ABPC flourished and American production money poured into the country. What had brought these circumstances about?

The key event was the abolition of the renter's quota in the 1948 Cinematograph Films Act. Only the exhibitor's quota remained, and there was no longer any statutory requirement for British distributors to distribute British films. This meant that they could establish looser links with producers. The old vertically integrated studio system was under extreme pressure, and began to break up as market power shifted to the distributors.

Distributors assessed the creative ingredients of a project, marketed the film and provided finance. The more canny ones realized that if they guaranteed only three-quarters of production costs, the NFFC would put up the rest. The decline of the vertically integrated combine removed some power from producers, but the new system of more flexible financing also offered them greater freedom to work on projects that suited their taste. The new arrangements meant that the production company had to bear most of the financial risk, which made them far less stable than the distribution companies. There were more production companies than ever before, because each producer/director team tended to have its own company, often specially founded for each film. The consequence of the new arrangements was far-reaching. Directors and screenwriters had less room to manoeuvre than before, yet the real source of power – the distribution company – was more distant from the production process.

The J. Arthur Rank Organization was the biggest of the distributors. Rank's first priority in the 1950s was to supply films for the company's cinemas. Since there were many hungry cinemas, quantity rather than quality was the keynote, and Rank and his henchman John Davis held their producers to £150,000 per film. Rank promoted family entertainment, which often led to anodyne product; besides aiming at moral improvement, he was also attempting to appeal to younger viewers as audiences became increasingly segmented. Moral agendas were balanced against market processes (Porter, 1997). Davis backed Rank's preference for films with conventional morality, which is piquant given Davis's six marriages and unsavoury divorce cases. But such was the scale of the Rank empire – three major production companies, plus some 23 one-picture companies and thirteen satellites – that it was impossible to control them all.

Rank's first production venture in the 1950s was British Film-makers (BFM), but none of its producers would pull together, and the organization was too immature to do anything but give them their head. Many

BFM films were quirky in their representation of women. Betty Box and Ralph Thomas's *Appointment with Venus* (1951) was a curious amalgam of animal husbandry and erotic love. It deals with the wartime career of pedigree Guernsey heifer Venus. As Goddess of Bovine Love, her milk yield is coveted by both British and Germans, while the Goddess of Human Love, Nicola (Glynis Johns), has German and British swains competing for the breeding stakes. John Bryan and Ronald Neame's *The Card* (1952) is a paean to entrepreneurial skills, and contains some unattractive roles for Valerie Hobson, Glynis Johns and Veronica Turleigh as frigid patron, grasping fiancée and dour mother respectively. Teddy Baird and Antony Asquith's *The Importance of Being Earnest* (1952) offers a rather camp interpretation of Wilde's play. Its manner foregrounds the homosexual aspects of 'Bunburying', and casts the redoubtable female characters to the emotional edges of the text.

BFM had no coherence in its cultural or sexual politics. Rank remedied this when he set up Group Film Producers, and he relied increasingly on Davis and Earl St John. They were both accountants at heart, with little understanding of popular taste, and they were keen to repeat profitable formulae. The first tranche of Group films was anodyne on the gender front – such as *The Kidnappers* (1953) and *The Young Lovers* (1954) – but there were two sets of exceptions. The first were films to which women made a significant contribution: *The Million Pound Note* (1953), scripted by Jill Craigie; *Simon and Laura* (1955), directed by Muriel Box; and *Doctor in the House* (1954) and *Doctor at Sea* (1955), both produced by Betty Box. The second exception to Group norms are two comedies which take an ambivalent attitude to the new consumerism: *Value for Money* (1955) and *An Alligator Named Daisy* (1955). They have different teams (Nolbandov and Annakin for the first, Stross and Lee Thompson for the second) and both star Diana Dors.

It is the transgressive Dors persona which dominates both films. Her very presence – feisty, vulgar, lascivious – calls into question the decent velleities intended to inform all Rank productions of this period. *Value for Money* deals with a northern businessman, Chayley (John Gregson), who makes a fortune from 'shoddy' (fabric recycling) and falls for brassy showgirl Ruthine (Dors). Chayley hears his dead father's portrait speak: 'Thy money will roll off every curve of her sinful body'. Ruthine makes a deal with nice girl Ethel (Susan Stephen). Both profit, Ethel by marriage to Chayley and Ruthine by a £5000 'breach of promise' payment. The film is a delirious satire on the world of goods and the emotions attending them, and Dors invests the whole film with a crackling cynicism.

An Alligator Named Daisy is about songwriter Peter (Donald Sinden), who is engaged to aristocratic Vanessa (Dors). Alligator Daisy falls in love with him: petshop-owner Prudence Croquet (Margaret Rutherford) blows down the beast's nostrils and divines that Daisy finds Peter attractive. He does the decent thing, buys her a pink ribbon, and forsakes Vanessa to marry a poor girl (Jean Carson) because she loves reptiles. The film is marvellously flexible in its treatment of class, and again Dors transforms the material by implying, through the bravura of her perform-ance, that desire and status are random.

Rank set up another production company (called 'Rank') in 1955, and this time Davis was more rigorous in exacting obeisance. Davis devised a cumbersome system whereby he and Rank first agreed the topic with the producer and financed pre-production. They only gave their financial support to a package of script, cast and director if it conformed to their views. The films of this third Rank production company have common themes. First of all there is a preoccupation with fatherhood. *Lost* (1956) deals with a little boy abducted by a crazed widow who has lost her baby. The original screenplay by Janet Green blames the mother for being a career woman (S14362).[1] It is the father and the male detective who show practical concern. Small script touches make women seem fallible: the silly females in the chemist ('Flaming Poppy or Chinese Orange?'), the little girl who misleads them all ('Zoë's a dreadful little liar. It seems ingrained in her'), the crazed widow (a Sister Ruth lookalike). By con-trast, it is the men who are more fitted for motherhood.

Jacqueline (1956) foregrounds a little girl's relationship with her father. He is feckless, but when his daughter takes him in hand, he becomes integrated into natural cycles. *The Spanish Gardener* (1956) is preoccupied with fatherhood too. It deals with an embittered diplomat (Michael Hordern), who has an obsessive love for his son and becomes jealous of the child's feelings for handsome gardener José (Dirk Bogarde). It is an emotionally raw film about nurture and loyalty, and constructed so that women are entirely irrelevant to both issues.

Many Rank productions from 1955 to 1959 are preoccupied with masculinity on a broader level. *Hell Drivers* (1957) debates appropriate levels of competitiveness, and *A Night to Remember* (1958) and *North-west Frontier* (1958) focus on male derring-do. The two costume films,

The Gypsy and the Gentleman (1958) and *A Tale of Two Cities* (1958), nuance masculinity differently, possibly because the first is directed by an American (Joseph Losey) and the second produced by a woman (Betty Box). Even the cycle of Norman Wisdom films can be interpreted as a sustained meditation on male anxieties. Like Arthur Askey, Wisdom evokes fears about size, and like Askey, he is allotted personable females. The Wisdom character is bullied by those bigger than himself – bosses, mothers, even his horse. 'Norman' is feminized, since both his body and his emotions are out of control. He is ultra-expressive, speaking as soon as he feels, and moving as soon as he speaks. The comedy works because he operates like a volatile woman, but looks like an overgrown boy.

Another category of Rank films can be classed as sexual tourism. In *The Black Tent* (1956), the aristocratic hero (Donald Sinden) finds that his dead brother has married a Berber girl; she bears a son, who is the rightful heir. The widow plays a vital role by being small, self-effacing and non-European, with chronic gaze aversion. The Japanese heroine of *The Wind Cannot Read* (1958) is the same. Sabby (Yoko Tani) falls in love with Dirk Bogarde. They marry, but she dies before her diffidence becomes irritating. *The Wind Cannot Read* was produced by Betty Box, but the script was written solely by Richard Mason, the original novelist, so Box had little room for manoeuvre. The film proposes Sabby as ideally feminine: biddable and tiny, she 'fits like a pair of old shoes'.

The smaller satellite companies attached to Rank were subject to some control. Rank and Davis would only give a complete distribution agreement when they had approved the whole script. For *White Corridors* (1951), Rank intervened to make sure the little boy did not die (MacFarlane, 1997, p. 325). Some directors found Rank's satellite conditions conducive, because they accepted Davis's gender remit. Robert Hamer, for example, made *The Long Memory* (1953) and *To Paris with Love* (1955). The first contained a bleak misogyny, and the second a world-weary prurience. Nonetheless some films were made under the Rank umbrella which implicitly challenged the company's strictures on gender matters. There were three avenues of evasion for the producer/director team: to display bloody-mindedness, to deploy low cunning with subliminal messages too subtle for Davis to read, or to concentrate on real historical events.

The leading exponents of bloody-mindedness were Powell and Pressburger. They made *Battle of the River Plate* (1956) and *Ill Met by*

Moonlight (1956) for Rank. They were in a bullish mood, and were soon at daggers drawn with Davis. The Manolo's Bar sequence in *Plate* required girls who could 'sing or dance or do acrobatics, or something' (Powell, 1992, p. 327). They are sinuous, decorative tarts whom Rank did not approve of. And in *Moonlight*, the women were only there by default, as Powell noted:

> I am a feminist. I love women, and I understand women, and I can't believe any story that has no feminine interest in it . . . women are in everything – bless 'em! Where were the women in *Ill Met By Moonlight*? You can't tell me that all those brave young men, British and Greek, playing tag with death every night of their lives, didn't inspire love and hatred, trust and betrayal. (*ibid.*, p. 361)

So women's invisibility is somehow a proof of their importance.

Also into the bloody-minded category comes *Sapphire* (1959), made for Artna films by Relph and Dearden. They were mature film-makers, and could be trusted to deliver something respectable. Nonetheless, *Sapphire* contains some unpredictable representations of women. The mixed-race heroine (whom we never see alive) is aware of the status of classical music and a white skin. The key scene is the murder confession by Sapphire's future sister-in-law (Yvonne Mitchell). Abandoned by her husband, she works in a dairy (milk, of course, signals nurture and whiteness). The scene argues the dire effects of sexual repression on the 'respectable' woman. We hear her outrage that Sapphire was fond of laughing and swinging her legs. The film suggests that sexual repression, racial prejudice and lower-middle-class tensions erupt with particular intensity in women.

Some small production teams evaded Rank controls by using low cunning, and smuggling in offensive script material. Pinnacle's *Tony Draws a Horse* (1950) is about an unruly boy whose mother (Anne Crawford) is a practising psychotherapist. Tony draws a well-endowed stallion on the wall. The disputed drawing is in indelible ink and occupies a prominent place. The film was produced by Brock Williams, who also worked on the scenario, and was based on Lesley Storm's play. As Williams was frantic with production tasks, Storm was brought in to script. She turned in a facsimile of her own play, risqué jokes and all.

Another 'low cunning' stunt was pulled by Sirius, a company set up by William Rose and Henry Cornelius to make *Genevieve* (1953). Davis accepted the project because it had NFFC money. He failed to notice that the *mise en scène* colluded with the script, to produce a positive image of feisty, consumerist females. The wife Wendy (Dinah Sheridan) is casual about housekeeping ('Proper lunch or proper dinner?'), is stylishly *au fait* with luxury articles like peppers, and is careless about eggs. Rosalind (Kay Kendall) is sexually experienced: there are veiled references to nights with the appalling Ambrose (Kenneth More). She has a slobbering female St Bernard, which is laudably indulged, and she gets drunk and plays a virtuoso piece on the trumpet. A more obedient Rank film would have censured such crimes; *Genevieve* celebrates them.

The direction of acting style was another evasion technique. Teddy Baird and Antony Asquith ran a small company called Javelin-Vic, which made two films for Rank, *The Woman in Question* (1950) and *The Browning Version* (1951). On the face of it, both projects looked innocuous: a murder thriller and a Rattigan play. But the team directed Jean Kent so as to infuse the female lead with unparalleled nastiness. *The Woman in Question* reconstructs the murdered woman from five different perspectives. She has no identity, but is the creature of others' imaginations. And in *The Browning Version* Kent's demeanour makes the original Rattigan heroine more ill-meaning and lascivious. Most of Asquith's other films presented women as predatory, and these continue the task.

The final example of 'low cunning' is to undermine a seemingly neutral topic from within by constructing a labyrinthine narrative. Independent Artists did this with *Bachelor of Hearts* (1958). This is about a German student at Cambridge (Hardy Kruger) who learns to smoke a pipe and wear a tweed jacket. Seldom have these seemed such Herculean tasks. So far so good: international feelings could be soothed by the film, and the hungers of Rank's European cinemas could be assuaged. No wonder Davis wanted it. But either scriptwriter Frederick Raphael or director Wolf Rilla (who gave his own Christian name to the hero) subverted the 'decency' of the project, by inserting an explosive sub-plot. Young Wolf is suborned to masquerade as a number of stereotypes – Angry Young Man, Muscular Christian – because the other students think that is what women want. And they do, murmuring 'you're so angry!' to his Jimmy Porter lookalike. So Kruger shifts from being the wholesome suitor of Sylvia Syms to being the priapic Janus of academe.

Other small companies used historical truth as an excuse for evading

Rank behests. Vic's *A Town Like Alice* (1956) dealt with real events in its treatment of a female Japanese prisoner-of-war group. It posits an essential femininity: whatever their age or class, the women are united by their desire for survival and the protection of children. Nationality is superseded by sisterhood. It is the Malay woman shopkeeper who disobeys her husband and gives the baby milk to Jean (Virginia McKenna). However, the female community does not permit unratified sexual behaviour. The loose Ellen (Maureen Swanson) gives herself to the Japanese for cigarettes. We never see her again.

Carve Her Name with Pride (1958) was conceived by its production team as a tribute to Violette Szabo, who worked in the Resistance for the Allies. Virginia McKenna took care to model her performance on Szabo (MacFarlane, 1997, p. 383). McKenna's accent is lower-middle-class London suburban, and it confers an ordinariness on the heroine. Received Pronunciation would have connected her with Establishment values. She floats free from them, and the love poem by Leo Marks which contains her code is so universal that it frees her from the limitations of history too. The combination of the love theme and the woman's voice caused the poem to be cut loose in the popular imagination from its original anchorage in war and pain. It became so popular that McKenna gave public readings in her own accent, one of which was set to music on the BBC's *Open House* programme.

After Rank, the next largest distribution company of the period was the Associated British Picture Corporation (ABPC). Its head was Robert Clark, a man of business rather than moral vision, who had no coherent ideology. He had a purely commercial attitude to the projects he distributed or produced, and some of them made a great deal of money.[2] Frederick Gotfurt, who was the scenario editor for ABPC, wanted scriptwriters' status raised so that they could specialize: 'It's a bad thing for writers to feel that they must become directors in order to get any kind of recognition for their work.' Gotfurt orchestrated a 'creative triumvirate' between producer, director and scriptwriter. He tended to prefer 'socially important films' for ABPC (Gotfurt, 1959). This meant that the company lacked lightness of touch: its comedies and musicals were leaden affairs. And the script was so much the dominant discourse at ABPC that visual languages (*mise en scène*, acting style) were overdetermined and lacklustre.

ABPC employed a woman, Kathleen Leaver, as its story reader. Leaver (who was married to the producer Robert Hall) 'kept a full-time eye' on television, stage plays and novels. She argued that 'taste goes in cycles', and that it was her job to predict the tide of cultural events.[3] In the late 1940s, ABPC had employed June Faithfull, Daphne Heathcote and Constance Newton as script supervisors, a more policy-based role than scriptwriting. Throughout the 1950s, Anne Burnaby played a key script-writing role in more important projects. Joan Henry, who was married to ABPC director J. Lee Thompson, also scripted her own novels for the company. So, a combination of marital coincidence and managerial *laissez-faire* resulted in the appointment of high-profile female employees, who had some effect on ABPC's project choice. However, it was reluctant to employ female directors.

ABPC was a horrible place to work: it was suggested that 'Abandon Hope, All Ye Who Enter Here' be inscribed over the entrance (Dryhurst, 1987, p. 234). Richard Attenborough recalled that it 'created nothing in terms of commitment' (MacFarlane, 1997, p. 36). Producers were interested in speed rather than aesthetic effect. Dressing rooms were spartan, and management were peremptory with their contract actors. They made money from other studios by loaning out its male contract stars (George Baker, Richard Todd). ABPC had few female stars apart from Sylvia Syms; actresses tended to be bought in from other studios (Diana Dors from Rank for *Yield to the Night*, for example). Management were more interested in making money by loaning Audrey Hepburn out to Paramount than finding good roles for her. They actually suggested that she star in a biopic of Gracie Fields.

The small companies whom ABPC distributed were a motley crew. Some were set up by aspirant newcomers: Mario Zampi's Transocean, for example. But mainly the ABPC satellites were bolt-holes for decaying talents.[4] Powell and Pressburger founded a little company to make *Oh . . . Rosalinda!!* (1955) for ABPC. The film, which was arch and mannered, revealed their high-art aspirations as overblown and their sexual politics antediluvian, whatever Powell's bank manager might say: 'What's the matter with the critics? What do the public want, anyway? Here are two lovely women, singing and dancing and acting – isn't that enough for them?' (Powell, 1992, p. 280). The answer was no, of course.

ABPC also offered a distribution umbrella to old dogs trying new tricks. Butcher's made *The Golden Disc* (1958) for them, which was an attempt to jump on the popular music bandwagon. It had a modern veneer – close-ups of Nancy Whiskey, and a nifty refurbishment of a Tea Shoppe into a coffee bar – but the gender arrangements were old-fashioned. It made a *rapprochement* between generations which was clearly intended to reassure panicking parents while giving youngsters entertainment.

ABPC's satellites were part of a hit-or-miss approach. However, Lee Thompson worked through some smaller companies within ABPC which did produce innovative work. The first was Marble Arch, which was set up by producer Victor Skutezky. Lee Thompson directed the X-certificated *The Yellow Balloon* (1952), which he scripted with Anne Burnaby. The film, which deals with a boy (Andrew Ray) who is being blackmailed, foregrounds the emotional turmoil of the mother (Kathleen Ryan), and gives a compassionate role to the divorced dance teacher (S1786). Lee Thompson then directed *The Weak and the Wicked* (1954) for Skutezky. It was based on the Joan Henry novel, and scripted by Burnaby, Henry herself and Lee Thompson. *The Weak and the Wicked* deals with women in prison, and focuses on gambler Jean Raymond (Glynis Johns). The project shows a cross-section of female casualties, and prison is presented as a humane organization which recognizes the inmates' essential femininity. Their gender binds them together. Jean rejects the Governor's suggestion that she is different because she is middle class:

> I'm a woman too. Maybe I've had a softer life than some of them, but do you think that it makes it any easier for me ... I tell you, there are no different prisoners, only those who are bright enough to know when they are beaten. (S1605)

Marble Arch also produced *It's Great to Be Young* (1956), a confident account of youth culture which has a modicum of sexual equality. Lee Thompson worked for ABPC with other companies. With Kenwood he directed *For Better, for Worse* (1954), which is quite like *Genevieve*, and *Yield to the Night* (1956). The latter is a crucial film, which is based on Joan Henry's novel and scripted by her. It concerns the last weeks in the death cell of Mary Hilton, who killed the woman with whom her lover was infatuated.[5] *Yield to the Night* foregrounds female desire in an unusually intense way. Mary is uncomfortably close to the viewer, and yet the film avoids sentiment and expressiveness. Her voice flatly records her terror of death, and the close-up of her face as she sees the sky for the last time is (as the script instructs) 'without any visible sign of emotion'. The murder is impassively committed: 'Mary fires with cold deliberation and a certain savage satisfaction. Four shots ring out – equally spaced and measured' (S1698).

With one exception: the repeated shots of shoes. The original Henry novel presents female bodies as a whole; there is no mention of feet or shoes, and her injury is to the thigh, not the heel, as in the film (Henry, 1954, p. 79). There are many visual references to stiletto heels, sensible lace-ups, slippers, skating boots and court shoes (Chadder, 1999), all of which follow the guidance of the script. It is not too fanciful to see Mary as Oedipus (Swollen-Foot), the blister on her heel a symbol of her hubris. With such a heavily inflected series of images, something is afoot. The shoes become the only site of expressivity in the whole film, and on a subliminal level they symbolize all those fierce needs that are being punished – the desire for passion, adornment and revenge.

Lee Thompson was involved with two other one-picture companies for ABPC: first, Godwin-Willis, which he used to make *Woman in a Dressing Gown* (1957). Lee Thompson produced with Frank Godwin, and he also directed; it was scripted by Ted Willis from his own TV play. However, the three were comprehensively shafted by ABPC head Robert Clark, who negotiated a labyrinthine deal which they were too naïve to see through (Willis, 1991, pp. 140–1). The film made a great deal of money which they never saw.

Woman in a Dressing Gown is a poignant film about housekeeping. Slatternly Amy (Yvonne Mitchell) loves husband Jim (Anthony Quayle) but is too disorganized to give domestic satisfaction. She is bullied by husband and son, and her spontaneity irritates them. Jim falls for tidy Georgie (Sylvia Syms), who flatters his ego. The film balances them against each other. The cool Georgie has her rights, as well as the wounded Amy, who wails when at bay: 'Having babies ruined my pretty figure!' Both husband and son are presented as beyond reform. The film finally sympathizes with Amy, by using a series of framing shots which stress her isolation.

With Allegro, Lee Thompson, Godwin and Willis made *No Trees in the Street* (1959), another pioneering drama. Yet again Clark ran financial rings round the hapless trio. *No Trees in the Street* dealt with the Bad Old Days in the 1930s East End, and the script offered an interesting role to Sylvia Syms. She aspires to be decent, but becomes a commodity when she is inveigled into becoming a gangster's moll. The film offers a bleak perspective on how it feels to be bought and sold.

So the minor companies attached to ABPC gave rise to some innovatory representations of women. Most were directed by Lee Thompson, and scripted either by women or Ted Willis. It is interesting to consider a Lee Thompson film of the period which was not made for ABPC, *Tiger Bay*. It has the same degree of radicalism in its presentation of females. Lee Thompson originally wanted to cast a boy in the main role, but was impressed by Hayley Mills and changed the casting (Mills, 1981, p. 342). *Tiger Bay* foregrounds the child's attachment to a murderer. On one level it is about a little girl's desire to acquire a gun (with all its phallic connotations), and on another it explores the disastrous consequences for the adult female lead who wants 'a body which is my own to give how and when I like'.

How did such radicalism fare in ABPC's own productions? Badly on the whole. ABPC output in the first half of the decade was anodyne, with a range of genres – crime, musical, melodrama, comedy – none of which were significant on the gender front or at the box-office. *The Franchise Affair* (1951), which deals with a mother and daughter wrongly accused of kidnapping, blames the nubile young 'victim', who turns out to be devious and unchaste. The exception to ABPC's dullish form was *The Young Wives' Tale* (1951), scripted by Anne Burnaby. This deals with undomesticated Sabina (Joan Greenwood), and her marriage to inconsiderate Rodney (Nigel Patrick). The script mounts a fierce attack on the sexual division of labour. Bruce (Derek Farr) makes breathtaking pronouncements: 'I'd like six children with a hearty buxom wife who'd adore me and the children and spend her time between the kitchen and the dairy and the nursery and the garden.' He admires Sabina because 'you had the courage to give up your profession and take on a job you hate, because you wanted to be a wife to your man'. *The Young Wives' Tale* ends with a feigned marital swap and total mayhem, while the radio intones: 'World security can never be achieved without peace at home. The Minister of Food said in Birmingham last night that the country can never repay the debt it owes the British Housewife' (S1500). Of course, such savage feminist irony did not do well commercially.

After 1955, ABPC's fortunes improved, but its performance was inconsistent. *The Dam Busters* (1955) was a major hit, but it owes its meaning to its avoidance of the feminine; indeed, the penetration of the dam and the ensuing torrents could be interpreted as a paean to ejaculation. *It's Never Too Late* (1956) deals with a housewife (Phyllis Calvert) invited to Hollywood to script her own novel. Although at home she finds little creative space ('I'm tired of being someone's wife, mother and daughter. I'd like to be me'), she needs the claustrophobic atmosphere and returns there to be exploited anew. It is a conservative film which could be interpreted as a cinematic *roman-à-clef* criticizing the petticoat rule in the ABPC scripting department. The company then tried a remake of the 1930s hit *The Good Companions* in 1957, but not even the direction of Lee Thompson could conceal the fact that the times were out of joint. The female roles could not survive the transition. *The Moonraker* (1958) was a competent Puritan/Cavalier film, but it failed to capitalize on the fertility of the theme, or make intelligent use of Sylvia Syms's talents.

In the second half of the decade, only films employing Burnaby or Lee Thompson were radical on gender matters. *No Time for Tears* (1957) was an original screenplay by Burnaby, and dealt with a children's hospital ward. The matron (Anne Neagle) operates as the mouthpiece of patriarchal values, exhorting God in morning prayers to 'help us to play the man'. But she is liberal, and adopts two unloved children. Burnaby's script warns against excessive commitment. A monologue by Sister Birch (Flora Robson) tells a probationer nurse about her own earlier feelings: 'He said his first words to me, he took his first steps into my arms ... they're all our children while they're here. Give too much love to one, and you're robbing the others.' The script argues that feminine nurture can be given by males. Dr Seagrove (Anthony Quayle) admonishes a student nurse:

> Give her a little love. I don't want you ever to accept crying as normal. Now this little lass may have a headache, and she's letting us know about it in the only way she can. That's what we call love [takes the child]. What we want is a jolly good cuddle. (S1652)

The child then calls him 'Mummy'. *No Time for Tears* argues that the powers of 'Mummy' can be invested anywhere, irrespective of gender.

Burnaby wrote the original screenplay for *Operation Bullshine* (1959). It describes an ATS group in World War II, and suggests that, far from being the 'Army's Groundsheet', the women were the Army's scourge. They secrete kittens in their cleavage, and wear curlers (one 'looks like the Medusa herself'). They resist normal female tasks like dishwashing ('I joined up to get away from this sort of thing'). The women are sexually voracious, descending on a German parachutist, who is thrilled at the prospect of erotic slavery. *Operation Bullshine* is a joyful celebration of female bad behaviour (S2778).

Lee Thompson directed and scripted *Ice Cold in Alex* (1958), a war film which deals with alcohol and enmity in the desert. It initially had official support, which cooled when it became clear that the film had 'little recruiting value'.[6] *Alex* offered an unusual role to Sylvia Syms, with scorching love scenes which were excised by the censor (Mills, 1981, p. 341). She plays a courageous nurse who expects to take an equal part in the struggle.

So the presence of Lee Thompson and some female scriptwriters resulted in ABPC and some of its satellites producing films which challenged anodyne representations of women. However, many middlebrow film-makers resented what they saw as the stranglehold of Rank and ABPC, and they grouped themselves around British Lion. Korda had bought British Lion in 1946, and he attached it to his own London Films. British Lion borrowed £3 million from the NFFC, but the money was spent by 1954, when the Treasury put it into liquidation. Korda took the role of executive producer throughout. From the completion of *An Ideal Husband* until his death in early 1956, Korda no longer took a hands-on approach (Kulik, 1975, p. 310). None of the 1950s films under the British Lion/London banner bore the stamp of Korda's authorship; the only film in which he directly intervened on set was Launder and Gilliat's *The Story of Gilbert and Sullivan* (1953), which shows some of the old flamboyance. *The Man Who Loved Redheads* (1955) has much in common with Korda's social comedies of the 1930s. Photographed by old Korda hand Georges Périnal, it deals with aristocratic adulterer Mark (John Justin), who falls in love with a series of redheads. The film has a veneer of sophistication atop prurience: a comatose woman will, we are told, 'be a great deal better on her back'.

In general, British Lion operated as the bolt-hole for producers and directors who wanted free rein for their creativity. Korda could not defend Powell and Pressburger from artistic disaster with *Gone to Earth* and *The Elusive Pimpernel*, because he was in hock to the Americans. He felt he had to give them their head with the garish *The Tales of Hoffman* – (1951) by way of recompense.

Normally, Korda's liberalism meant that British Lion's creative personnel were left unhampered. Ian Dalrymple and Jack Lee were encouraged to follow their documentarist bent in *The Wooden Horse* (1950), and Ralph Richardson was given his only crack at directing with *Home at Seven* (1952). Each of these replicates the sexual agenda of their production team. Bigger directors worked with British Lion too. Carol Reed made *The Outcast of the Islands* (1951), and the exotic settings liberated him sufficiently to make a (for him) unusually sensual film, in which the hero's erotic obsession intensifies in proportion to his dusky beloved's incomprehension of his motives. David Lean made *The Sound Barrier* (1952) and *Hobson's Choice* (1954) for Korda. In *The Sound Barrier*, Ann Todd, as the pilot's wife, wanted to make an emotional plea for him not to fly: 'I felt that women, when they have something important to say, are inclined to get rather fierce. It's an animal thing. I felt she would be frightened and in her fear would bang him on the chest.' Lean refused the excessive emotion: 'no man would stay in the audience. They'd just walk out' (Brownlow, 1997, pp. 289–90). Lean won, and the film's emotional coldness is the result.

Frank Launder and Sidney Gilliat developed a brand of comedy which nuanced female energy in an unexpected way. *The Happiest Days of Your Life* (1950), *The Belles of St Trinian's* (1954) and *Blue Murder at St Trinian's* (1957) all deal with little schoolgirls who strike terror into the hearts of everyone; they are self-willed and amoral. The older girls are the same, but with a fierce sexual appetite. The gymslips for both groups are the same size: they cover the importunate wriggling bodies of the little girls and display the hungry limbs of the big ones. The films contain some wonderful cameos. Miss Fitton, as played by Alistair Sim in both the *Trinian's* films, is both male and female, simpering and ruthless. The headmistress in *The Happiest Days of Your Life* (Margaret Rutherford) is a marvel of doggedness. Joyce Grenfell, who plays in all three films, is the sublime apotheosis of a hundred Brown Owls. Her gait is clumsily one-sided, right arm and leg moving together, and her voice is intensified by speaking on the out breath ('Sammy – could it be Wedding Bells?'). These films are a rueful celebration of unruly females, and they suggest that deep in the psyche of compliant women lurks the spectre of the Old Girls. In *The Belles of St Trinian's*, these harpies are so intent on victory that they resort to African tribal dress and adopt the *testudo*, the Roman technique of battle. Anything goes.

Launder and Gilliat's school comedies were the only part of their *oeuvre* to celebrate the Lady of Misrule. Beneath their other 1950s films lay a streak of puritanism. Their more serious political comedies, *The Green Man* (1955) and *Left, Right and Centre* (1959), allot ordinary roles to women, and their thriller *Fortune Is a Woman* (1957) places female duplicity at the heart of the intrigue. *Lady Godiva Rides Again* (1951) is about a beauty queen who resorts to nude posing, while the barker intones: 'she is simple as Joan of Arc, mysterious as Mona Lisa, barefoot as the Constant Nymph'. She retreats into marriage, where she thankfully admits that 'Mummy doesn't know anything', except for the rhyme learned during her modelling days: 'Home-Loving Hearts are Happiest'. *Lady Godiva* argues that stupid women are best at home, and clever ones should be avoided.

British Lion was effectively leaderless from Korda's death until 1958. The government formed a new company, British Lion Films Limited, but its liabilities made production difficult. In early 1958, the NFFC invited Launder and Gilliat and the Boultings to become directors of the company.[7] This enabled the Boultings to continue the highbrow trajectory they had embarked upon in 1940. Their 1950s films interrogate institutions, and find venality and virtue in equal proportion. Women are marginal to all the debates; they are a decorative irritant in the social machine, and a symptom of its ills. For the Boultings, women are society's pit canaries.

Private's Progress (1956) begins its tale of Army life by having the hero (Ian Carmichael) drop his trousers. A prolonged close-up of his pendulous face is accompanied by the doctor's voice-over intoning loudly: 'THAT's nothing to be ashamed of, Son!' Such unproblematical dealings with masculinity also inform *Brothers-in-Law* (1957) and *Carlton-Browne of the FO* (1959). *Lucky Jim* (1957) replicates the emotional structures of the original novel: Jim (Carmichael) is riven by fear and desire when faced with women. The only significant addition to the novel is the boxer bitch. She howls loudly at the music, gets drunk and makes embarrassing displays of affection: a true Boulting female. Only in *I'm All Right Jack* (1959) is there any advance on the vacuous model, and that is because Mrs Kite (Irene Handl) and Aunt Dolly (Margaret Rutherford) are ageing conservatives combining against union power.

The post-Korda regime at British Lion operated a blunderbuss technique: fire enough pellets, and some of them might hit. Accordingly, the range of female representations was extremely broad. It contained Muriel

Box's sophisticated *Truth about Women* (1958), as well as the rambunctious *Happy Is the Bride* (1958). The best index of British Lion's eclecticism was *Passport to Shame* (1959), in which French girl Malou (Odile Versois) is lured into prostitution. The film traded on the Wolfenden Report and was a response to Eros's *The Flesh Is Weak* (1957). *Passport to Shame* suggests that there are 'good' girls like Malou, who can be inveigled into trade through love, and 'bad' girls like Vicki (Diana Dors), who enjoy their work. Malou is small; Vicki is gloriously large. This doubleness is mirrored in the spatial arrangement of the two adjacent houses, the respectable home and the house of ill-repute. The latter is burned down and the good woman survives. British Lion's wish to be a non-judgemental distributor brought it some strange bedfellows.

If we now turn to Ealing, we can see the effects of the new distribution system on a small studio. Balcon had entered into a distribution arrangement with Rank in 1947, but it only began to bite in the 1950s, when John Davis intervened in its day-to-day business. Balcon's papers show the many humiliations he had to bear. Rank put up 50 per cent of the production costs, in return for worldwide distribution rights. Davis whittled down Balcon's average production budget from a reasonable £180,000 to a much lower sum, and he interrogated Balcon about canteen expenditure and plywood costs.[8] He even insisted on altering the tone of *The Ladykillers* because it was insufficiently appreciative of the police.[9] Davis's letters have a hectoring tone, and Balcon clearly felt his aesthetic judgements were being undermined. Small wonder that he wanted distributors to 'be ancillary to a major production organisation'.[10]

John Davis's views on gender representation constituted no challenge to Balcon. Indeed, they probably gave him extra ballast. Balcon had an antipathy to feminine subject matter anyway, preferring what he called 'the typical stiff-upper-lipped English type'. He complained to Jack Hawkins that 'the publicity line seems to be that unless an actor is in some kind of a clinch with a female, it is all rather unexciting and dull'.[11] The only Ealing film to deal with womanly topics was *The Feminine Touch*, which exercised moral rigour towards its female protagonists. Balcon 'thoroughly enjoyed it and was most moved by certain sequences'.[12]

Balcon was opposed to any women entering direction. He told Kay Mander 'quite flatly that women couldn't handle film crews and anyway,

WOMEN IN BRITISH CINEMA

there weren't any suitable films for women to direct' (ACTT, 1983, pp. 69–70). He turned Jill Craigie down too: 'There is no immediate possibility of our working together on a picture. I mean, of course, in your capacity as a director ... our conversation may be worthwhile, if you are willing to postpone your ideas about directing.'[13] Balcon rejected any possibility that Ealing output should be nuanced for female audiences. Craigie suggested that changes in women's lives be addressed:

> Can you honestly say that any of our directors, even Sandy [Mackendrick], gets under the skins of their women characters? Has your wife or your daughter ever said anything to you about British films – I mean during the last 6 or 7 years – 'that is me, that is how I would have felt under those circumstances'? ... there is a young female market. They buy the records, they go out for their entertainment. Their goal is, very naturally, marriage ... the main conflict in the mind of these young girls is whether to hold out for their dream man, who is rather like a movie star, or settle down for reality, which is nothing like what they were aiming at. Our films are made as though we're completely unaware of this new generation. What the young girls are up to affects their mothers, their landladies, the shops, the courts, everyone in society.[14]

Balcon's silence towards this impassioned cry is the loudest in British film history. Ealing's pattern of gender representation throughout the decade is a testament to his deafness to the female voice. During the postwar period, some Ealing films had placed women in the centre of the narrative. Now they were shoved further towards the margins, with fresh admonishments.

Ealing output in the 1950s can be classified into four types: Power Structures, New Commodification, Boys' Games and Wartime Glories. Power Structures deal with the mechanisms of social control. In *The Blue Lamp* (1950), the key relationships in the film are between Dixon (Jack Warner) and his son-substitute (Jimmy Handley), and between Dixon and his criminal enemy Tom (Dirk Bogarde). There is no emotional space left for relationships with women. Accordingly, the moll Di (Peggy Evans) is shown as unreliable, though fascinated by Tom's 'gun'. Mum (Gladys Henson) is granted the privilege of deference.

I Believe in You (1952) deals with trainee probation officer Henry (Cecil Parker) and the work he undertakes with Matty (Celia Johnson).

All the deviants are female: the drunken aristocrat, the crazed astrologer, the paranoid cat-lady. The prostitute is of special interest. She owns a white standard poodle (indisputable proof of moral turpitude) and pays no income tax. Women are outside the community; they can only enter it if, like Matty, they sacrifice their desires. *The Long Arm* (1956) falls into the same pattern. The detective Tom Halliday (Jack Hawkins) is 'a broad, well set up man. Mastery of his work has given him an air of authority' (S154). The man's body *is* the social institution.

New Commodification films present consumerism as a tragedy, and attempt to replace it with a revived moral order. The women are shown to be more vulnerable to the new hedonism. In *Dance Hall* (1950), the Palais is presented as the site of unratified sexual exchange. Women who dance together are ordered to 'come out of that jungle'. The young wife's predicament is sympathetically presented, and she complains, 'you want me to stay at home and be bored, bored, bored!' (S55). But ultimately she is forced to forgo her dancing pleasures.

Other Ealing films indicate that women are most susceptible to consumerism's charms. *Meet Mr Lucifer* (1953) suggests that the Devil's television prevails most powerfully on young wives, since they are more acquisitive. *The Love Lottery* (1953) argues that consumer culture is increasingly 'based on the frustrations of women'. Fans pursue the film star (David Niven), and he dreams of being torn to pieces by 'great grisly acres of women lurking around and trying to pick up the scent'. Even *Touch and Go* (1955) contains a covert debate about modern things and their people. A modernist furniture designer (Jack Hawkins) wants to emigrate to Australia. He is taught that it is wrong to make purely modernist things, and wrong to persuade people to want them.

The Man in the White Suit (1951) is preoccupied with consumerism too. Sidney Stratton's (Alec Guinness) invention puts a stop to the cycle of consumption, decay and replacement, as the old landlady (Edie Martin) realizes: 'what's to become of my bit of washing when there's no washing left to do?' *The Man in the White Suit* takes a very pessimistic view of consumption, but also of the reforming powers of creativity. Indeed, Ealing loads the dice against those who countermand consumerism. In *The Ladykillers* (1955), the burden of saving the old order is laid on an elderly lady in spats who loves her parrots. Her sweet battiness is unequal to the task.

Boys' Games films celebrate masculine gadgetry and ritual. *The*

Magnet (1950) and *The Lavender Hill Mob* (1951) fall into this category. So do *The Square Ring* (1953) and *The Maggie* (1954). Of particular interest is *The Titfield Thunderbolt* (1953), which shows men behaving like schoolboys with train sets. One scene shows a duel between a steamroller and a train in which the protagonists bellow taunts derived from games. Another scene shows Hawkins (Sid James) in a pub, watching a TV western in which a bar-room tart is told to 'scram, Baby'. A short dissolve elides the tart with a respectable lady collecting for charity, whom Hawkins dispatches: 'not today, Miss'. The films suggest that those incompetent in the discourse of games are outside the real community of ritual.

Wartime Glories – the Ealing war films – are an extension of Boys' Games. *The Cruel Sea* (1953) intensifies the misogyny of the Monserrat novel, and *The Ship That Died of Shame* (1955), though a well-found vessel, is 'like a ideal woman. She does what you want, when you want it.' And in *Dunkirk* (1958) it is the women who believe Lord Haw-Haw: 'All the same, he may be right.' This was because Balcon thought it right that 'there are no women characters of any importance'.[15] Ealing war films inhabit a more exclusively male terrain than anyone else's. Balcon would have liked to make more, but Davis feared the likely effects on foreign takings:

> they are not acceptable in a very large number of countries which form part of our basic markets. The reason is obvious. Either a defeated people do not wish to be reminded of the victor, or an occupied people do not wish to be reminded of the horrors of occupation.[16]

There remains the case of *Mandy* (1952). It has the same preoccupation as *The Divided Heart* (1954): namely, mother-love. *Mandy* presents 'excessive' mother-love as a problem. Headmaster Searle (Jack Hawkins) thinks Mandy's deafness is compounded by the fact that she is 'wholly dependent on the mother'. Unlike the original novel, a substantial proportion of the film's narrative is taken up by the possibility of the mother's infidelity. The husband (Terence Morgan) eviscerates himself with his suspicions, until his father advises that he had best behave as if his wife (Phyllis Calvert) were blameless, and try to think that 'Kit isn't like that'. *Mandy* is a lacerating film about a vulnerable little girl, but its emotional power is vitiated by its suspicion of her gender.

The old school – the major producers of the 1930s and 1940s – were now in decline. Herbert Wilcox did well with *Odette* (1950) and *The Lady with the Lamp* (1951), because there was still some mileage left in Neagle's earlier image. The first was about Odette Churchill's sufferings as a spy, and the second about Florence Nightingale's experiences in the Crimea. Neagle's demeanour was appropriate, but as the decade progressed, Wilcox was unable to adapt her manner. She co-starred with Errol Flynn in two sad reprises, *Lilacs in the Spring* (1955) and *King's Rhapsody* (1956). Wilcox teamed Neagle again with Michael Wilding in the dismal *Derby Day* (1952), in which she merely had to be unsuitably dressed. Otherwise, Wilcox miscast her in *My Teenage Daughter* (1956) and *The Lady Is a Square* (1959). Neagle's older personae signalled disappointment, instead of the rage or insouciance which are alternative modes of greeting the Grim Reaper.

Korda too no longer functioned as a cinematic author in the 1950s. The sexual and class politics he had espoused in films – the kitten-princesses and the aristocratic symbolism – were no longer appropriate. British Lion operated as a fulcrum for those escaping from the constraints of Rank and ABPC; Korda was their facilitator, not the provider of intellectual sustenance.

Powell and Pressburger's partnership foundered under the new distribution arrangements. Under Independent Producers Ltd, The Archers's films had devised a world of cultural élitism in which women had played an important symbolic role. This was too frail to withstand the rigours of the 1950s marketplace, and the partnership broke up.

Although older producer/directors could not deal with the sea-change in social and sexual behaviour, various other small outfits did attempt the task. Hammer produced the most consistent body of films. From the early 1950s, it struck deals with American distributors, and was aggressive in its handling of them. Hammer was street-wise in its choice of topics, and greased its path on the world markets by employing ageing American stars (Brian Donlevy, George Brent) at the behest of the distribution companies. Hammer was unusual in the degree of power exerted from above. Executive producer James Carreras, producer Antony Hinds and associate producer Antony Nelson Keys exerted tight control, and even rigged up microphones to keep tabs on what was happening on the studio floor. Producers kept a firm hand on the scripting process, and wrote many themselves; the script was the master discourse. The visual languages and the gender politics of Hammer films depend on the script guidelines.

Hammer's representation of women varied dramatically according to genre in the 1950s. In the modern-dress films, females contain and resolve contradictions. In *The Last Page* (1952), the heroine (Diana Dors) shifts from guiltless ingénue to ruthless blackmailer to helpless murder victim. In *Danger List* (1957), the culpable carelessness of the female pharmacist is atoned by the death of the sick wife. Women have a straightforward narrative function in the science fiction films, *Spaceways* (1953), *The Quatermass Xperiment* (1955), *X the Unknown* (1956) and *Quatermass II* (1957). However, at the symbolic level, the films evoke anxiety about sexuality: male in the first *Quatermass*, and female in *X the Unknown* (Hutchings, 1993, pp. 48–9).

It was with the historical horror films that Hammer began to exploit the symbolic resonances of their female characters to the full. They prepared the ground for the sustained treatment of female sexuality which Hammer undertook in the 1960s. In *The Curse of Frankenstein* (1957), *Dracula* (1958), *The Revenge of Frankenstein* (1958) and *The Mummy* (1959), Hammer films display a nervous preoccupation with the body: its orifices, its blood, its organs. In the Frankenstein films, both male and female protagonists are comprehensively eroticized. In *Dracula*, both heroines enjoy the vampire's unconventional style of coitus. They are transformed by his unratified penetration, which destroys them as moral beings. Only penetration by the stake of the celibate Van Helsing (Peter Cushing) can restore them to the moral mainstream. *Dracula*'s treatment of sexuality and its discontents is predicated on an aristocratic symbolism similar to Gainsborough's. Dracula has all the flair of a Byronic hero, who destroys what he loves and who brutalizes what he respects. The female figures are presented without any such social gloss; they are outside history, class and time.

In *The Mummy*, the dangers encapsulated by women move onto centre stage. The maimed John (Peter Cushing) loves Isobel. She is the double of Princess Ananka, the beloved of the maimed Karis (Christopher Lee) of old. The most intense passage in the film describes the death, dis-embowelling and mummification of Ananka. John's voice-over intones the ritual about the baths of natron and removal of the organs, while before our eyes her young body retains its charm. She is both mother and beloved, alive yet dead, and the most powerful perturbation in the text.

Other independent film-makers represented female sexuality as a dis-
ruptive force, but used different strategies. The New Wave – a loose
grouping of younger directors comprising Tony Richardson, Lindsay
Anderson, Karel Reisz, Jack Clayton and others – originally called itself
Free Cinema. With hindsight Free Cinema now seems formalist and self-
indulgent, its documentaries narrowly élitist and traditional in their
gender politics. The feature films made by New Wave practitioners were
innovatory in their subject matter, and were homogeneous in tone and
approach in spite of being made for different companies. They were, of
course, exclusively contemporary in their interests.

The early New Wave films responded to consumerism with a bitter
misogyny. *Look Back in Anger* (1959), made by Woodfall from John
Osborne's play, describes a sustained programme of abuse which masquerades as love. Osborne's sympathies are with Jimmy Porter, and the
textual dynamics make Alison (Mary Ure) collude in her own brutal-
ization. The game of 'bears and squirrels' confers a furry sentimentality
onto a relationship founded on loathing. *Look Back in Anger* is about
male inadequacy in the face of female vulnerability: 'I want to be there
when you grovel . . . I want the front seat. I want to see your face rubbed
in the mud.' Jimmy dislikes being engulfed by Alison's body: 'It's not that
she hasn't her own kind of passion. She has. The passion of a python. She
just devours me whole every time as if I were some over-large rabbit.' As
Germaine Greer famously remarked, women have very little idea how
much men hate them. There is nothing in 1950s cinema which is so
instructive in this regard as *Look Back in Anger*.

Tony Richardson's production of the play softens the original a little.
This was due partially to BBFC censorship. However, the misogyny of the
original was unchanged, since the censors were preoccupied by 'language' (Aldgate, 1995, pp. 74–9). And anyway, Richardson was more
interested in the intensity of Jimmy's emotions than in their social or
sexual effects.

Woodfall's film of Alan Sillitoe's novel, *Saturday Night and Sunday
Morning* (1960) also had a rocky censorship ride, largely because of the
abortion scene. Directed by Karel Reisz and scripted by Sillitoe, the film
makes space for Brenda (Rachel Roberts) to express her desires: 'Eh,
Arthur, what a time we had last night!' But eventually she is surplus to
requirements, since she is older and pregnant (the abortion is successful in
the novel). Brenda is abandoned by Arthur for a younger woman.

The *mise en scène* of *Saturday Night and Sunday Morning* oppresses the male characters, and it makes the claustrophobia impinge intensely on them. The Seatons' kitchen (actually Sillitoe's mother's house) is tightly framed, with choking close-ups of Arthur as he rebels against limitation. None of the female protagonists are shot in this way. The same spatial arrangements and shooting style obtain in *Room at the Top* (1959). This had the same cameraman, Freddie Francis, and was directed by Jack Clayton for John and James Woolf's Remus company.

Room at the Top, like *Saturday Night and Sunday Morning*, is about the declining marketability of older women. In John Braine's original novel, Joe Lampton expresses love for his older mistress Alice Aisgill, and contempt for millionaire's daughter Susan Brown, whose body he uses as his high road to 'the Top'. The Remus film equalizes the balance. Although Joe (Laurence Harvey) still loves Alice (Simone Signoret), the script gives houseroom to others' insults to her. And Susan (Heather Sears) is allowed to verbalize her pleasure in a sexual act which was perfunctory for her partner.

The film is transformed by Signoret. Like so many women before her, she is transfigured by her love for a man who is her emotional inferior. In her bodily play, Alice is luminous and erotically inventive; Joe is wooden and self-serving. *Room at the Top* was probably intended to administer a corrective to Old Bags and Young Tarts; but the effect of Signoret's performance unbalances that, and the film instead evokes a profound pity: pity for Alice's willingness to confer her love on an unworthy object, and pity for Joe's inability to disregard her age and lack of status. Signoret herself was well aware of these resonances in the role (Signoret, 1978, p. 220).

If we now turn to less ambitious projects than the New Wave, we can see that some small companies produced films which were more progressive on the gender front. Eros, for example, which was a small distribution outfit, made *The Flesh Is Weak*, in which Marissa (Milly Vitale) is lured into prostitution by her love for a gangster. The film's publicity material suggests that producer Stross took out extra insurance against personal injury, so concerned was he that gangland bosses would take revenge on his disclosures. As Marissa puts up increasing resistance to her exploitation, her clothes become astonishingly elegant. Her stylish wardrobe functions on a symbolic level, and her sartorial transformation signals a will to exert power.

Eros also made *Serious Charge* (1959) about a vicar falsely accused of homosexuality. This film too contains assertive women who dominate the text. The repressed spinster (Sarah Churchill) loves vicar Anthony Quayle. She declares her love, and eventually fakes a rape in order to incriminate the vicar's enemy. The vicar's mother (Irene Browne) is iconoclastic. She is an avowed atheist, a sexual liberal and an outspoken cynic, telling the spinster: 'You wanted to go to bed with my son. The trouble is, you went about it the wrong way.' The mother then encourages her to flaunt herself more discreetly, and her advice is presented as sensible.

Female stereotypes were quite rigorously constructed in the 1950s, and room to manoeuvre was minimal. Eunice Gayson bitterly told aspiring actresses: 'Don't be a brunette. Don't have sex-appeal. Don't be independent.'[17] *Picturegoer* mounted a series of articles about British actresses' lack of range. For Maurice Elvey, 'our girls wear sex like a fur coat, self-consciously and awkwardly . . . they are frankly too lady-like to let their real feelings show'. Journalist Dick Richards argued that studios had 'a crazy, criminal contempt for women players . . . the glamour gals have the pulling power – if they are allowed to exert it. But they are getting so used to playing second fiddle and merely decorating male-adventure stories that they are throwing in the sponge.' Ivan Foxwell argued that war films limited women's acting opportunities: 'such stories hardly offer chances for the development of glamour, do they?' And Joan Sims complained: 'Can't a girl be funny without being turned into a scarecrow? . . . They're not content with making me look like the battered back of a tram. They make me look a glutton as well.'[18]

Directors, of course, could affect actresses' roles: Brian Desmond Hurst shot scenes in *Scrooge* (1951) to favour Kathleen Harrison and disfavour Alistair Sim. But in general, roles were determined by distributors, producers and scriptwriters. Some persuaded 'respectable' actresses like Yvonne Mitchell to pose for glamour stills. Those too old for such tricks went to the wall. The death of Margaret Lockwood's career was a clear consequence of decisions made higher up, whatever audiences might want.[19] Lockwood herself was 'sick of being haggard and wearing dramatic make-up and killing somebody or other'.[20] Roles as Mary Magdalen and Tess of the D'Urbevilles were mooted for her, but Rank's underlings scuppered them (Hurst, n.d., p. 141).

The categories of roles were more watertight than they had been in the

1940s. Once actresses were typecast, there was little chance of trans-ference into other personae or genres. Virginia McKenna, for example, wanted to extend her range, hating the appellation 'English Rose'. This proved difficult, and she was fortunate to land the lead role of *A Town Like Alice*. But if you had open features, shallow-set eyes and short curls like Susan Stephen, Peggy Cummins or June Thorburn, you stood little chance of being anything other than an MoI reprise: a virtuous potential homemaker. Such were the production constraints that it was impossible to try the ironic 'undercutting' techniques some actresses had used in the 1930s.

Of course, the industry required other types than MoI reprises. Whor-ish Hussy roles were much in demand, and they had to be tall, blonde, large-breasted and appear sexually hungry and stupid. Belinda Lee and Liz Fraser fell into this category. So did Yana, who was sexier than Ealing expected: as a result, they refused to feature her in publicity pictures.[21] Sabrina had made a television career out of her bosom and her silence: 'All I did was walk on and be made fun of.'[22] In films her Lancashire accent was dubbed and in *Stock Car* (1955) she was used 'for good-natured laughs' by director Wolf Rilla, who thought her figure was 'too far forward or something'.[23] The most important Whorish Hussy, of course, was Diana Dors, who was combative and feisty, with a mocking awareness of her image:

> I am, by English standards, a fairly flamboyant character ... I am paid large sums of money not because I look and act like the girl next door, but because my name is linked immediately with mink, fast cars and pink champagne.[24]

Dors complained about the range of roles she was offered, and was critical about the British industry in general: if Helen of Troy were in British movies, producers would have cast her 'as a juvenile delinquent'.[25] She did, however, enjoy being lusted after: 'to be looked at as if you were a chocolate éclair does wonders for a girl's ego'.[26] Dors was a sort of Lady Docker of the screen, eliciting *Schadenfreude* responses of disapproval and envy.

British film narratives of the 1950s required 'outsiders' to express forbidden repertoires of desire. Foreign Floosies were recruited in droves to play characters with negotiable morality. Milly Vitale, Brigitte Bardot, Odile Versois, Yvonne Furnaux and Marla Landi were exotic in a different way from 1930s imports. They were tousled, experienced and mainly blonde; their narrative function was to operate as sexual proxies for respectable British girls. Foreign girls' eroticism and accent placed them outside the class arena, of course. In general, 1950s cinema juxta-posed native females in a critical relationship to sexy outsiders. Eccentric, respectable women were positively positioned in film narratives: actresses like Edie Martin, Katie Johnson, Irene Handl, Margaret Rutherford and Joyce Grenfell had more room for technical manoeuvre than the sexpots, whose narrative function was fixed. But the eccentrics were all neu-tralized by their age, which confers absurdity onto their desires.

The structure of the industry in the 1950s had precise effects on the function of women in film texts. The bigger distribution companies (Rank and ABPC) had so many satellites that total control was impos-sible, and some liberal and challenging interpretations of females were inserted by devious means. British Lion's blunderbuss distribution tech-nique had some unpredictable effects too: in a sense, it liberated the Boultings and Launder and Gilliat to follow their star, in terms of gender representation. Paradoxically, the most conservative images of women issued from the most innovative films – those made by Hammer and by the New Wave film-makers. That had important consequences for images of women in 1960s cinema.

Notes

1. Quotations identified by numbers with the prefix S (e.g., S123) refer to the BFI's collection of unpublished scripts.
2. *Laughter in Paradise* (1951) was the *Kineweekly* Top Moneymaker of its year, as was *The Dam Busters* (1955).
3. Kathleen Leaver, 'Reading for a living', *ABC Film Review*, July 1955.
4. Into this category fell Walter Mycroft's Bow Bells, which made *The Woman's Angle* (1952) and Herbert Wilcox's Everest, which made the grisly *Wonderful Things!* (1958) starring Frankie Vaughan as a Catalan fisherman.
5. Henry's novel came out before the Ruth Ellis case. Ellis shot her lover in premeditation, and was hanged. The film was released a year after the hanging. So the Ellis case fed into the reception of the film, but not necessarily into the making of it.
6. PRO WO 32/16026, War Office memo, 31 July 1957. See also memo of 15 May 1957.
7. See MacFarlane (1997), pp. 75–6, and a very full account by Sidney Gilliat in *Positif*, no. 406, December 1994.
8. See exchange of letters in early 1954 in H/119, Balcon Collection, BFI Library.
9. *Ibid.*, H/134, Davis to Balcon, 23 December 1954.
10. *Ibid.*, I/235, memo, 18 June 1959.

11. *Ibid.*, I/20, letter to Jack Hawkins, 20 September 1956.
12. *Ibid.*, letter to Pat Jackson, 16 March 1956.
13. *Ibid.*, I/45, letter to Jill Craigie, 14 June 1958.
14. *Ibid.*, Craigie to Balcon, 12 January 1958.
15. *Ibid.*, I/46(a), Balcon to Leslie Norman, 19 March 1956.
16. *Ibid.*, H/138, Davis to Balcon, 18 October 1955.
17. *Picturegoer*, 28 April 1956.
18. *Ibid.*, 28 July 1956; 25 January 1955; 2 April 1955; 7 May 1955.
19. See readers' letters in *Picturegoer*, 16 September 1950; 10 February 1951; 17 March 1951; 28 November 1953; 29 January 1955.
20. *Picturegoer*, 12 March 1955. See also *Woman*, 25 March 1955.
21. *Picturegoer*, 12 February 1955.
22. *Ibid.*, 12 November 1955.
23. *Ibid.*, 25 June 1955.
24. *Ibid.*, 24 March 1956.
25. *Ibid.*, 12 May 1956.
26. *Ibid.*, 15 October 1955. See also *Sequence 7*, Spring 1949.

5

The 1960s: Delusions of Freedom

The 1960s was a period in which social change in Britain appeared to be accelerated: the Profumo affair, the election of the Labour government in 1964, the public protests about Vietnam, the suspension of capital punishment in 1965, and the Race Relations, Sexual Offences, Obscene Publications and Abortion Acts all modified people's perceptions of individual freedom. The transformations in class-consciousness and sexual permissiveness were not, perhaps, as extensive as some people hoped, and earlier discourses of social probity and sexual chastity were by no means called into question by the majority. But the 1960s was an unusually self-conscious decade, and cultural forms played a crucial role in establishing new agendas and possible realms of consciousness. This was grasped by the influential article on 'London, the swinging city' in *Time*, which during its tour of British sub-cultural forms insisted that 'the girls have become as emancipated as the boys', and that they 'lead fulfilled sex lives'.[1]

The cinema was part of the self-mythologizing tendency of the period, and celebrated specific aspects of the social transformation. It fed directly into the fantasy of national vitality, and was partially responsible for the myth of Swinging Britain. Some 1960s film critics fell for the notion that film reflected changes in the *Zeitgeist*. Philip French argued that

> The future historian might see the move enacted in symbolic terms in *Billy Liar*. In retrospect the high point of the picture is the nouvelle vague-ish promenade through the Northern high street by Julie Christie as Liz, harbinger of short skirts, discotheques, the pill and what you will.[2]

But in fact the Swinging Britain myth bore little relation to many people's lived experience. If anyone did interpret the myth as a reflection of reality, they might fairly have expected the whole country to be populated by young girls with visible knickers and flexible morality, who were good at sprinting along pavements. However, they would have been disappointed. Those who thought art had straightforward consequences might have expected the sales of lilac photography paper to skyrocket after the orgy scene in Antonioni's *Blow-up* (1967). They would have been crestfallen too.

British films of the 1960s were in fact far more prescriptive towards women than they had been in the 1950s. The structure of the industry and the cultural capital of its leaders and workers in that decade produced images of women which were varied and occasionally liberal. But 1960s cinema drew the boundaries between sacred and profane females in an unexpectedly rigid way. It judged women either as Keepers of the Flame (safe but dull), or as Courtesans (willing penetratees, but heartless). There were important exceptions, of course, but on the whole, the emotional repertoire of women on the 1960s screen was pitifully truncated. There were four reasons. First, as I shall show in Part II, women left the industry in droves, and the perspectives offered by many female screenwriters and directors were lost. Second, John Trevelyan liberalized BBFC practices in a gradual yet radical manner (Aldgate, 1995). The new freedoms temporarily blinded some film-makers to anything but sexual action. Third, some of the 'grammar school boys' in the cultural and film industries now had more confidence than before, and their preoccupations with masculinity had freer rein. Fourth, the economic structure of the British film industry changed drastically. By 1970 it was moving into what seemed like a terminal phase.

The distribution arrangements which had worked so well for Rank and ABPC began to unravel. They brought in the 'barring' system of booking, holding successful films over for weeks and ignoring a heavy backlog of films which they deemed of minority appeal. Rank and ABPC also began to require exhibitors to pay a higher proportion of their box-office gross. This led to rebellious murmurings among the exhibitors. In addition, there was a chronic fall in audience numbers, and seating capacity fell by more than half as cinemas closed. As the decade progressed, the boundary between the British and the international film industry became increasingly blurred, as virtually no film could recoup its costs without some success in the American market. The American majors invested spasmodically in the British industry in the 1960s, until at one time they accounted for some 90 per cent of capital invested. Of course, American-financed films, even those preoccupied with the British way of life, had different cultural capital and textual effects from the native product.[3] But anyway, American cash was withdrawn at the end of the decade with indecent haste, and with catastrophic effects on the native industry.

All this led to an unusually volatile situation in which, rather like the 1930s, entrepreneurs in the business would try anything once, even if the project was culturally shallow-rooted. *Girl on a Motorcycle* (1968) and *Gonks Go Beat* (1965) are examples of such shallow-rooters, but there were many more.[4] Inexperienced and irresponsible funding encouraged risk-taking strategies which plumped for bandwagons, quick returns or downright silliness.

During the 1950s, ABPC had, rather by accident than design, provided creative space for female scriptwriters and proto-feminist representations. The company had produced some films which asked startling questions about the sexual status quo. All this changed in the 1960s. The company's financial problems caused it to cut back on production. ABPC only made one popular film in the 1960s, *The Young Ones* (1961), which was the Top Moneymaker in 1962. This starred Cliff Richard in a hey-kids-let's-put-on-a-show extravaganza. It contains some oedipal by-play between Cliff and his father (Robert Morley), and its gender arrangements are symmetrical. Good girl Toni (Carole Gray) has manageable hair and a flat chest. Bad girl Dorinda (Sonya Cordeau) has ebullient hair and breasts. Poor Cliff has no choice at all.

ABPC made a policy decision to concentrate mainly on comedy films, which was unwise considering its personnel expertise. It had made some important prison films in the 1950s, but the experience was forgotten in such farragos as the convict comedy *The Pot Carriers* (1962). One of its comedies starring Charlie Drake, *Petticoat Pirates* (1961), gave significant roles to women, but it was a hamfisted enterprise. ABPC had lost its way with popular cinema.

Rank fared badly too. Under its helmsman John Davis, the organization had promulgated anodyne family films in the 1950s. All this changed in the 1960s. The company tried a variety of modes and genres, which vitiated its former clear patterns of gender representation. Accordingly, Rank attempted high-culture vehicles: *The Royal Ballet* (1960), *Der Rosenkavalier* (1962), *Romeo and Juliet* (1966), possibly aimed at female aficionados. It continued with the *Doctor* films produced by Betty Box –

Doctor in Love (1960), *Doctor in Distress* (1963) and *Doctor in Clover* (1965) – which became progressively coarser. They ended in a lip-smacking priapism which gave a new frisson to the 'internal examination'. Three Morecambe and Wise comedies were made, in which female roles were stereotypical; ditto for four Norman Wisdom vehicles.

Davis, with increasing desperation, tried specialist sub-genres: a spy spoof, a nun melodrama, a Catholic western. But the day of the compliant house director was fading fast, and often only quirky ones were available for hire. Roy Ward Baker, for example, made *The Singer Not the Song* for Rank in 1961; this was an extraordinary film, although he claimed that 'it broke my heart' (MacFarlane, 1997, pp. 51–2). Set in Mexico, it deals with an intense relationship between Father Keogh (John Mills, wearing an uncertain Irish accent and a cassock that looks like a frock) and bandit Anacleto (Dirk Bogarde, wearing black leather, a white palfrey and a Byronic sneer). Their mutual fascination leads to their violent deaths, and Father Keogh gasps his last with his hand clutching Anacleto's leather groin.

But *The Singer Not the Song* is not quite 'as camp as Christmas' (Bourne, 1996, p. 152). Rather, it is a testament to the cultural pickle Davis was in, and to Baker's anarchic inventiveness. The film displays a chronic inconsistency in its treatment of women as well as men. In the original novel by Audrey Erskine Lindop, the heroine Locha is a plain child who falls in love with Father Keogh; narrative time is given to her mother, a woman with astonishing erotic needs who inhibits her child's desires. The film script by Nigel Balchin excises the mother, which unbalances the emotional proportion, and converts Locha into a sexually hungry devotee. To complicate matters further, Davis cast Mylène Demongeot as Locha. In high sex-kitten mode, she teeters through the text wearing an assortment of flock nylon headscarves and sultry looks. The sheer inconsistency of her role throws attention back onto the male leads, to whom Baker, in some desperation, clearly gave their head. *The Singer Not the Song* shows that under certain circumstances, *schtick* leads to *shlock*.

Baker's heart was not broken for long, since he directed *Flame in the Streets* for Rank in the same year. This is the story of a union activist (John Mills) whose daughter wishes to marry a black schoolteacher. Yet again, the representation of women in the film was determined by management's attitude to the original source. The film was based on Ted Willis's play, which he had adapted into a popular television version. The film script caused Willis 'anguish', since he was forced to transfer the action from high summer to mid-winter. More crucially, Davis cast Brenda de Banzie as the working-class wife, and she was presented 'with painted fingernails, clothes that might have been bought in Bond Street, and an accent that owed more to Mayfair than to Bermondsey' (Willis, 1991, p. 146). So the clout of her bitter words to her husband is vitiated: 'you even made love to me as though you were taking a quick drink'.

A more confident director, Val Guest, made two films for Rank. He had already refined his ideas about generic convention and the representation of women with *The Day the Earth Caught Fire* (1961), which he also produced and scripted. This film conflated the themes of global catastrophe and female desire. The earth is in meltdown and so is heroine Janet Munro, inflamed by the temperature and the amorous attentions of Edward Judd.[5] Guest liked to construct narratives in which women's feelings were thoroughly integrated into the main narrative. He made *80,000 Suspects* for Rank in 1963. The main story about a smallpox epidemic is skilfully woven with a sub-plot about the hero's wife and mistress, who are constructed with admirable complexity. Guest then directed *The Beauty Jungle* (1964) for Rank, which is about a secretary (Janette Scott) who is groomed into a beauty queen. She becomes a ferocious opportunist, and it is a stronger female role than any other Rank films of the period. We must attribute that to Guest, not to Davis.

In the 1950s, the satellite companies attached to Rank had been under considerable pressure, and they resorted to evasive tactics to get their textual way. None of that was necessary in the 1960s. To begin with, Davis was diversifying out of film production. But more importantly, he was beginning to offer mere distribution arrangements rather than direct funding, and he made few demands on the independent producers. Accordingly, some 37 one-picture companies plied Rank with distribution trade during the 1960s. Few of the films were either profitable or significant, except for *The Day of the Triffids* (Security, 1962), and *The Ipcress File* (Lowndes, 1965), which were both conventional on the gender front. Allied Film-makers (AFM) were distributed by Rank, but they had their own remit. Another larger company was Independent Artists, which released, among others, *This Sporting Life* in 1963. By no stretch of the imagination could this be construed as a Rank film, since (according to one reviewer) it was 'Krafft-Ebing in a rugby shirt'.[6] Rank distributed Adder Films's *Carry On* cycle from 1966, by which time it had become gloriously smutty. There can be no stronger proof of the breakdown of Rank policy than the shot of the row of raised kilts in *Carry On up the Khyber* in 1968: let a hundred penises bloom. A long trajectory of 'decency' had come to an end at last.

The history of British Lion in the 1960s is a woeful tale too, but this time of government bungling and wasted energy.[7] We saw in the last chapter that British Lion had served as a permissive catch-all for independent film-makers, and that it had backed some adventurous projects. In the 1960s, the Boultings and Launder and Gilliat were drawn into administration, and made fewer films. Launder and Gilliat continued the same trajectory as before, but *Pure Hell of St Trinian's* (1960), although energetic in its treatment of the banshees, was derivative, copying the diamond-necklace-in-the-football motif from Will Hay's *Boys Will Be Boys*. Their other 1960s films were equally lacklustre. Small wonder that Gilliat advised: 'Whatever you do, don't go into management.'[8]

John and Roy Boulting did not develop from their 1950s position, in which, as I argued, women operated as society's pit canaries. On the face of it, their *The Family Way* (1966) is about impotence in the younger generation and unrecognized homosexual desire in the older one, and the handling of such material in an unsensational way is an innovation. But even such a frank film defines the women as bystanders at the sexual feast. All they can do is complain about what is denied to them. British Lion's economic structure did not encourage creative breakthroughs on the gender front for the Boultings. Whether they wanted them or not, of course, was another matter.

The demise of Ealing had left Michael Balcon rootless. His connection with producer Maxwell Setton led to the inception of Bryanston Films, which was intended to be an unofficial ministry of independent film-makers. Bryanston had a complex 'revolving credit' system, and released its few films through British Lion (Balcon, 1969, pp. 194–5). Woodfall Films was an autonomous unit within Bryanston, and, in a well-documented débâcle, Bryanston lost Woodfall through its failure to fund *Tom Jones* (1963). This indirectly contributed to its downfall.[9]

Bryanston's 1960s productions are a testimony to the longevity of the Ealing ethic. Decent, liberal, sexually conservative – all its films sat well within the framework of Ealing. *The Battle of the Sexes* (1960), which dealt with the depredations of a 'castrating' American efficiency expert (Constance Cummings) on old-fashioned business, is a combination of themes from Ealing films of the 1950s. *Sammy Going South* (1964) is a reprise of *Scott of the Antarctic*, but with a child as hero. *Sammy*, like *Scott*, is preoccupied by what must be sacrificed in order to be a man – tenderness, expressivity, trust. Although competent, *Sammy* and the other Bryanston pieces were cinematic dinosaurs. The company died giving birth to the newly invigorated Woodfall, which had more aggressive sexual politics.

Herbert Wilcox ceased making films in the late 1950s, and other older producer/directors were either bankrupt or dead, their styles of gender representation having died with them. Michael Powell's career as a mainstream director came to a catastrophic end with *Peeping Tom* (1960). The history of its reception is too well known to rehearse here. Suffice it to say that the story of the scopophiliac film-maker with the penetrative camera had reviews of unparalleled ferocity, particularly from female critics.[10] Powell's film career never recovered, but *Peeping Tom* was rehabilitated by later critics. These revisions were undoubtedly a consequence of that selective version of Freud which was modish in some British academic circles from 1974. It suited some people's book to co-opt *Peeping Tom* into a proof of the link between scopophilia and mainstream cinema. The film could be hailed as a misunderstood masterpiece, while serving to reinforce the culpability of the epistemological habits of the cinematic apparatus.

The film certainly is (as many male critics have suggested) powerful, compassionate and self-reflexive. But it needs to be said that, morally, *Peeping Tom* is a loathsome film. It colludes with, and celebrates, men's physical power over women. Its compassion is reserved for the perpetrator of the sexual crime rather than for his victims, who are forced to watch their own faces as they are impaled on his spike. The self-referential quality of the narrative – the little jokes about filming, the casting of Powell himself as the ogre father – is unctuous.

Peeping Tom resulted from the lifting of constraints or inhibitions. Censorship controls were shifting radically by 1960. But more importantly, Powell's collaboration with Pressburger had ended, and his intellectual partner for the new project was Leo Marks, who wrote the script. With hindsight, it is clear that Pressburger had operated as a brake on Powell's preoccupation with male pathology. Powell initially tried to pass the buck of *Peeping Tom*'s débâcle onto Pressburger (MacDonald, 1994, pp. 381–2). But it would not stick, so he fingered Marks instead (Powell, 1992, pp. 392–6).

Powell interpreted Marks's script so as to anchor the themes of blindness and mutilation firmly within the female body. In one of the first full-length nude shots in British mainstream cinema, protagonist Mark (Carl Boehm) makes a camera set-up of a professional model. Due to her twisted pose, we see it all: breasts, buttocks, shaven *mons veneris*. All, that is, except her face, which is turned away. She is eviscerated immediately afterwards. When Mark approaches his first prostitute victim, the camera pulls back to a dress-shop window. It is full of female body parts – heads, legs, a torso – which display frippery, and female guilt and mutilation are ineluctably linked. But especially in the maternal body. The child Mark is filmed visiting his mother's deathbed: her hands and torso are seen, but her face – the most expressive body part – is cut from the frame.[11] Helen's blind mother (Maxine Audley) constitutes the most intuitive challenge to Mark. But her white stick is explicitly without a 'point', and cannot compete with his camera, which can both see and kill.

Peeping Tom enacts the terror of a little boy in flight from the monster. The monstrous thing has many forms: it is the lizard running up his trouser legs, and the random glance of passers-by. But the most monstrous thing is the unmutilated maternal body, on which he is compelled to make his 'Mark'.

We should now turn to film-makers who managed to make a profitable settlement with the new economic and social conditions. Some of them were old hands in the business, but they were inventive. Even so, there was no automatic correlation between entrepreneurialism and radical sexual politics. AFM, for example, was set up by Michael Relph, Basil Dearden, Bryan Forbes and Richard Attenborough in 1959. They were financially connected with Rank, but intellectually independent. In the films produced and directed by Attenborough and Forbes – *Whistle Down the Wind* (1961), *Seance on a Wet Afternoon* (1964) – the issue of gender is not foregrounded. Relph and Dearden's AFM films, on the other hand – even the seemingly neutral *Life for Ruth* (1962) – are absolutely preoccupied by 'separate spheres'. *The League of Gentlemen* (1960) is structured around a male group bonded together by their social and sexual deviance. The women are adulterous or better dead: 'I'm sorry to say the bitch is still alive', as the group leader remarks of his wife. *The Man in the Moon* (1960), which Relph co-scripted, deals with breezy William Blood (Kenneth More) who makes a career from his rude good health. William is guarded in his relationships, especially with besotted stripper Shirley Ann Field. His competitive approach to other men is temporarily sabotaged when Leo (Charles Gray) is brainwashed into liking him with excessive fervour. The plot resolves the heterosexual embarrassment by marrying William to his stripper and producing triplets.

Indeed, the purpose of Relph and Dearden's *Victim* (1961) was to resolve heterosexual embarrassment too. This film, which became celebrated for its pioneering treatment of homosexuality, shifts male desire to centre stage by consigning female desire to the emotional periphery. The script by Janet Green places the guilt onto the spinster, whose homophobia, greed and sexual frustration motivate her blackmail of the gay protagonists. Raymond Durgnat suggests that her homophobia is based on her view that men 'are the disgusting loving the disgusting. . . . She is a distant cousin of the women of SCUM' (Durgnat, 1997, p. 84).

In any case, the spinster is the 'sick' centre of the film. Its 'cold' centre is Laura Farr (Sylvia Syms), wife of the closeted barrister Stephen (Dirk Bogarde). The costume designs present Laura as a virgin or a nun. In the most important sequence, she wears a large white 'puritan' collar, which obscures her breasts and throws an innocent light onto her face.[12] The script, and Syms's acting style, suggest that here is a woman who has never caught fire. The set dressing evokes an austere world devoid of feminine clutter. In the showdown between the Farrs, the ornaments on the mantelpiece behind Stephen come into focus as he confesses: a row of little soldiers. Staffordshire dogs would have been just as appropriate, but the little grenadiers are identical, stiff, manly and therefore desirable.

The artistic autonomy at AFM permitted Relph and Dearden an enhanced degree of control over scripting and *mise en scène*, and they developed a gender politics which was only liberal towards men. Anglo-Amalgamated was another small company in which director/producer teams could have their head, and with different textual effects. It was an independent outfit owned by Stuart Levy and Nat Cohen, who moved from second features to more adventurous fare. They backed *Peeping Tom*, but pulled it from the circuits once the scandal broke. Cohen feared that if he were accused of handling pornography, he would lose his chance of a KBE in the Honours List.[13] In general, though, Anglo-Amalgamated supported its personnel. Its most important team was Joseph Janni and John Schlesinger. Janni was a producer of some sophistication, who imported earthy insights from Italian neo-realist cinema: 'In those days, England had forgotten she possessed provinces. She denied that her people ever had a sex life: sex was regarded, if it was regarded at all, as an exclusively Continental pursuit' (Walker, 1974, p. 109). John Schlesinger was an openly gay director who valued rapport with his actors (MacFarlane, 1997, p. 513). The combination of Janni's and Schlesinger's talents produced films which concentrate more on the pains than pleasures of sexual love, and which contain women who are punished for departing from the norm; not by society (that is the 'liberal' part of the texts), but by themselves.

Anglo-Amalgamated offered 100 per cent finance for *A Kind of Loving* (1962). Janni had invited playwrights Keith Waterhouse and Willis Hall to script Stan Barstow's original novel. Neither script nor completed film disturbs the disposition of the novel, which concentrates exclusively on Vic's (Alan Bates) predicament as he impregnates his girlfriend and marries her. The film single-mindedly evokes Vic's insecurities (the breath-smelling shot) and his sensations: 'I've always thought you had beautiful breasts.' Ingrid (June Ritchie), on the other hand, always expresses vulnerability and pain: 'something that ought to have happened, hasn't happened'. With her dragon mother and her preference for TV gameshows, Ingrid is the inarticulate baggage which impedes Vic's progress. In the sad ending, the couple grope each other hopelessly in a municipal hut.

Billy Liar (1963) was also scripted by Waterhouse and Hall, this time from Waterhouse's novel and their own stage version. The film, like its sources, gives very funny access to the hero's fantasy. The real world of Billy (Tom Courtenay) is tedious: no wonder he wants to 'LOOOSE himselfah in LONDONAH'. But the imaginary utopia he constructs is derivative and primitive, rather like the Brontë children's Angria/Gondal. It is a place where primal urges of killing, recognition and revenge can be satisfied. In Billy's dream-work, there is no need to deal with the complexities of sexual desire, except in the most rudimentary way. *Billy Liar* is about the inability of the masculine imagination to encompass the free female. Liz (Julie Christie) is never inside Billy's fantasies, and finally she abandons him to them.[14] With no visible means of support, she floats free above the world of goods in pursuit of her own quixotic desires. The film enacts a Venus-and-Mars separation. The males are tribal and sexually timid, the females individualistic and wilful. There can be no common ground between them.

Darling (1965) continues the same theme. Schlesinger shared the scripting with Frederick Raphael and Joseph Janni, and the film is a sour meditation on female duplicity and media hype. Its structure relies to an unusual extent on the heroine's voice-over, which it both requires and undercuts. Diana (Julie Christie) moves from man to man, but not for pleasure. The script is evasive about her motivation, which seems to be a mixture of curiosity and boredom. She has a brief attention span, both intellectually and emotionally, whereas the males are dogged. They may be dull, but they know who they are, and that is the nub of the film. It is not necessarily the case, as Carrie Tarr (1985) suggests, that *Darling* represents anxieties about women in the permissive society. Rather, Diana evokes a version of the Eternal-Feminine (instinctive, illogical) which the film-makers find irritating, and which the exasperated males in the text can never accommodate.

Far from the Madding Crowd (1967) could be made to fit nicely within that paradigm, which is doubtless why Schlesinger wanted to film it. It was not funded by Anglo-Amalgamated, but was produced by Janni and scripted by Raphael. It transformed Hardy's novel into a debate about feminine wiles and freedoms, and enacts a dour pessimism about heterosexual love. Bathsheba (Julie Christie) plays at being independent; her kittenish ways are ineffectual in the real world of men. By casting such a strong, complex actor (Peter Finch) as Bathsheba's suitor, her performance is impossibly squeezed. At the end, the stolid Gabriel Oak (Alan Bates) drones: 'whenever I look up, there you will be'. Poor Bathsheba; never has monogamy seemed such a life-sentence.

The New Wave, whose inception had been in the 1950s, continued apace. Woodfall Films underwent a radical change in its fortunes in 1962 when United Artists agreed to finance it, and for once financial security and avant-garde style went hand in hand (Walker, 1974, pp. 260–1). At the end of the 1950s, *Look Back in Anger* and *Saturday Night and Sunday Morning* had focused exclusively on male burdens. So did *The Entertainer* (1960) and *The Loneliness of the Long Distance Runner* (1962). In the latter, the dour integrity of the hero (Tom Courtenay), and the hopes and anxieties focused on him, make it a masculinist text. The same could be said of *Tom Jones*. Its hero (Albert Finney) is a true child of the Enlightenment, in his pragmatic acceptance of the laws of rationality and the pleasures of circumvention. *Tom Jones* is a film about a hell-raising boy growing up, although this is concealed by the tricksy shooting style. Tom progresses, via rough trade and lascivious eating scenes, to a sober yet sexual marriage. Just like Arthur Seaton, in fact, only with more charm.

Those Woodfall films in which women had a major writing role do not conform to this pattern. *A Taste of Honey* (1961) was based on Shelagh Delaney's play, which she scripted for Woodfall. The play presented both Jo and her mother Helen as unruly women, and refused to censure their sexual fecklessness. Delaney's script takes the same position, but gives more narrative space to Helen. It inserts a school lesson on Keats: 'Jo is listening enraptured by the poem, completely caught and spellbound by it.' And the lovemaking is romanticized: 'Jimmy takes Jo's coat and spreads it slowly on the ground. He kneels and holds out his hand to Jo. Very slowly she kneels beside him. There is music, the special sort of music that belongs to Jo.' The structure is improved by balancing location sequences: the funfair 'is meant as a deliberate contrast to the earlier sequence in Blackpool'. Delaney gives detailed instructions about the settings: Jo sees 'black monuments and statues erected to the great men of the past'. Moreover, Delaney intensifies the strength of the women: 'I feel wonderful. I feel I could take care of everything, even you' (S328).

The final film owes as much to Delaney's reorientation of the play as it does to Richardson's direction. However, his mode of working encouraged Rita Tushingham and Dora Bryan to present those on the periphery of society as being absolutely central to themselves. Jo and Helen are lascivious and poor, but they know that they are anyone's equal. *A Taste of Honey* invokes a utopia in which the outcasts – blacks, homosexuals, tarts – are at the heart of society, and it gives a radical spin to Woodfall's output. *A Taste of Honey* must be defined as a feminist text above all. The female generations control the action and, in the end, expel the men.

The Girl with Green Eyes (1964) does not have the same social radicalism, though it is liberal enough on sexual matters. It was scripted by Edna O'Brien from her novel *The Lonely Girl*, which was loosely slung and florid. Her script is an improvement – tight, economical and incisive. It locates the heroine Kate (Rita Tushingham) far more precisely in her social milieu. Both novel and film are fascinated by the paradox that innocents are often more sophisticated than their mentors. Eugene Galliard (Peter Finch) is a roué who regards commitment as a moveable feast: 'With this ring I thee bed and board for such time as you remain reasonable and kind'. The text turns round when he tells Kate, 'I liked you better before you started thinking'. *The Girl with Green Eyes* is a classic 'Dreams of Leaving' text: it is about abandoning home and a repressive relationship, told from an exclusively feminine perspective. Kate finally muses to herself: 'I have changed. I go to school at night and meet different men' (S967). And better ones, perhaps.

The Knack ... and How to Get It (1965) was a great success for Woodfall. It was directed by Richard Lester and based on Ann Jellicoe's play. Jellicoe's earlier *Sport of My Mad Mother* was avant-garde and preoccupied by male loathing for the mother-figure. *The Knack* deals with the maelstrom of the desire felt by Tolen, Colin and Tom for the innocent Nancy, whom they intimidate until she imagines she has been raped (in spirit, of course, she has been). Jellicoe's play had both feminism and verbal pyrotechnics, and she argued: 'I write this way because the image that everyone has of the rational, intellectual and intelligent man – I don't think it's true' (Taylor, 1962, pp. 69–70). She conceived *The Knack* as a corrective against sexual exploitation:

> The play is against this leather fetish sort of thing and against the sadism that it implies. One of the characters, Tolen, is used as an extreme example of a case where sex is used as a power compensation. So *The Knack* is really a lecture on sexual attitudes ... it is not a play about sex. It is a play about how you should treat people. (McCrindle, 1971, pp. 245–6)

Jellicoe's play was radically revised in Charles Wood and Richard Lester's script, which was both literal and exploitative in its presentation of women. It shows the women queuing to be serviced by Tolen, 'all dressed uniformly in white sweaters – they are photographed in diffuse over-exposure to give fantasy quality'. The 'Brechtian' subtitles from Tolen's lecture are: 'WOMEN ... NOT INDIVIDUALS ... JUST TYPES ... SURRENDERING ... MAN MUST DOMINATE'. And when Nancy faints in terror, the boys feel for her pulse: 'Have they got it in the same place as us?' (S2445). The script evinces a grudging admiration for Tolen, and the other male characters are too ineffectual to counterbalance him.

The Knack was interpreted by George Melly as 'optimistic. It believed in pleasure at its most intense. It proposed love and fucking because it felt that this was more pleasurable than fucking without love' (Walker, 1974, p. 263). But the pleasurable side for Nancy was underplayed by the script, and the film uses the camera close-ups as a weapon to humiliate her. *The Knack* is an interesting example of a feminist original which has been converted into an aggressively masculinist text. All the running through the streets, pushing beds and yelling cannot conceal that *The Knack* is a deeply repressive film.

Hammer was also conservative in the textual functions it allotted to women. Its top-down style of management meant that producers' control over the script made that the master discourse. The studio's preoccupation in the 1950s had been with the uncontrolled body; by the 1960s, that body had become exclusively female. Hammers of this decade are primarily concerned with taboos (cannibalism, necrophilia, incest, lesbianism) and rituals (garlic, masses, stakes, black magic). The films rest on oppositions between dark and fair, animal and human, the quick and the dead, male and female. Social contradictions have been replaced by archetypal ones, as a means of defusing audience anxieties.

Some Hammer films of the 1960s are preoccupied with female blood. In *Plague of the Zombies* (1965), both the heroines suffer deep cuts inflicted by the Squire. Each time he engages in voodoo rituals, the wounds bleed copiously, and the blood signifies the women's status as sacrificial victims. In *Countess Dracula* (1970), the menopausal heroine (Ingrid Pitt) is rejuvenated by virgins' blood after her own has ceased, and its viscosity enables her to become, as it were, her own daughter and to make love to her own prospective son-in-law: a transgressive act for which she pays dear. In *Blood from the Mummy's Tomb* (1971) the plot centres round the body of the dead Egyptian Queen Tera. On her death, her right hand is severed by the priests, who hope to inhibit her influence. Archaeologists attempt to control Tera's power, and each time one of them dies, the stump, seen in prolonged close-up, bleeds afresh. The blood symbolizes her occult and inhuman power.

In all these cases, oozing female blood has a different function from the male blood which spurts in, for example, *Dracula Prince of Darkness* (1965). It seems likely that menstruation is signified. This biological phenomenon, of course, operates as a site of danger and taboo in some cultures, and particularly in our own. The Hammer films of the period evoke this distaste, and present female blood as polluting and 'uncanny'. These are very visceral films.

Other Hammer films of the period are interested in female power and its dangerous excess. *She* (1965) is a prolonged meditation on the appropriate punishment for overreaching females. In Rider Haggard's original novel, in the mythical country 'the women are what they please. We worship them, and give them their way because without them the world could not go on: they are the source of life' (Haggard, 1915, p. 120). But the Hammer film draws the line much more sternly between sacred and profane women. The protagonists penetrate the land of Ayesha (She-Who-Must-Be-Obeyed) through the legs of a giant statue of her. Entry into her dangerous country, where nothing has changed for thousands of years, is coterminous with entry into the mother of all, the consumer of all, and the lover of all, whose appetites will not be gainsaid.

The predatory Ayesha (Ursula Andress) is strongly contrasted to the nurturing Ustane (Rosenda Monteros), who succours the hero. Ayesha has Ustane thrown into a burning chasm (its vaginal significance is rather overplayed) and we see her remains: a dry dust, which is shocking but not disgusting. Ayesha returns to the immortalizing flame a second time, and this act of hubris results in her return to the mortal condition. Her putrescence is wet and malodorous. The dry, nurturing dust of Ustane is clearly preferable to Ayesha's polluting slime. Here and elsewhere in Hammer films, divinely beautiful female bodies were the site of danger. Perhaps in order to reduce their charge, Hammer began to put them on their Christmas cards instead of a robin.[15]

The Witches (1966) is an interesting extension of the immortal-woman theme. It deals with a cult led by the local scholar-sorceress (Kay Walsh). She believes that older women 'relish the thought of a secret power, especially when their own normal powers are failing'. Accordingly, she devises a ritual in which she dresses in the skin of a virgin and wears antlers, thus assuming both eternal life and male attributes.

Females in Hammer films are strange and sometimes literally unearthly. In *Quatermass and the Pit* (1967) the female scientist (Barbara Shelley) is descended from Martians, and as she appropriates the scanning equipment, she moans like a woman in orgasm: immediately objects fly about and extraterrestrials appear on the monitor. Hammer films of this period often contain women acutely on the cusp between different modes of being. In *The Reptile* (1965) the heroine sways between being a woman and a giant lizard; in *Frankenstein Created Woman* (1967) she swings from dark cripple to blonde avenger, and from female to male; in *The Gorgon* (1964) she shifts from life-bringing virgin to death-bringing crone at the very moment of the full moon. And in the extraordinary *Dr Jekyll and Sister Hyde* (1971), Ralph Bates concocts an ovary cocktail and becomes his 'sister' (Martine Beswick). This powerful Freudian reading of Stevenson's tale suggests that the unspeakable Hyde is Jekyll's feminine side, which is dangerous when released and threatening when challenged.

The acute instability of the female function in these films opens up a space in which women's power and difference can be examined. Each of the unstable heroines is rendered immobile once the pendulum effect has been safely neutralized. The heroines of the Frankenstein cycle display no such instability, and those of the Dracula films are predictable: their sexuality is always unleashed after the first bite. This is because these films have other agendas: they examine the issues of gentlemanly competence and aristocratic symbolism, and female issues are secondary. But the patterns of gender representation at Hammer make it one of the clearest cases of studio authorship. An important edition of *Femmes Fatales* argued that its films were 'feminist fables sans soapbox', since they contained female repressors who surrendered to their ids.[16] What is more likely is that Hammer producers were responding *negatively* to contemporary changes in female mores, and constructing films which were meant to operate as a corrective.

As the 1960s progressed, many production companies faltered. Once companies shed their autonomous identity, the studio-as-auteur notion loses its usefulness. Some other explanatory models are more useful than others when this happens. Genre, for example, is not particularly fruitful here, and does not permit us to make fine distinctions. The function of women in most 1960s musicals is unremarkable. High melodrama, a mode which foregrounded villainous females, was dead. Comedy was too heterogeneous to allow us to draw clear patterns, except in the case of the sub-genre of *Carry On* films, which, with the same producer, director and stars, formed a coherent ensemble.

The *Carry On* films' representation of women varies according to the scriptwriter. The scripts by Norman Hudis, from *Carry On Sergeant* (1958) to *Carry On Cruising* (1962), concentrate on institutions in which a degree of social verisimilitude is appropriate.[17] The women do not disrupt the narratives, because the aim is social consensus. They are either beautiful (Shirley Eaton in *Sergeant* and *Nurse*, 1959) or efficient (Hattie Jacques in *Nurse*, Joan Sims in *Constable*, 1960). But in no case does desire *for* the women or by them impede the smooth narrative flow. All that changed when Talbot Rothwell began to script, from *Carry On Cabby* (1963) to *Carry On Dick* (1974).

Rothwell's scripts are parodic, building on audiences' film memories. More importantly, they are absolutely focused on sexual desire and its often absurd consummation, and women take an active part in its pursuit. In *Carry On Spying* (1964), Agent Daphne Honeybutt (Barbara Windsor) is the cleverest of the spy team, and in *Carry On Cleo* (1964), all the women, from Amanda Barrie as Cleopatra to Sheila Hancock as Senna Pod, have the time of their lives. In *Carry On Screaming* (1966), the female Undead Valeria (Fenella Fielding) smokes with desire and inhales her lover. And in *Carry On Doctor* (1968), Matron Hattie Jacques, seducing Dr Tinkle (Kenneth Williams), promises that 'You won't be disappointed. The young birds may be tender, but the older ones have more flavour.' His rejoinder is coarse (to do with stuffing turkeys), but the point has been made: women should speak their desires, even though their men are poltroons.

Carry On Cabby is particularly significant. Peggy (Hattie Jacques) is neglected by husband Charlie (Sid James), and founds a female taxi company in revenge. Her miniskirted GlamCabs drivers have compliant expressions, but their rebellious inventiveness is the centre of the film. The most interesting character is Flo (Esma Cannon), a feisty pensioner who wears trousers, takes risks and is more intelligent than the men.[10] In the end, Peggy is rescued by Charlie and, pregnant, returns to the family. It is a comic Saturnalia after all, and order must be restored. But here and in other *Carry Ons*, the women have a better time than in New Wave films.

So there is some, albeit limited, mileage in genre classification. More can be learned about patterns of gender representation by considering the ways in which some popular fictions were recycled. The *Fu Manchu* films are a rich quarry. Produced by Harry Alan Towers, they were all based on Sax Rohmer novels: *The Face of Fu Manchu* (1965), *The Brides of Fu Manchu* (1966), *The Vengeance of Fu Manchu* (1967), *The Blood of Fu Manchu* (1968) and *The Castle of Fu Manchu* (1970). They were

European co-productions made in East Asia or Spain, and were distributed by the major German company Constantin. Towers was the only British film-maker to trade exclusively with Germany, and he cast top German stars in all the films to maximize their chances at that box-office. He scripted them all, often under the pseudonym Peter Welbeck.[19] Towers's films now seem a bewildering mélange of sets, accents and personnel, but they crucially reactivate debates about the Inscrutable Orient which had been asleep since the 1930s, reconstituting it as the birthplace of the Fatal Woman. Tsai Chin always played Fu Manchu's daughter Lin Tang, and the films emphasize her ruthlessness, whereas in the novels she is more sympathetic. Lin Tang has mesmeric powers (unusual in a film female) and an impassive demeanour; she can do anything to anyone, since she has no moral code except obedience to her father. Lin Tang's moral vacuum presented problems for Tsai Chin, who felt that the films were racially as well as sexually demeaning: 'There are professional chinks and niggers as there are professional virgins ... but I signed the contracts though I searched my conscience.'[20]

Tsai Chin is always juxtaposed with a Nordic female, often played by Towers's girlfriend Maria Rohm, who bears different messages of male flattery. In *The Revenge of Fu Manchu*, Rohm (who needed a good orthodontist) played a nightclub singer whose ditty insisted that 'any kind of man is better than no man at all' – a *non sequitur* clearly intended to comfort the males in the audience.

Towers had an interest in Amazonian domination, as instanced by his marvellous *Sumuru* (1967). His rewriting of the Rohmer novels to foreground inscrutable women doubtless issued from some private knot, but en route he developed residual cultural forms into outstanding images of female power. He played both sides against the middle by inserting a submissive white girl into the equation.

The Bond films reinterpret popular fiction too. Cubby Broccoli and Harry Saltzman bought the film rights to Fleming's novels, which had some cachet among male middle-class readers.[21] After problems with initial financing, the films eventually proved enormously profitable. Fleming's hero was aware of the status attached to certain consumer durables. Women in the novels had some autonomy: Honeychile Rider in *Dr No* (1962) knows enough about marine life to extricate herself from a crab sandwich, and Pussy Galore in *Goldfinger* (1964) is a committed lesbian. But the films nuance gender difference more crudely. Sean Connery was cast because 'he looked as though he had balls'.[22] The Bond films of the 1960s cut sexuality loose from its connections with class, which are so evident in other films of the period. The film Bond understands about packaging, but he also intuits an essential femininity, which is submissive and dim. Honeychile rises from the sea like Venus, beautiful when wet, 'like a sea-lion', according to Broccoli (Walker, 1974, p. 188). She knows a conch from a razor shell, but that is all she knows, except how to accommodate the mighty weapon of 007. In *From Russia with Love* (1963), the heroine is simply a sexual playmate with a taste for pastel negligées. And in *Goldfinger* the dead body of Jill Masterton (Shirley Eaton) becomes the gold standard, and Pussy Galore (Honor Blackman) forswears girls after one joust with Bond. In *Thunderball* (1965), bad girl Fiona (Luciana Paluzzi) resists Bond's attempt to change her sexual politics, and she is horribly dispatched. All the Bond scripts of this period have a very rigid 'girl formula' into which female roles must fit.[23]

The Bond films evoke a utopia where all personable females speak with the same voice.[24] They are Playboy Bunnies without the ears, and their reward for sexual compliance is instant orgasm. The Bond films present this as a fair exchange, since their sealed world insulates the females from inconveniences like work or motherhood. But the Bond girls walk a tightrope. If they are a wrinkle too old, a whisper too assertive, they are consigned to the outer darkness inhabited by Rosa Klebb and Miss Moneypenny, and only their underwear is left behind.[25] The Bond films lay down the boundaries of permissible desire in an unusually rigorous way, and in order to do so they radically redraw the map of the popular fictions on which they were based.

There are other ways of categorizing the representation of women, and it is here that the sexual politics of the director becomes significant. In *Sight and Sound* in 1959, a range of directors were asked what projects they would instigate, given a free hand. The general response was of anxiety and lack of ambition.[26] In the 1960s, however, directors had more confidence in their own ability to impose their signature on their work, since they were now less likely to be hampered by an intractable studio machine. David Lean and Lindsay Anderson are clearly directors of this type. It is difficult to argue up some directors to the status of auteurs. For example, the case for Basil Dearden as a solo auteur breaks down if we consider *Khartoum* (1966) and *Only When I Larf* (1968), which are the only films of the period on which he worked without

Michael Relph. Their partnership produced films with a common gender and social politics, and Dearden's solo efforts were quite unlike the rest.

Robert Hamer was a different case. A sour misogyny pervaded all Hamer's earlier films, ironic masterpieces though some of them were. *School for Scoundrels* (1960) was Hamer's last film and his most characteristic. With some gusto he undertook a film interpretation of Stephen Potter's *Gamesmanship*, which was greatly to his taste. Potter's books are an attempt to apply the theory of possessive individualism to every crevice of the individual life, but Hamer chose to concentrate on sexual competition. Hero Ian Carmichael steals Janette Scott away from Terry-Thomas by wiles and lures, and the whole is predicated on her gullibility.

Karel Reisz made a strong argument for his own status as an auteur:

> Essentially I always make the same film, wherever and however I'm working. All my films . . . are about a central character who is in some way on the edge of sanity, seen partly from his or her own point of view, partly, none too sympathetically, from the outside.[27]

This may be a *post hoc* judgement, but it holds good for *Saturday Night and Sunday Morning*, in which Arthur, though sane, is certainly repellent. *Morgan – A Suitable Case for Treatment* (1966) contains a hero who, though insane, is amiable (MacFarlane, 1997, p. 479). The heroine of *Isadora* (1969) is both fey and unpleasant. What is interesting about all Reisz's protagonists is that, male or female, they are equally ruthless. Other people are fodder for their fantasies, and their egotism surpasses all gender boundaries.

A more solid case can be made for Joseph Losey's auteurist signature on gender matters. He had a rigorous understanding of the class system, and saw his women as economically determined. Their cultural and sexual pleasures were predicated on their class position:

> But sexual power, intellectual power, intrigue – it seems to me that this quality of exercising power over an essentially man's world has produced certain qualities in the female. And that these have lately been carried over into marriage, particularly upper-bourgeois marriage . . . (Ciment, 1985, p. 212)

This fuelled Losey's French-Italian production *Eve* (1962) and many of his 1960s British films. In *The Servant* (1963), Susan (Wendy Craig) is a prisoner of her upper-class mental habits. Vera (Sarah Miles) is also blameless, since she is on erotic autopilot: her class expectations have given her no room to manoeuvre. But anyway, Losey's main contention was that 'the strongly matriarchal aspect of English society' impinged more negatively on men (*ibid.*, p. 232). This view fed into the homosexual theme in *The Servant*. The focus in *Accident* (1967) is also on the upper-class male psyche, this time of that particularly British type of academic who operates in the subjunctive mood. Fiercely competitive, intellectually anal, Stephen (Dirk Bogarde) is fascinated by women on whom he can make no impact. The women in *Accident* have realized it is impolitic to show their feelings. The impassive Jacqueline Sassard was chosen by Losey because 'she has these eyes which were windows, which you could look through. . . . She is simply a catalyst for all the other things' (*ibid.*, p. 264). The wives (Vivien Merchant and Ann Firbank) see all but say nothing. The mistress (Delphine Seyrig) dines with Stephen under a sign which says, 'Have your meals here and keep the wife as a pet.' Losey suggests that the women's painful repression is a structural part of the social fabric. *The Go-Between* (1970) makes the same point. Marian (Julie Christie) is brutally arrogant in both her prime and her dotage, but her selfishness is a rebellion. In his 1960s films, Losey never blames the women; he blames the system which creates them.

Modesty Blaise (1966), of course, was a different case. Losey conceived it as a parody of spy thrillers, and he chose Monica Vitti because of her art-house cachet. Artistically the film went askew because Losey failed to recognize that certain genres are acutely predicated on masculinity, and are ludicrous if straightforwardly transposed to the feminine. The Bond mode is about male power, while Modesty, however athletic she may be, is an unfortunate combination of Peter Pan and Greta Garbo.

Ken Russell, too, had a recognizable style and sexual politics. All his work pays rigorous attention to period, and to the discomforts of unconventional desires. The problem is not with the visual discourse of the films, which is sumptuous; the difficulties arise with the script or soundtrack. In *Women in Love* (1969), for example, Russell did not have the sense to change Lawrence's words, so that Alan Bates intones to Jennie Linden: 'There is a golden light in you, which I wish that you would give me.' And in *The Music Lovers* (1970), the extreme match between sound and image is ludicrous. 'My dear, meet Mr Borodin,' bawls the pander mother to the nymphomaniac Mrs Tchaikovsky (Glenda Jackson); at once *The Polovtsian Dances* swell over the soundtrack. Such shortcuts imperil the development of a coherent position on either sexuality or art.

Nonetheless, Russell did attempt the task in his 1960s work. In *Women in Love*, he directed Glenda Jackson and Jennie Linden so as to evoke the complexity of their characters' erotic feelings. The problem was that Russell was attracted by sexual imagery which he presented without nuance. The wrestling and sex scenes recall one of the eternal verities: namely, that male buttocks at ramming speed are an unedifying sight. It was the same problem with *The Music Lovers*. The Tchaikovskys' wedding night in the railway carriage could have been a piquant combination of sexual coyness and vibrating locale. Russell chose to confront the composer's terror of the vagina by alternating inserts of a cavernous red crinoline (with castrating metal hoops) with shots of Mrs Tchaikovsky coming to a rolling boil. It was enough to put even the heterosexuals off.

There are, of course, films of the period which elude all categories: films which show women in a thoughtful light, or which problematize female issues, or simply just show women having a good time. There are not many, at least not scripted by male writers, but there are some. *Four in the Morning* (1965), for example, is important. It has a tripartite structure about a dead female body washed up in the Thames, a woman (Ann Lynn) whose relationship founders because her lover is too laconic, and a wife (Judi Dench) whose beloved baby is strangling her life. It is a film which evokes a gasp of emotional pain as it enunciates the traps in which women are caught. Ann Lynn struggles to explain that her man's emotional inarticulacy kills her spirit; Judi Dench tears at the web of need which her child weaves. The whole is intercut with shots of the female corpse. Naked, anonymous, its meaning is debated by officials.

Four in the Morning was originally conceived as a documentary about the Thames (Murphy, 1992, p. 84), but the mood and technique raise it into feminist art. Films in other modes also create spaces in which female freedom can be addressed. *Smashing Time* (1967), for example, is a satire on Swinging London, and is witty, inventive and liberal. Yvonne (Lynn Redgrave) and Brenda (Rita Tushingham) come down from the provinces and wreak havoc among the glitterati. *Smashing Time* celebrates their guilt-free indulgence in sex, unusual clothes and plain speaking. Yvonne and Brenda sample, exploit and then abandon Swinging London; they can snatch happiness without regret. The film owes its radicalism to a marvellous script by George Melly, which contains social gargoyles Charlotte Brillig and Bobby Mome-Rath.

Smashing Time never relaxes into realism; the script prohibits it. The same holds good for the films based on Joe Orton's comedies, *Entertaining Mr Sloane* (1970) and *Loot* (1970). The scripts are unremittingly anti-naturalistic, swooping from hyperbole to malapropism. Of course, the agenda of Orton's work is fiercely homosexualist, and since his women are not desired, they can prey upon the world with their energies intact. Kath (Beryl Reid) and Fay (Lee Remick) may be trollops and harridans, but at least they belong to themselves.[28]

In the 1950s, female stereotypes and acting roles were determined by the producers, distributors and scriptwriters. The chaos in the industry in the 1960s meant that while some constraints were lifted, new ones were imposed: the predilections of the director, the limitations of the original popular novel, the avant-garde style. The seven-year contract was dead, and actresses were now adrift on the market, often negotiating one-picture deals. A whole tranche of actresses entered the cinema who were classically trained and whose main allegiance was to the theatre. Janet Suzman, Maggie Smith, Judi Dench, Glenda Jackson, Vanessa Redgrave and others accepted film roles as an incidental part of their acting training, and chose parts with such care that they could not be typecast.

However, the industry still required recognizable social types. In the 1950s, Whorish Hussy roles were in demand; in the 1960s, the industry needed sex-kittens instead. They were blonde too, but small, feisty and sexually entrepreneurial. Barbara Windsor, Judy Geeson, Adrienne Posta and others played heroines who were mainly working class and sexually careless. They all exhibited unpredictable movement, swift changes of gaze and fast blink rates. Gillian Hills's role in *Beat Girl* (1960) is a good example of the sex-kitten mode. Her sexual anxieties have been displaced onto her hair and clothes, whose mussed appearance signals erotic arousal. Significantly, the Foreign Floozies of the 1950s are redundant in the new decade; the native sex-kittens fulfil their function.

More crucially, the 1960s film industry required actresses who could evoke changes in contemporary mores, and indicate some of the complexities of sexual freedom. It is in this light that we should interpret the careers of Julie Christie, Rita Tushingham, Lynn Redgrave, Hayley Mills, Susannah York and Sarah Miles. These actresses played characters who were unhampered by convention, and were more serious than the sex-kittens: they thought issues through.

What is notable about most actresses' accounts of 1960s conditions is that they rarely felt exploited. The new freedoms of choice removed the sting from undignified roles. The actresses working at Hammer, for example, never felt demeaned by their roles. Ingrid Pitt thought she had autonomy in her performance style, given the constraints of the roles: 'a hairdo set in concrete and a set of teeth long enough to sever [my] own carotid without really trying'. Veronica Carlson, Caroline Munro and Hazel Court enjoyed the latitude permitted by the studio. Barbara Shelley gave a particularly robust defence of Hammer's treatment of women, arguing that the producers were feminists who liked portraying powerful females.[29]

The 1960s industry was mainly concerned with the regulation of heterosexual freedom, and the challenges posed by contraception and female emancipation. However, there were some minor debates about lesbianism. In *The L-shaped Room* (1963), Cicely Courtneidge plays Mavis, an old music-hall hand. Bryan Forbes inserted the scene of Mavis's reminiscences to Jane (Leslie Caron) about her dead woman partner: 'I did have a friend. We lived together for years. A real love-match it was ... it takes all sorts, dear.' This was, as Stephen Bourne suggests, a tender and respectful scene (Bourne, 1996, p. 165). But Mavis is old, lonely and bereaved. Lesbianism is more positively presented in *The World Ten Times Over* (1963), which deals with Ginnie (June Ritchie) and Billa (Sylvia Syms) who are in love and each other's support. Syms tried to flag up lesbian style through her choice of clothes – the leather coat – but the film was hampered by censorship conditions.[30] In general, the industry was robustly heterosexist in its presentation of lesbians. There was one film which portrayed homosexual love with tenderness and dignity, but that was *The Leather Boys* (1963), where the emotion was between men.

We can conclude that the 1960s industry was much more rigorous and less permissive towards females than it had been in the 1950s. Then, some combative personae or artists had been able to slip through gaps in the texts or productive practices, in order to evade patriarchal models. In the 1960s, those gaps were closing fast, with the onset of the new auteurism and the decline of the big combines. Most importantly, the innovative, emergent film types were particularly conservative on gender matters, and that boded ill for the 1970s.

Notes

1. *Time*, 15 April 1966.
2. *Sight and Sound*, Summer 1966. The girl on whom Waterhouse had modelled 'Liz' was herself transfixed by Christie's panache, and 'for the rest of her life she tried to identify herself totally with the made-up Liz' (Waterhouse, 1995, p. 203).
3. John Russell Taylor discussed the issue with some subtlety in *Sight and Sound*, Spring 1974.
4. Jack Cardiff directed the first film, and he described it as a traduced technological and erotic *tour de force*: Cardiff (1996), pp. 242–3.
5. Guest commented that Munro wanted to get rid of her earlier virginal image: 'In the Disney films, they used to make her tie her boobs down for all her parts, to make her look like she had none. We got *those* out, to start with!' (Weaver, 1994, p. 117.)
6. *Sight and Sound*, Summer 1996, quote by Philip French.
7. See Murphy (1992), Walker (1974), Boulting in MacFarlane (1997), and Sidney Gilliat's *Positif* article (no. 406, December 1994). The British Lion material in the Board of Trade files at the Public Record Office is a real Grimpen Mire for historians. *Caveat lector!*
8. Unpublished letter from Gilliat to British Council, in the possession of Vincent Porter.
9. See the files on Bryanston in the Balcon Papers at the BFI Library, and the accounts in Walker (1974) and Murphy (1992).
10. See C. A. Lejeune in the *Observer*, 10 April 1960; Nina Hibbin in the *Daily Worker*, 9 April 1960; Isobel Quigley in the *Spectator*, 15 April 1960; and Dilys Powell in the *Sunday Times*, 10 April 1960.
11. Gruesomely enough, Powell cast his own wife and son in these parts.
12. There are references to 'puritanism' in the script. Laura, who is childless, deals with a disturbed child who defaces a drawing of his mother.
13. *Evening Standard*, 21 November 1997.
14. The only time 'Liz' appears in a fantasy sequence, it is not Christie but Topsy Jane, the original actress who shot a few scenes (Waterhouse, 1995, p. 202).
15. See an interesting article on Raquel Welch in *Loaded*, no. 50, June 1998.
16. *Femmes Fatales*, vol. 6, no. 1, July 1997, p. 3. See also Svela (1991), for a feminist indictment of Hammer.
17. Hudis went in search of 'copy' at Slough police station and lifted incidents from his wife's nursing experiences (Hibbin and Hibbin, 1988, pp. 83, 16).
18. Cannon was Australian, but only in this film was her accent allowed to emerge. Presumably, the twang intensified the image of a game, lively female.
19. I am grateful to Tim Bergfelder for some information on Towers. For an extraordinarily bland account of his own life and relationships, see Towers (1949). For material about Towers's problems with Equity, see Lee (1977, p. 249).

20. Tsai Chin (1988), pp. 144–5. For an interesting interpretation of her work, see Polly Toynbee in the *Guardian*, 21 July 1988.
21. See Murphy (1992), pp. 112–13, 218–19. See Walker (1974), pp. 181–98. For an interesting contemporary take on the films, see Ronald Bryden, 'Spies who came into camp', *Observer*, 7 August 1966.
22. Walker (1974), p. 187. To appreciate the different symbolic function of male and female genitalia, imagine that Broccoli had praised Andress because 'she looked as though she had ovaries'.
23. *Playboy*, June 1967.
24. James Chapman (1999) argues that the Bond girls in this period are even dubbed by the same voice.
25. See *Financial Times*, 12/13 September 1997, on the sale of Bond memorabilia: 'There is very little from the Bond girls, apart from a pair of knickers that Shirley Eaton might have worn ... '.
26. *Sight and Sound*, Spring 1959.
27. *Sight and Sound*, Spring 1974.
28. Orton's earlier work throws interesting light on his representation of women: see *Between Us Girls* (1998), which was written in 1957.
29. *Femmes Fatales*, vol. 6, no. 1, July 1997, pp. 14–15, 22, 25, 26, 30–1.
30. Interview with Sylvia Syms by Stephen Bourne in *Gay Times*, June 1989.

6

The 1970s: Financial and Cultural Penury

During the 1970s, the Labour Party made radical improvements to the everyday lives of women. With the support of a group of feminists pushing from the party's left wing, the Equal Pay Act and the Sex Discrimination Act were on stream by 1975. Measures improving pension rights and child benefit were also passed. By the early 1970s, contraception was freely available to unmarried women, and the so-called sexual revolution was under way. There were many theoretical advances in feminism, and a broad shift in consciousness about what it might entail. However, the British film industry of the 1970s was in no condition to respond to the changes in women's lives and consciousness. This was not because of ill-will, but because of penury and cultural decline.

The first problem the industry encountered was the sudden exit of American capital. MGM cancelled *Man's Fate* a week before shooting; it closed its British studios in Borehamwood in 1970 (Bart, 1990, p. 40). Columbia's profits were drastically down by 1969; so were those of 20th Century Fox and Universal. A credit squeeze was on, and the American majors had to bear the cost of the loans they had taken out for their earlier high-budget productions. American investments in British films fell by nearly three-quarters, from £31.2 million in 1969 to £8.3 million in 1971. The transatlantic finance which had funded enterprises such as *Tom Jones* in the previous decade shrivelled up. Worse, there was little native funding to replace it. Britain's entry into the EEC in 1973 provided no benefits in that regard.

The NFFC's record in the 1970s was poor. It only loaned £4 million for 31 feature films throughout the decade. In 1972 the Conservative government forced it to set up a consortium, with some degree of success, and in 1976 the Labour government established the National Film Development

Fund, but with straitened funds. Dickinson and Street have rightly suggested that this particular 'combination of state support and private enterprise discouraged experiment, and in the end films of the high-budget category were backed' (Dickinson and Street, 1985, p. 241). Certainly the shifts from the extremes of Conservative to Labour cultural policies impinged very badly on the industry.

By 1973, the situation was critical. In July, only six British films were in production. Pinewood and Shepperton lay empty for several months. The situation was made more critical when, in November 1974, the new Labour government decided to tax the highest earners. Many British stars of international status, such as Sean Connery and Michael Caine, became overseas residents. Film-makers such as Schlesinger, Lester and Reisz left Britain too. The spaces vacated were not, of course, filled by women artists. Film culture was simply impoverished when the established players left.

Such economic and legislative constraints brought cultural consequences in their wake. We saw in the previous chapter that the link between distribution and production companies was coming unravelled, and that the studio system was dying. The 1970s witnessed its death. Rank virtually ceased film production, and British Lion was caught in the toils of Vavasseur, a company primarily interested in property investment and screen advertising. Its residual film interests were bought out by EMI in 1976. The artistic deaths of the old guard also occurred in this decade. Launder and Gilliat ended sadly with *Ooh ... You Are Awful* (1972), a film about tattoos on girls' buttocks, and the Boultings' last offering was *Soft Beds, Hard Battles* (1973).

The case of EMI is an interesting index of the extent of the sea-change in British film culture. Originally a music recording company, it took over ABPC in 1969, and set up co-production with MGM. Bryan Forbes was appointed head of EMI-MGM, but was summarily relieved of his post in 1971, when Nat Cohen took over production. Cohen ran Anglo-EMI, as it was now called, with an eye to international markets. He persuaded Lord Brabourne, Mountbatten's son-in-law, to intervene with Agatha Christie to permit some of her novels to be filmed (Walker, 1985, pp. 129–32). Accordingly, *Murder on the Orient Express* (1974) and *Death on the Nile* (1978) were made, with enormous profit.

These films are proof of the cultural crisis in the industry. They painstakingly represent the visual surface of an earlier period without examining the structures of feeling which informed it. They are essentially lessons in textile appreciation. Both films venerate the class system of the original novels, because their fixed values can be embodied in a *mise en scène* which is remarkably static. But more importantly, *Murder on the Orient Express* and *Death on the Nile* replicate and validate the fixed gender roles favoured by Christie. The women in the films are locked into rigid caricatures. In a period when women's lives were being transformed, the most expensive and profitable film texts were insisting on the efficacy of the old gender arrangements.

The expertise of British film craftsmen and special-effects artists was much in demand in the 1970s with films such as *Superman* (1978) and *Alien* (1979). While legally British, these could not be construed as part of British culture; their intellectual and financial capital was entirely American. As in the 1950s, the Americans specialized in costume dramas when filming in Britain, and this coincided with a reduction in their overall investment. And again like the 1950s, the American costume films foregrounded masculine sensibilities, even when the subject matter seemed to require the reverse. Columbia-Warners' *Nicholas and Alexandra* (1971) consistently favoured male perspectives and eyeline matches; MGM's *Lady Caroline Lamb* (1973) was really a justification for Byron.[1] Universal's *Mary Queen of Scots* (1972) had a wooden narrative. The only costume film to deploy the glories of the genre fully was *Barry Lyndon* (1975), which owed more to Stanley Kubrick's bloody-mindedness than to his backers. Kubrick's script was an intelligent version of Thackeray's novel, and replicated the equanimity of the original.[2] *Barry Lyndon* deployed the costume genre in the Gainsborough mode – as a means of balancing complicity and power between men and women.

Kubrick's film was sensual and radical, with its roots deep in film culture and the historical imagination. Such flexibility was beyond British film-makers in the 1970s. They were now hampered from creative engagement with those costume or fantasy genres which had formerly been a British specialism. *Royal Flash* (1975), for example, was parodic and mannered. Scripted by George MacDonald Fraser from his own book, the high point of its comedy was the sexual awakening of the Duchess (Britt Ekland). On her wedding night she is clamped into a rigour of sexual terror. After the overnight ministrations of the impostor Duke (Malcolm McDowell), she becomes an erotic tornado. Such infelicities of tone also bedevil the awkward *Psychomania* (1973), in which male and female motorcyclists kill themselves in order to achieve sexual nirvana while still wearing their helmets. Fantasy was notoriously prone to financial and distribution problems, even when filmed by British directors with an impeccable understanding of the genre. *The Wicker Man* (1974) is a case in point. Anthony Shaffer's screenplay was accepted by British Lion, filmed in Scotland and directed by Shaffer's working partner Robin Hardy. When British Lion was sold in 1973, the new owners loathed the completed film, had it drastically cut and distributed it as a second feature to *Don't Look Now* (1973). British Lion then sold the distribution rights to National General, which immediately went bankrupt; Warners subsequently acquired the film and shelved it. When Hardy tried to reconstruct his film by reinserting the negative trims, he found that they had been used as landfill for a motorway.[3]

These disasters meant that *The Wicker Man*, the most sexually radical film of the decade, was hardly seen by anyone. It dealt with a pagan community in the Western Isles, which required a virgin sacrifice for its crops; it lured policeman Howie (Edward Woodward) from the mainland for this purpose. At the end, the ritual sacrifice is exacted in spite of the rational Howie's insistence that the crowd should 'Think! Think!' *The Wicker Man* was iconoclastic in its presentation of women. The older women – the schoolteacher, the librarian, the vanished girl's mother – are enthusiastic gatekeepers and purveyors of paganism. But its most powerful erotic charge is carried by Willow (Britt Ekland). She functions as the community's sexual litmus; she initiates young boys and invigorates old ones, and is celebrated for her appetites. The bawdy song 'The Landlord's Daughter' constructs her as a goddess of desire, without shame or artifice.

Willow's attempted seduction of Howie takes the form of a sensual dance, rather like Kanchi's in *Black Narcissus*. Ekland has been directed to move in such a way that her body echoes the décor. Her room contains corn dollies and candles, besides other objects replete with sexual symbolism, and her mobile body is both yielding and aggressive. As Willow strikes the connecting wall of Howie's room with the flat of her hand, the blow is both a stimulus and a caress. The dance is one of the most remarkable sequences in the film culture of the period, since Willow acts erotically both for herself and for the community, and neither are shortchanged.[4] But this innovative film reached few audiences and failed at the box-office, because of the venality and unpredictability of those in financial control.

Other films, potentially just as radical, never reached the screen at all. *Trick or Treat* was a novel by Ray Connolly, which he and Michael Apted tried to film in 1975; £400,000 was lost in the process. It dealt with two girls who fall in love and decide to have a baby together, by using the husband of a friend. Connolly's account of the scripting process is hilarious. He describes how, when in a restaurant, he and Apted acted out the sexually explosive scenes charting the girls' relationship:

> Apted put an arm out towards me: 'For God's sake, Kathy . . . ' The restaurant was now an audience of ears, alert to the conversation and to my name. 'Don't touch me', I yelled. 'I don't want your hands . . . your fingers, near me'. 'I don't understand', he said. 'What's wrong?' I shook my head but he kept on, 'Tell me, darling . . . ' A waiter hovered over us waiting to take our order. He was looking at us strangely. 'I'm pregnant', I said. Then I started to cry.[5]

Connolly and Apted had signed with Goodtimes Enterprises, a small independent company with limited funds. The NFFC backed out of the project, and additional funding was offered by Hugh Hefner's *Playboy* films division. But Hefner wished to control the casting, which proved disastrous. Shooting was stopped due to irreconcilable differences between actresses, scriptwriters and production personnel over the degree of nudity and sexual action.[6]

Trick or Treat was a débâcle, but there were many other innovative films which never got off the drawing board at all. In such dire circumstances, only a few smaller production outfits managed to maintain a coherent profile on gender and other matters; but the quality of their product was undistinguished. Tigon made a series of shlock/horror films such as *Mongo* (1970) in which the heroines played overblown roles, and Amicus filmed a series of episodic portmanteau pieces which were punitive towards erring females: *Tales from the Crypt* (1972) and *From beyond the Grave* (1974) were both moralizing and sensational. Hammer's treatment of gender issues was much less nuanced than before. During the 1960s, the studio had broached female sexuality in a manner which half-celebrated and half-feared it; as the 1970s progressed, it was less ambivalent. The Karnstein cycle concentrated on the dangers of female desire, focusing on the lesbian vampire Carmilla. In *The Vampire Lovers* (1970), Ingrid Pitt plays in a major key throughout, creating the terrifying spectacle of a woman who can give and receive pleasure without the benefit of males.[7] The theme is continued in *Lust for a Vampire* (1971) and *Twins of Evil* (1971). The lesbian heroines embody the supposed dangers of female narcissism and its challenges to patriarchal order. Indeed, Peter Hutchings suggests that most 1970s Hammer films display anxiety about the increasingly flimsy status of masculinity (Hutchings, 1993, pp. 165–84). One of the most interesting films in this regard is *The Satanic Rites of Dracula* (1973), which contains a scene in which a young girl is ritually stabbed. The close-up of the bleeding wound looks remarkably like a vagina. Through the good offices of the male celebrants of the ritual, her wound is healed: before our very eyes, the orifice is safely sealed and, raised from the dead, the girl turns and gives the camera a complicitous smile. The sexual difference of women has been disavowed.

Hammer also embarked on a series of comedies based on TV series – *That's Your Funeral* (1972), *Love Thy Neighbour* (1973) and *A Man about the House* (1974) – which replicated the sexual conservatism of the television originals. *On the Buses* spawned several Hammer sequels such as *Holiday on the Buses* (1973), in which the plain bespectacled Olive (Anna Karen) is the butt of her abusive husband and family. Hammer had been opportunistic in its filming of radio programmes during the 1950s, and now it returned to its entrepreneurial roots. The difference was that its original sources were now crude, socially and sexually divisive, and cruel; the Hammer films merely intensified them.

The fare of some other specialized production companies declined in quality too. The 1960s *Carry On* films had provided a space for female Saturnalia, but in the 1970s the cycle became increasingly conservative, since the formula was insufficiently flexible to produce innovative work. *Carry On* lust became perfunctory, and the films expressed a sour mistrust towards females. In *Carry On up the Jungle* (1970), Terry Scott as the Jungle Boy espies a pair of breasts from afar. His facial control is exemplary: first of all astonishment, then jealousy, then rage as he squeezes his own flat chest and tries to emulate what he lacks. Such panic fuels *Carry On Girls* (1973), in which the feminist Augusta Prodworthy (June Whitfield) protests against the bathing-beauty contest. Her followers are lesbians and gorgons, and her invented rituals are supposedly an index of her repressed desires: 'Rosemary – fetch the candle!' The range of roles permitted to *Carry On* females is narrower than before. Consider the narrative function of Renée Houston as Agatha Spanner in *Carry On at Your Convenience* (1971). She vanquishes the union strike by publicly spanking her grown son, and is empowered by her age; but it has withered her, and she is reduced to playing strip poker with Charles Hawtrey.

The James Bond films were formula films too, but with bigger budgets. United Artists had given Eon almost unlimited funding on *Diamonds Are Forever* (1971) and *Live and Let Die* (1973) once the profitability of the Bond films was established. However, the funding crisis in the British industry even impinged on the Bond films after the mid-1970s. *The Spy Who Loved Me* (1977) was hedged around by legal problems about the use of SPECTRE as a plot device, and it foregrounded more gadgetry and visual spectacle as a consequence. The women in the film cannot compete with Atlantis and the Temple of Karnak, and they are the subject of racy innuendoes – 'tell Bond to pull out', 'keeping the British end up, Sir'. *The Spy Who Loved Me* does contain a heroine who is brave, resourceful and patriotic. Barbara Bach as the Russian agent manages to do all her British counterpart can do; except in bed, of course. The same holds good for the heroine of *Moonraker* (1979). Lois Childs plays Dr Goodhead (which is presumably what she gives). She is technologically competent and sexually compliant – 'I think he's attempting re-entry'. Yet ultimately she is dwarfed by the hardware. The gadgetry has replaced the female body as the source of fascination.

One route open to smaller film-makers was to make cheap sex films, which was facilitated by changes in certification regulations. Soft-porn films for theatrical distribution increased throughout the decade, and the bonanza continued until the early 1980s when official controls became more rigorous. In a wilting market, sex films were the only reliable way of firming up box-office figures: *The Wife Swappers* (1969), for example, made more money than the trumpeted reissue of *Spartacus* (McGillivray, 1992, p. 56). The dominance of skinflicks affected erstwhile career directors: Wolf Rilla was forced into the soft-porn market with *Secrets of a Door-to-door Salesman* (1973) and *Bedtime with Rosie* (1975).

Skinflicks of the 1970s were ostensibly shot for mixed audiences, but the aim was indubitably male arousal. The female protagonists in films such as *Adventures of a Plumber's Mate* (1978) are anonymous and passive. *Percy* (1971) and *Percy's Progress* (1974) are male what-if soliloquies: 'what if I lost the appendage I value most, what if that which I gain instead surpasses my wildest dreams? Someone else's penis was better than mine, but now it *is* mine.' Such priapic wish-fulfilment also fuelled glossier productions like *The Stud* (1978). In the opening sequence Tony (Oliver Tobias) rises from a one-night stand and surveys the trophies of sexual war: letters and photos, rows of shirts from grateful females. Tony kisses his own face in the mirror: 'You handsome bastard!' These are emotionally impoverished films, which evoke a sexuality devoid of tenderness.

The more profitable sex films had a comic edge, and many of the 1970s sex comedies contain males who are risibly alienated from their own bodies. *Confessions of a Window Cleaner* (1974) and other films in the cycle placed the uncouth Robin Askwith in situations which tested his perseverance. The issue was not whether he enjoyed the sexual act, but whether he could complete it in untoward circumstances. The sex comedies were films of chronic emotional detachment, in which the males displayed bewilderment about fleshly hydraulics, and an ill-concealed irritation if anyone failed to come up to scratch; consider the heroes' chagrin in *Confessions of a Driving Instructor* (1976) when Miss Slenderparts turns out to be Irene Handl. The standards by which women's bodies were judged in these films are unforgiving. Portly Roy Kinnear, as the jailed pornographer in *Eskimo Nell* (1974), bewails the fact that his new film must star the prison governor's wife: 'nice woman; terrible tits'.

The sex films of the 1970s attested to a profound unease about women's autonomy, and they often focused on ambiguous female protagonists. The narratives of both *Girl Stroke Boy* (1971) and *I Want What I Want* (1972) struggle to reassign the cross-dressing protagonist to one gender category. *The Virgin Witch* (1970) corrects a heroine who, as a lesbian and a witch, has transgressed two forbidden boundaries. These skinflicks are light years away from a liberal erotic art whose business is mutual stimulus and release from inhibition. In the 1970s, the sex film's function was titillation for males first, and instruction for females second: tickle and teach.

In the 1970s, directors established in the 1960s encountered profound problems in the marketplace. John Schlesinger's last British film of the decade was *Sunday, Bloody Sunday* (1971). This film continued the trajectory Schlesinger had set in motion in the 1960s, in which he rehearsed the pains of heterosexual love. There was some acrimony between Schlesinger and scriptwriter Penelope Gilliat; he felt that she misunderstood the characters' motivations (MacFarlane, 1997, p. 513). *Sunday, Bloody Sunday* nuanced the three-way relationship so that Alex (Glenda Jackson) has to play a poor hand; after all, what she has to offer is so much less interesting, because it is sexually ordinary.

David Lean too continued his career with difficulty in the decade, making only *Ryan's Daughter* (1970). This was Lean's most sexually radical film, in which for the first time he celebrated female desire and charted its social interdictions. *Ryan's Daughter* was conceived by Lean and playwright Robert Bolt as a version of *Madame Bovary*, but with a more humane and libertarian spin (Brownlow, 1997, pp. 553–4). Displaying a confidence rare in the period, the film deals with the indefatigability of romantic love, and focuses on the emotional complexity of the heroine (Sarah Miles). A series of lyrical love scenes, lit and dressed in an imaginative manner, suggest that she has little option, once roused by the wounded VC, than to succour him with her body. *Ryan's Daughter* is a subtle examination of female erotic temperament and its repression by social controls. No one recognized that, however, since industry responses were motivated by envy. One unnamed director, 'was absolutely incensed that David had been given X million dollars. He said he could make three films for that budget. He was incensed that he had essentially stolen it from other film-makers. That was the general feeling at the time' (*ibid.*, p. 583). Critics loathed the film for its excessive romanticism, and one American critic bewailed its 'idea that an Irish girl needs a half-dead Englishman to arouse her'.[6] Lean was so discouraged that he did not make another film for fourteen years.

Joseph Losey relaxed his earlier analytic exposure of the British class system and women's place in it. His films became more overtly political with *The Assassination of Trotsky* (1972) and *Galileo* (1976). The connection between sexual and political agendas, which had worked so well for Losey in the 1960s, was broken, and the films suffered in consequence. *The Romantic Englishwoman* (1975) had scripting problems, and was affected by Losey's dislike of the star, Glenda Jackson (Ciment, 1985, p. 340). *A Doll's House* (1973) was limited by Jane Fonda's performance (Walker, 1985, p. 125). But more disastrously, Losey squabbled over the script with the other lead, Delphine Seyrig, who thought it gave an inadequate account of Ibsen's feminism. Eventually 'a kind of really horrible war developed between the men and the women' working on the film.[9] In consequence, the finished text was lumpy and incoherent.

During the 1960s, Ken Russell had developed a style of authorship which combined visual flamboyance with poor scripting. This intensified in the following decade. All Russell's 1970s films were composed of two separate discourses – a visual one which was stylish, but *about nothing*, and a verbal one which was self-indulgent. Women in Russell's 1970s films operated as a Plimsoll line of sexual excess: they indicated how full the social boat could be loaded before it sank. *The Devils* (1971) converted the most undefiled members of society into the most polluted: the nuns' sealed orifices are penetrated by crucifixes, incinerated thigh-bones and assorted body parts. The nuns are a *tabula rasa* which displays society's repressed scrawl to advantage. Russell's 1970s films aspire to grand opera in their mood, but lack its emotional finesse. The divas in *Tommy* (1975), for example, do everything with vigour and volume: Tina Turner belts it out as the Acid Queen, Ann-Margret as Mother luxuriates in the torrent of chocolate and baked beans spewed from the television. But decibels, whether musical or emotional, are rarely an end in themselves. In many ways, Russell's quietest film of the period, *Savage Messiah* (1972), was his best. He envisaged it as 'just two people in a room talking', and managed to present gender relations as neither boring nor disgusting.[10]

The 1970s industry permitted some newer directors to develop an individual voice. They all had executive control over the scripts, since there were no longer author-producers or studio systems to insist otherwise. Ken Loach's realist *Kes* (1970) and *Family Life* (1971) insisted that, in inimical conditions, social groups would turn and rend the weakest members: children in the first film, women in the second. Mike Leigh's *Bleak Moments* (1972) was also realist, but with a more intuitive approach. He thought that the 1970s British film industry was in such a parlous condition that real cinematic work was only possible for television (MacFarlane, 1997, p. 361).

Other, less realist, directors co-opted women into their broader agendas. John Boorman's *Zardoz* (1974) deployed different female types as a means of signalling agreement with more traditional, organicist values: the ageing of Consuela (Charlotte Rampling) is preferable to the brittle

Vortex immortality of May (Sara Kestelman). For Derek Jarman, the sexual politics and plot of *Sebastiane* (1976) precluded even the presence of women. But interestingly, Jarman's later 1970s work combined formal avant-garde qualities with a radical liberalism towards both sexes. The females in *Jubilee* (1978) are fierce and autonomous, and they have escaped emotional bondage. Nicolas Roeg's use of female roles varied according to the project. *Performance* (1970) was too preoccupied by exploration of the male protagonists' feminine side to trouble itself with the real thing; in *Don't Look Now*, the explicit love scene takes care to balance male against female pleasure; in *The Man Who Fell to Earth* (1976), the issues raised were much broader than those of sexual politics.

In previous chapters, I traced the female stereotypes which cinema required, in order to assess the demands on actresses. In mainstream British cinema of the 1970s, it is no longer possible to sketch the ebb and flow of performance styles in this way. This is because the systems of authorship which had obtained before – production or distribution companies – were no longer extant. Directorial voices in mainstream cinema were muffled too. Russell, Losey, Schlesinger and others were under such financial pressure that their *Weltanschauung* was out of kilter with the period, and often with their own previous work.

This meant that patterns of female identity in 1970s cinema were acutely unstable. There was some coherence within genre films – the *Carry Ons*, for example, or the sex films – but in general the industry could not undertake one of the important functions it had fulfilled before: the production of stylized meditations on emergent social forms. The cultural transaction the industry had performed – that of reflecting back to society a range of distorted or seeming-real images – was nullified. Actresses perforce had to be content with slim pickings, and not fret if cultural forms made little sense in the face of radical social change. This is not to say, of course, that some actresses did not manage to have significant careers – Glenda Jackson and Britt Ekland spring to mind – but their personae or trajectories were hampered.

This general instability of female representation can be exemplified by Diana Dors. In sexpot mode, she appeared in a range of 1970s films such as *The Amorous Milkman* (1974) and *Confessions of a Driving Instructor*, although her narrative usefulness was impeded by her age and her voluptuous size. When it came to finding her serious roles suited to her considerable talents, the 1970s film industry gave her parts which tee-tered between unconvincing extremes. In *Nothing But the Night* (1973), for example, Dors seems to be playing a crazed mother intent on trying to kill her child; as the narrative progresses, however, it is revealed that she is in fact a Madonna trying to protect her own. The instability causes the role to implode, and her last close-up is as a dead Guy Fawkes figure: the miscreants have dealt with her contradictions by burning her like a witch.[11]

It looks as though the cultural shipwreck of the 1970s industry had dire consequences for the representation of women. Never before had their lives appeared so truncated or their pleasures so perfunctory. For once, the economic base does appear to determine the cultural superstructure, and in a brutal and unreflecting manner.

Notes

1. See an interesting interview with the star Richard Chamberlain in *Films and Filming*, October 1972: 'Lord Byron had a beauty and magnetism and sexuality which really set women on their ears.'
2. See an article on the film by Frank Wiswell in *Films and Filming*, October 1977.
3. See Lee (1997), pp. 436–9, and the *Guardian*, 8 January 1999. *The Wicker Man* achieved cult status some years after its release, of course.
4. For the director's view of the individual/society relationship, see *Cinéfantastique*, Winter 1977: 'the idea that it is necessary to sacrifice people for the good of other people is never far from human consciousness'.
5. *Sunday Times* Colour Supplement, 5 September 1976. See also Connolly (1985), pp. 227–40.
6. For an account by Kathleen Tynan, one of the scriptwriters, see *Evening Standard*, 3 June 1976.
7. For an interpretation of Pitt's work, see *The Independent*, 11 August 1997.
8. This was Pauline Kael in the *New Yorker*, 21 November 1970.
9. Ciment (1985), pp. 330–1. For Seyrig's version of the script struggles, see Britton (1991), pp. 65–6.
10. *Films and Filming*, October 1972. It contained a cameo role of a suffragette, played by Helen Mirren.
11. There is an interesting piece on Dors's later career in *Films and Filming*, February 1973.

7

The 1980s: 'The British Are Coming'

The 1980s were marked by a cultural and political revolution whose consequences are still evident. Margaret Thatcher was in office from 1979 to 1990, and inculcated a regime of astonishing brutality, pronouncing that 'there is no such thing as society'. She designed a militantly individualistic culture to replace notions of consensus and public responsibility. She could not, of course, have survived so long without a modicum of support from the country at large – by those who espoused the same system of petty entrepreneurialism, and who knew the price of everything but the value of nothing.

Thatcher brought in a series of measures to create a flexible labour force, which led to casualization and an increase in unskilled female labour. As the 1980s progressed, the gap widened between work-poor households, in which neither partner was working, and work-rich ones, in which both were employed. As an intellectual force, feminism was in some disarray from the early 1980s. The forces of Thatcherism had dissipated leftism too, which exacerbated the sense of crisis among the intelligentsia.

The film industry confronted the issues raised by Thatcherism in an uneven way, because it was forced at last to confront the free market totally unprotected. The government passed the new Films Act in 1984/5, which finally got rid of the Eady Levy and privatized the NFFC. This had a disastrous effect on funding, which was now more parlous than ever before. Directors had to float on the current of commerce, and some of them found favour with the men in suits. Indeed, many of the new directors and producers had begun in advertising (Auty, 1985, p. 58). Perhaps that helped them to appear salesworthy.

A huge fillip to independent film production was provided by Channel Four Television, which was established in 1982. It instigated new forms of collaboration with producers via Film Four International and its investments in British Screen, and its tactics did release fresh capital.[1] Without Channel Four, a whole tranche of excellent films would never have been made. But competition was so fierce that barnstorming marketing skills were more necessary than before, and more diffident directors, or minor-key projects, had difficulties. The BFI Production Board backed projects which seemed too avant-garde for mainstream financiers – *Burning an Illusion* (1982), *The Draughtsman's Contract* (1982), *Ascendancy* (1983), *Caravaggio* (1985), *Distant Voices, Still Lives* (1988), and others. The aims of the BFI were laudable, and certainly films were funded which would otherwise have had no chance of reaching the screen, but the Production Board had a penchant for films with an academic flavour, which displayed their credentials with a degree of martyrdom. Since women were not a minority social group, it was less inclined to favour films about them.

There are no consistent patterns of gender representation in films sponsored by Channel Four or the BFI. Everything depended on the director and his (and it was almost always *his*) control over the script and the production team. The crucial determinant was the degree to which he could appear to be totally convinced by the viability of his project, when in front of a selection panel. The ways in which women were represented in Channel Four or BFI films were therefore unpredictable. The same cannot be said for Goldcrest Films, the most important independent production company of the decade. Well orchestrated and profitable though they were, Goldcrest's films were utterly neglectful of women. Its chief executive later accepted that the company's films were a straightforward reflection of the cultural and gender capital of the producers:

> Just as in the entire Goldcrest management team and board of directors there was found to be no place for a woman, so in Goldcrest's films there were few substantial parts for actresses. Indeed, it is striking how few parts there were for black people, bohemians, muscle-men, intellectuals – any kind of person, in fact, with whom the Goldcrest executives could not themselves strongly identify. Many of the pictures tell the same story, of an essentially middle-class man, whose honour, fortitude and decency enabled him to triumph against the odds.[2]

Jake Eberts, Goldcrest's founder, had a predilection for what he called 'low concept' films, which were 'true stories ... based on historical fact' (Eberts and Ilott, 1990, p. 33). The facts were carefully selected, of course.

David Puttnam, one of the executive producers at Goldcrest, recognized his own and the company's gender bias: 'I don't understand women's motivations, which means that I don't know how to address the scripts, the castings etc. Women's reactions are extremely arbitrary to me.'[3] Accordingly, *The Killing Fields* (1984), although morally irreproachable, was essentially about a male bond. Puttnam noted that

> It starts off with an exciting relationship which goes down through a kind of visual and energetic period to reach a crisis, a tragedy, a parting of the ways. Then the curve flows up again to a reunion. That curve is as good as you're ever going to get for a movie. You can't ask for more. (Yule, 1988, p. 229)

The Emerald Forest (1985), although ecologically sound, was fundamentally about a father–son search and the superiority of a tribal culture whose courtship ritual was prefaced by a blow from a club. *The Dresser* (1984) is about a fulfilling relationship between a flagging actor and his body servant, while the lead role in *Gandhi* (1982) was given to a white actor (Ben Kingsley) because 'as far as the Goldcrest board and management were concerned, Kingsley, unlike Gandhi himself, was one of them' (Eberts and Ilott, 1990, p. xv). At the end of the film, the British flag is lowered and the Indian and Pakistani ones are raised: the final shot is of Gandhi spinning at his wheel. Overtaken by history, he ends up as a homespun philosopher.

Goldcrest's obsession with the male gender was consistent throughout, regardless of the director. In *Greystoke* (1984), in which it collaborated with Warners, Bob Towne's original script employed the romantic ending traditionally associated with the Tarzan tale: Jane swings through the jungle with her agreeably taciturn mate. However, director Hugh Hudson, with the full support of management, excised the woman. According to Terry Semel:

> He felt it was better for them not to have a romance. It got rewritten to the point that it was no longer about Jane and Tarzan, but about Tarzan and the ape tribe. It was all about men. He didn't even want to call her Jane. (Eberts and Ilott, 1990, p. 354)

The main relationship is between the simian aristocrat and his senile grandfather.

Or consider the sequence of the young men running along the beach in *Chariots of Fire* (1981), which is used as a framing device to open and close the film. The community of athletes travels effortlessly, containing and supporting all male incomers and belief systems: beautiful and self-sufficient, the *kouroi* move as one. And what other national cinema, in what other period, would have found the money to make a film of *Another Country* (1984), which deals with a petulant sixth-former whose decision to betray his country is based on the school's refusal to let him wear a sprigged waistcoat and be called a 'God'?[4]

Whatever the bleak economic realities behind the hype, Goldcrest was largely responsible for the myth of the British film renaissance. This was bought wholesale by many journalists and critics, and by some of those employed in the industry, notably scriptwriter Colin Welland, who famously declared when *Chariots of Fire* won an Oscar: 'the British are coming!'

Well, *some* of them. The women were probably faking it. On the face of it, British film culture of the 1980s was marked by images of masculinity of an unusually exclusive and aggressive type. Non-Goldcrest films such as *Withnail and I* (1984), *My Beautiful Laundrette* (1985), *Prick up Your Ears* (1987), *We Think the World of You* (1987) and many others portray an exclusively male world in which women are an irrelevance. Such films should be interpreted as a species of gender triumphalism: part of their intention is to discomfort and marginalize the female presence. They spring from a laudably liberal impulse to express the desires of a homosexual group hitherto almost invisible in mainstream cinema. But in the venal culture of the 1980s, this impulse was vitiated, and often fed into texts whose business was not to celebrate men but to denigrate women. It has been argued that 1980s British cinema was preoccupied as never before with national identity. However, it was preoccupied with masculinity in a new way too. This was facilitated by the style of the new funding arrangements, and was doubtless fuelled by the complex emotions evoked by Thatcher herself: admiration, loathing and fear of the Monstrous-Feminine.

Thus, several films by different directors expressed anxiety about unruly women. *The French Lieutenant's Woman* (1981) replicated the fear of the wilful Sarah which motivated John Fowles's original novel.

The Missionary (1983) was soured by mistrust of the philanthropic Lady Ames (Maggie Smith). *Dance with a Stranger* (1984) presents Ruth Ellis as a tight-lipped hysteric whose predilection for emotional abuse makes her downfall inevitable. *Scandal* (1989) is a sustained meditation on the havoc wreaked by so-called female promiscuity. Other films of the period concentrate on powerful mothers who dominate their sons, such as *Hope and Glory* (1987). Thomas Elsaesser argues that all such films are 'exorcising male childhood traumas, and all involve a highly ambivalent reckoning with the mother's sexuality'. He quotes Boorman's diary, on which *Hope and Glory* is based:

> While my father went to the war, he left me with a house full of women, with no male to curb the female excesses. The inexplicable and sudden tears, then the crass conspiratorial laughter at some sexual allusion ... and the stifling embraces when a boy's face was pressed into that infinite softness, falling, falling, inhaling all those layers of odours only scantily concealed by lily of the valley.[5]

Some directors intended their films to offer an explicit critique of Thatcherism, but the projects were suborned by the sheer power of the ideological sea-change. Lindsay Anderson's *Britannia Hospital* (1982), for example, was conceived as a coruscating satire on the inroads of Thatcherism into state provision, but it was derailed by the seeming inevitability of the process. The film's narrative enacts a horrified fascination, rather like that of a rabbit by a stoat. The hyperbolism of the male managers and surgeons pales before the conviction of the chief nurse (Jill Bennett). Pale, blonde and insanely devoted to her cause, she is clearly a miniature Margaret. Richard Eyre came similarly unstuck with *The Ploughman's Lunch* (1983). He meant it to display the shipwreck of Thatcherite attitudes, with the saurian protagonist (Jonathan Pryce) displaying gross moral turpitude. But the spectacle of everyone, male and female, internalizing the sexual politics of the marketplace was an intoxicating one. Stephen Frears's *Sammy and Rosie Get Laid* (1988) had a similar dynamic. He saw it as 'an attempt to bring Margaret Thatcher down. It clearly failed. It's actually very overt in its attempt to rally the troops.'[6] The director's intentions in *Sammy and Rosie Get Laid* were paradoxically scuppered by the strength of the female lead (Frances Barber). Hanif Kureshi's script gave a central role to Rosie's motivation, and the direction and acting style present her as a feisty female who pursues her own path while wearing an array of dazzling outfits. Rosie is a social, sexual and sartorial *bricoleuse*, and she is able to profit from the chaos and misery of Thatcherite culture. The other female leads are also empowered by the new society. The older Alice (Claire Bloom) feels free to take a lover, though doubtless she might have reconsidered had she heard him say that 'she's got another ten years' wear in her'. For the young lesbians (Meera Syal and Suzette Llewellyn) the *laissez-faire* atmosphere is liberating. The males, on the other hand, are nonplussed and even infantilized by it (Barber, 1993, p. 230).

Some 1980s directors were more ambivalent about Thatcherism. David Hare, for example, was first fascinated and then repelled by the effects of Thatcherite policies on the female psyche. In *Wetherby* (1985), which he both scripted and directed, Jean Travers (Vanessa Redgrave) is exposed to a stranger's suicide. With cinematic hindsight, we find that it was partially her fault, since she was liable to graceless couplings with inappropriate partners. The censors found *Wetherby* troubling because of its 'pervasive atmosphere of violence', but Hare thought it was really about 'what loneliness and repression and real sexual need feel like'.[7] With *Paris by Night* (1985), Hare became more intensely preoccupied with female ruthlessness. Clara (Charlotte Rampling) is a Conservative MEP, and Hare's original intentions for the film were unexceptionable. He wanted to show how: 'If you watch women in politics, they're not integrated into the activity; they're moved around it by the men. They're guests, but they're not *it*.' He wanted repeated shots of Clara waiting, because 'it's the men's rhythm time'.[8] But Hare became increasingly alienated by Clara. He presents her as dogged by a troublesome associate, whom she effortlessly topples over a Paris bridge to a watery grave. Clara wants to have it all, but the film suggests that her position makes it impossible for her to give anything. Her husband turns to drink; her child is fobbed off with nougat; all her lover can find to say is 'you're my first naked Tory'. Clara comes to symbolize the energy and moral dubiety of Thatcherism:

> The whole appeal of Thatcherism is that she came along and said that things were simple. People were so relieved to hear that. She told us that it was all right to stand up for Number One, and that if you did, nothing terrible will happen to you.[9]

Clara has to be neutralized in order to strike the Mother dead, symbolically speaking. 'Something terrible' must be her punishment.

Hare then scripted *Plenty* (1988), which dealt with a heroine (Meryl Streep) so committed to getting her own way that tranquillizers and suicide are the only appropriate coping mechanisms. *Strapless* (1988), which Hare both wrote and directed, continued the theme of female desire in a more uneven way. Lillian (Blair Brown) is a forthright doctor who is swept off her feet by the cosmopolitan Raymond (Bruno Ganz). He is a man's idea of what women want – a suave lounge lizard who believes in sex after marriage and who has a Royal Flush of credit cards. Alas, Raymond is a rotter. A sadder, wiser and poorer Lillian concludes that she feels richer in heart if not in pocket. She is comforted by the dress designs of her sister Amy (Bridget Fonda), who has made a strapless frock that will stand up on its own. The logic of Hare's narrative is that women prefer artificial cantilevering over emotional support. Bras have been burned for less.

Other, older directors came to the end of their creative careers in the 1980s, continuing the trajectories they had begun earlier. David Lean had moved into a more 'feminine' mode in the 1970s, and with *A Passage to India* (1984) he radically revised and scripted Forster's novel. Lean played down the metaphysical dimensions of the novel, and chose instead to give the female roles more resonance.[10] Mrs Moore (Peggy Ashcroft) is shown as an 'old soul', and becomes the hidden, radiant centre of the film, providing spiritual and moral power. In the novel she is a more neutral figure. And instead of presenting Adela (Judy Davis) as a puritanical spinster, as in the novel, Lean converts her into an honest but confused girl whom India catapults into sexual awareness. The key scene Lean inserted into the screenplay was of Adela cycling into the jungle and finding temples covered with erotic carvings. No sooner is she aroused by them than she is panicked by the monkey hordes which issue from the temple. Desire and fear are combined in her response, and her admirably complex sensibility is foregrounded.

Ken Russell too continued along the path he had laid down earlier. Throughout the 1970s, he had directed energetic films which displayed women in throbbing mode. In the 1980s, Russell's films placed women at the outer margins, where they function as sites of interdiction and terror. In *Gothic* (1987), the doomed evening chez Byron kicks off with a thrashing seizure thrown by Claire (Miriam Cyr); we are informed that she is prone to fits at 'times of the month'. Other gynaecological cata-strophes are interpreted as proof that women are biologically dangerous. The last shot is of a pitiful stillborn baby; water shimmers over it and distorts its appearance, so that it becomes Frankenstein's monster. Russell develops his position in *The Lair of the White Worm* (1988), in which Lady Sylvia (Amanda Donohoe) is an aristocratic vampire whose spittle lays waste the world of men.

Barry Keith Grant (1993) has suggested that Russell's 1980s films offer a radical critique of patriarchy, and that, poised between realism and fantasy, they deliberately display its contradictions. From the evidence of *Salome's Last Dance* (1988) in particular, it seems more likely that Russell is caught in patriarchy's toils and that, though an enraged prisoner, it affords him some erotic consolations. *Salome's Last Dance* is conceived as a play-within-a-play, and offers a blunt interpretation of Wilde's original text.[11] Russell has the same actor (Douglas Hodge) play both Bosie and John the Baptist. This gives rise to some gross by-play when Salome (Imogen Millais-Scott) squats over the Baptist's severed head. Immediately afterwards, she is pierced fore and aft by a javelin (she is crushed by the soldiers' shields in Wilde's play). Her death is presented as the consequence of her forcing John/Bosie to confront the vagina. The tiny Millais-Scott is directed to appear as a nymphomaniac with silver ankle boots and an athletic tongue. Poor Stratford Johns (Herod) resembles Lindsay Kemp in high-camp mode, and the whole film proves that little girls should be heard and not seen.

So far, I have examined production companies and directors and have established clear patterns of gender representation. If we now interrogate genre as a determining structure, we face difficulties; fixed generic bound-aries were in acute flux in the 1980s, and the old-style categories were no longer deployed. Adventure or crime films, for example, were now mixed with musical or satirical elements. The only adventure sub-genre to remain stable was the Bond films, and it was by now a homogenous and predictable phenomenon. *For Your Eyes Only* (1981), *Octopussy* (1983) and *View to a Kill* (1985) were fixed in an ironic mode which accorded ill with the hardware. All the Bond women were titillating cyphers, often with a proto-feminist overlay.

The art-house films pose different problems. Peter Wollen (1993) has valuably mapped the field of modernist and art-house film, and has suggested that the main art-house protagonists Peter Greenaway and

Derek Jarman constituted opposite ends of the aesthetic spectrum. Certainly the two are light-years apart in their sexual politics. Greenaway claims to be interested in fleshly textures (MacFarlane, 1997, pp. 242–3), but his films are unremittingly cerebral and evoke a sour distaste for the body. His *The Draughtsman's Contract* requires extensive cultural competence from the audience – Baroque style, debates about perspective, Catholic heresies, whether the wigs are accurate or not. All well and good: but the manner of the film, nitpicking and self-congratulatory, catapults us into the Land of Postmodernism, in which retro-chic dominates and style takes precedence over content.[12] The sexual politics of the film are by no means liberal. The journeyman artist Neville (Anthony Higgins) belabours Mrs Herbert (Janet Suzman) with violent sexual attentions. It may be that Greenaway intended her and her daughter to deploy Neville as a stud, to impregnate them and subvert patriarchy (Walsh, 1993). Whatever the reason, the textual effect is of an unrelieved nastiness, and one wonders whether it is possible to dwell within the environs of a dungheap and still smell sweet. The same issue arises with *The Cook, the Thief, His Wife and Her Lover* (1989). It is intended to operate as a satire on the worst excesses of Thatcherism, with the protagonist (Michael Gambon) symbolizing its venality and greed. But Greenaway collapses together consumerism and the everyday consumption of food. This is a problem, since the first has to do with the metaphoric value of goods and the second with innocent appetite. A second elision then takes place between food and sex, with the woman (Helen Mirren) operating as the fulcrum of all the systems of mastication and exchange. In herself she is nothing.

Jarman, on the other hand, gave the art-house film a more radical spin. In the 1980s, Jarman was of course preoccupied with the repressive effects of Thatcherism, as *The Last of England* (1987) and *War Requiem* (1989) show. But his more overtly gay films also make a space for women, and they appear in a positive light. In *Caravaggio*, the focus is on the art, loves and mutual betrayals of those outside the law; this includes profane women, the courtesans and tumblers, whose beauty and agility are celebrated. In an important scene, Caravaggio (Nigel Terry) rests from painting *Profane Love* as his acrobat model disports herself. With extraordinary flexibility and control, she pivots until she does the splits and her foot nestles behind her ear. At this moment, she looks intently at the globe and then back, with a mocking expression, at Caravaggio and the audience. She could enfold or engulf the world. And *The Garden* (1990), whose main business is a meditation on the Established Church's violence to gays, provides a resonant place for women. Christian imagery is deployed and radicalized throughout, with the Mother of God (Tilda Swinton) surpassingly beautiful and yet able to repel boarders by a nifty line in kick-boxing. The mother-figure is sexualized as well. The long table scene, redolent of da Vinci's *The Last Supper*, is peopled by women, each playing a single note on her wineglass. The glass harmonica makes the music of the spheres: 'what spirits are they conjuring?'[13] And an older woman dances the flamenco on that same table: passionate, controlled, she teaches the steps to her son. Women appear variously in *The Garden* as angels, lovers, mothers, artists and (perhaps most significantly of all) just ordinary beings joyfully gathering mushrooms. Jarman is a film-maker for women as well as men, and in his virtuosity, compassion and radicalism, is an artist for all time.

If we turn to the genre of costume film, we see that it too was fragmented and heterogeneous. This was not the case in earlier periods. In the 1980s, films deployed the past for nostalgia, for exhortation, for firming up debates about national identity, and for escapism. The past was mainly a commodity, rarely used for critical or radical purposes.[14] With perhaps one exception: the Merchant–Ivory films of the decade. Andrew Higson suggests that they are as conservative as the other 'heritage' films (Higson, 1993, pp. 109–10). But the potential radicalism of the original texts is, to my mind, maintained and even intensified. The input of scriptwriter Ruth Prawer Jhabvala was crucial, and as we shall see, her sense of structure and female character struggles for dominance over the décor. Jeffrey Richards is right to suggest that the Merchant–Ivory films constitute 'a continuing and comprehensive critique of the ethic of restraint, duty and the stiff upper lip' (Richards, 1997, p. 169). This critique also entails a focus on the ills of patriarchy, and instead proposes a feminization of culture.

In general, then, 1980s film culture resembles earlier historical periods: the images of women can be categorized according to production company and director, although genre is more problematical. Most 1980s cinema interpreted female identity as threatening and lubricious. There were a few honourable exceptions. Jarman, as I have shown, progressed towards a lyrical celebration of female beauty and strength. There were a few other films in the fantasy mode which made a similar accommodation. Ken McMullen's *Zina* (1986) presented a stylized mosaic of female experience.[15] Neil Jordan's *The Company of Wolves* (1984) concentrated on the menarche, and presented a young girl's transition to adulthood via a series of expressionist cameos which drew on fairytales. The film, of course, owes an enormous amount to Angela Carter's original tale and script. On one level, *The Company of Wolves* provides a checklist of the desirables of Thatcherism – the country house, the Volvo, the guard dogs – but on another level, it profoundly disrupts its certainties. The archetypal narrative of Red Riding Hood is subverted into a tale celebrating sexual love and the 'Hairy Stranger', whose arrival inspires both terror and desire. It avoids discursive realism wherever possible.

But mainly, it is to the realist mode that we must look for risk-taking images of women in the 1980s. This constitutes an important break in practice, since innovatory representations in mainstream cinema had hitherto been in the costume or comedy mode. Realist films in (say) the 1960s had provided bleak interpretations of women's lives and consciousness. In the 1980s, a range of films were made which dealt with recognizable lifestyles and dilemmas. Their directors all took great care to match different textual discourses together – décor, costumes, music – and they all made a minor adjustment to realist practice by encouraging a style of performance from their female protagonists which challenged the expected norm. Some female leads were directed so as to *under*act: in Bill Forsyth's *Gregory's Girl* (1983), the young footballer Dorothy (Dee Hepburn) displays a pawky indifference which baffles the hero. In *Another Time, Another Place* (1983), Phyllis Logan as the wartime heroine makes restraint into a fine art. This breaks open in the love scene with her Italian swain, in which her face is seen in orgasm in a prolonged close-up: refined, expressive and passionate, her sensuality is all the more poignant because it is clearly aroused by an unworthy mate. Another 'repressed' performance occurs in *A Letter to Brezhnev* (1985), in which Elaine (Alexandra Pigg) falls in love with a Russian sailor and, against all odds, has the courage (or folly) to migrate to him. Pigg's performance is a marvel of restraint, whereas her friend Teresa (Margi Clarke) is the boisterous reverse. *A Letter to Brezhnev* is interesting because the two female leads are exactly balanced: one slightly above, one slightly below the realistic norm. The result is a film which presents female desire as entirely reasonable.

Educating Rita (1983) does the same. This time the technique is to allow the female lead to let rip, and to *overact* in recognizable circumstances and institutions. Rita (Julie Walters) implicitly suggests, through the bravura of her performance, that it is possible to break through the wall of habit and to requite one's needs. The same goes for the much-maligned *Rita, Sue and Bob Too* (1986), which contains deliberately overblown performances from Siobhan Finneran as Rita and Michelle Holmes as Sue. *Rita, Sue and Bob Too* was dismissed by critics as a sexploitation film, perhaps because it was advertised as 'Thatcher's Britain With Its Knickers Down'. But in fact it was a feminist comedy, based on Andrea Dunbar's play about two girls from a dilapidated council estate who decide that one good man between two is better than none. Bob may be married, but he is solvent and an indefatigable lover. Dunbar herself insisted the girls were fully able to take responsibility for their actions; any moral offence caused had to do with the spectacle of girls willingly removing their own underwear.[16] Alan Clarke's film can be interpreted as old-fashioned libertarianism, but the whole focus is on the ribald girls, their friendship and their raucous desire for a 'jump'. One scene is of particular interest. Sue is rogered by Bob in an unpromising setting: in a car, in cold weather with her friend looking on. Nonetheless, her pleasure is intense. Bob asks whether she enjoyed herself: the answer is a huge grin and an emphatic 'yes'.[17] Underclass denizens Rita and Sue may be, but their desire for autonomy and fulfilment are equal to anyone's.

Mike Leigh's 1980s work was modified realism too. His *High Hopes* (1988) and *Life Is Sweet* (1990) both contained stylized performances which threw the theme of female identity into sharp relief. Leigh had been unable to obtain BFI funding, because 'I'm a man who doesn't have a script, won't say what it's going to be about, and doesn't want to discuss the cast – not by any standards a viable proposition!' (Fuller, 1995, p. xvi). His subject matter was disarmingly ordinary: 'what my films are about in essence are just basic things like living and dying and surviving and work and relationships and families' (MacFarlane, 1997, p. 362). Of course, Leigh's preoccupation with family life has an inevitable consequence for his female characters, who are all judged by whether they are mothers or not.

Leigh's method was to get the actors to concentrate on a person they knew, and then to slightly exaggerate one characteristic (Coveney, 1997, p. 71). This was a technique most fruitfully used in *High Hopes*. Two of the female leads are overblown: Laetitia Boothe-Braine (Lesley Manville) is materialistic and interlocutionary ('Have you got all your original features?'). Valerie (Heather Tobias) is hysterical and insecure ('You be Michael Douglas – I'll be a virgin'). The hyperactivity of their performances opens up a space for Ruth Sheen as Shirley to develop a character of extraordinary power and stillness. In one scene Shirley tries to persuade her partner Cyril (Philip Davis) that they should start a family. Cyril is reluctant, and the conversation takes a downward drift. Suddenly Shirley's eyes fill with tears, as she is torn between her love for Cyril and her need for a child. It is all done with the minimum of fuss and searching movements, whether physical or emotional.

Life Is Sweet has the same arrangements. It concentrates on the women in an ordinary suburban family. One twin daughter is a lesbian, employed and well adjusted; the other is an agoraphobic bulimic with a taste for heterosexual bondage. The second twin's emotional disarray prompts her mother Wendy (Alison Steadman) to a revealing conversation, in which she urges her daughter to know that she is loved. It is a moment of painful and dignified intimacy, in which Wendy presents herself as wife, mother and moral being and insists that, in spite of all, life is worth a candle.

In the 1980s, many actresses were required to produce a very tight, neurotic style of performance. Roles were created which necessitated a display of the pains of repression, and which required women to act as miniature Thatcherites in their deportment and morals. Miranda Richardson's performance in *Dance with a Stranger* and Charlotte Rampling's in *Paris by Night* were examples of these, in which the bodily behaviour was controlled and the back and neck rigidly clamped. In general, the alternatives to mini-Margarets were sketched in with little attention to detail. Actresses who were inscribed with the qualities of self-determination and autonomy (Julie Walters, Pauline Collins) tended to be physically undisciplined and unpredictable in their gaze patterns and body language. The only actress to be used to challenge this pattern was Tilda Swinton, who turned in some powerful performances in which her ambiguity was signalled by a still gaze and extreme physical composure. This had to do with the power of Jarman's avant-garde style, which reached a maturity and a confidence unmatched by anyone else's in the period.

Overall, images of women in 1980s British cinema were extremely mixed. Goldcrest and many of the heritage films (except Merchant–Ivory) portrayed females either as a threat or as a neutral void. Many directors wished to take issue with Thatcher's politics, but they remained fascinated by her authoritarian persona, and that is reflected in their films. The only films to explore female consciousness in a mindful way were mainstream ones in the realist/naturalist mode (and that was a major innovation, given realism's dismal history in sexual politics) or avant-garde ones by Jarman, whose outer-darkness position allowed him to take risks.

Notes

1. For material on Channel Four, see Quart (1993), Giles (1993) and Walker (1985). See also *Sight and Sound*, Spring 1984, for material on the relationship between film and television. John Hill (1999) contains much excellent material on legislative and economic matters.
2. Eberts and Ilott (1990), pp. xiv–xv. This passage was written by Ilott, but with the full co-operation of Eberts, Goldcrest's long-time chief executive. For other material on Goldcrest, see Yule (1988) and Walker (1985).
3. *Time*, May 1989.
4. In Eberts and Ilott (1990), p. 132, Eberts discusses the complex funding arrangements thought to be necessitated by the film's overtly homosexual theme.
5. *Monthly Film Bulletin*, October 1988.
6. Interview in Dixon (1994), p. 232. The whole interview is very instructive for Frears's attitude to Thatcherism. See also Kureshi (1987) for a comparison with Frears's collaborator.
7. *Film Comment*, September 1985, pp. 22, 20. See also *Stills*, February 1985.
8. *Films and Filming*, June 1989.
9. *Ibid.*
10. See Brownlow (1997), pp. 643–83, for a detailed account of the scripting and filming. Judy Davis was worried about Lean's bad reputation with female roles.
11. Russell's son translated Wilde's French text, which was originally turned into English by Lord Alfred Douglas. The screenplay for the film was by Ken Russell.
12. This posturing pseudo-philosophy, which encouraged its devotees to think that puns and quotation-hunting were a substitute for real intellectual labour, had some currency in the period.
13. See Jarman (1991), pp.199–200, for an account of the scene.
14. For debates about the heritage film, see Higson (1993, 1996), and Monk (1995, 1999).
15. See an interview with McMullen in *Monthly Film Bulletin*, May 1986.
16. *Time Out*, 2 September 1987.
17. For an interesting account of the film, which was shot on Steadicam, see Kelly (1988), pp. 171–81.

First a Girl (1935) Jessie Matthews. BFI Films: Stills, Posters and
Designs © Carlton International Media Ltd.

Me and Marlborough
(1934) Cicely
Courtneidge. BFI Films:
Stills, Posters and
Designs © Carlton
International Media Ltd.

The Gentle Sex (1943)
Lilli Palmer and Joyce
Howard. BFI Films: Stills,
Posters and Designs ©
Carlton International
Media Ltd.

The Wicked Lady (1945) Margaret Lockwood and James Mason. BFI Films: Stills, Posters and Designs © Carlton International Media Ltd.

Caravan (1946) Jean Kent. BFI
Films: Stills, Posters and Designs ©
Carlton International Media Ltd.

Miranda (1948)
Glynis Johns. BFI
Films: Stills, Posters
and Designs ©
Carlton International
Media Ltd.

Value for Money
(1955) Diana Dors.
BFI Films: Stills,
Posters and Designs
© Carlton International
Media Ltd.

Muriel Box directing a
film in the 1950s.
Author's private
collection.

A Town Like Alice (1956) Virginia McKenna. BFI Films: Stills, Posters and Designs © Carlton International Media Ltd.

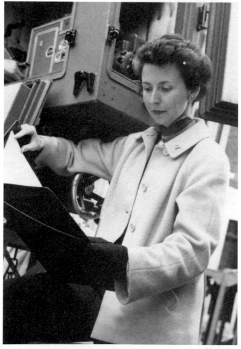

Wendy Toye on location in London filming *Raising a Riot* in the 1950s. Courtesy of Wendy Toye.

She (1965) Ursula Andress. BFI Films: Stills, Posters and Designs © 1965 Hammer Film Productions Ltd.

Smashing Time (1967) Lynn Redgrave and Rita Tushingham. BFI Films: Stills, Posters and Designs.

The Wicker Man (1974) Britt Ekland. BFI Films: Stills, Posters and Designs ©
Canal + Image UK Ltd.

Educating Rita (1983) Julie Walters and Michael Caine. BFI Films: Stills, Posters
and Designs © Carlton International Media Ltd.

PART II
WOMEN'S WORK

8

Producers

In the 1930s British film industry, women were rarely present in the upper echelons. Lady Yule was the only woman involved at the financial level. She was instrumental in setting up British National in 1934, with an eye to propagandizing the British way of life. She liaised with John Baxter and with J. Arthur Rank, but intervened very little in day-to-day filming. The industry was dominated by major producers who owned the company collateral, and none of them were women. There were a few female producers of a more hands-on type, but they worked on low-status items. Nell Emerald produced the quota quickies *Murder at the Cabaret* (1936), *Terror on Tiptoe* (1936) and *Dr Sin Fang* (1937). Gina Carlton produced *The Last Waltz* for Warwick in 1936, and Dora Nirva *The Street Singer* for British National in 1937. All these films were low-budget items, and did not lead to career advancement.

During the war, the only feature producer was Elizabeth Hiscott. She produced four maritime thrillers which her husband Leslie Hiscott directed, but the films themselves were unremarkable.[1] In the postwar period, Mary Field produced films for Gaumont-British Instructional (she had, of course, been directing nature programmes and children's documentaries since the 1930s). The real change for feature production came in late 1946, when Rank appointed Sydney Box as head of production at Gainsborough. Sydney then offered his sister Betty the opportunity to run the Islington studio. Betty Box had a broad definition of the producer's function: to choose the subject, to appoint the director, to organize the scripting, to cast the actors and to arrange post-production. She felt she was 'a very good housekeeper' in her ability to keep to budgets (MacFarlane, 1997, p. 85). Betty Box described herself as 'a near feminist'. She appointed other women when she could, and felt that 'I have had to put up with more because I am a woman. If I wanted an increase in my fee, I would be told "What do you need more money for when you've got a rich husband?" [2] Box was resolutely middlebrow, and lacked confidence in her own cultural capital. In a 1950s interview she argued that

> I'm no highbrow. What I look for is a rattling good story, plenty of laughs, plenty of situations and, most importantly, good casting. ... There can be no such thing as a purely woman's picture. The ingredients that make up a good film and good entertainment are plot, acting, setting, actors. If these are good, then the public will pay. [3]

She was still making the same connections in 1991:

> I wanted to make the popular kind of movies that people like myself wanted to see. I didn't believe that I was artistic enough to make great epics. I liked and still like films about characters – not action-motivated films. [4]

Box's postwar projects can be divided into two categories, melodramas and comedies. The melodramas all have some sexual titillation, combined with moral conservatism. *Dear Murderer* (1947) is about an adulterous wife (Greta Gynt) who makes liberal use of her sexual favours until her husband (Eric Portman) murders her current lover. Considerable narrative time is given to Portman's gentlemanly violence until, in a key travelling shot, the wife is seen looking into a triple dressing-table mirror. From that moment, the film focuses on her vanity and deviance, as she kills her husband because he interferes with her pleasures: 'You've got to die so that I may go on living as I want to live.' *When the Bough Breaks* (1947) is about an unmarried mother (Patricia Roc). The script treats motherhood in a social-realist manner, but the acting style and music have a strongly melodramatic flavour. *The Blind Goddess* (1948), for which Betty Box was the executive producer, is a melodrama with noirish overtones. It deals with the devious Lady Brasted (Anne Crawford) and her crooked husband. Betty insisted that significant modifications be made to the original script by Muriel and Sydney Box, which emphasized the heroine's moral turpitude. In the original script, Lady Brasted really did take a lover, whereas she only pretends to in the finished film. She was also unscrupulous: 'I was brought up in the gutter. I too have taken risks. I kept myself alive by stealing ... I loved him and that was why I was ready to lie and forge and steal for him' (S13922). The character in the final film is far more ambivalent. The original script foregrounded two mythical figures in a statuette, the Blind Goddess (Justice) and the Blind God (Eros). The final film version pays this scant attention, possibly because Betty Box thought that the issue was handled in too highbrow a manner by Muriel.

None of Betty Box's melodramas had much success at the box-office. The only exception was *So Long at the Fair* (1950), which was moderately successful. It also deals with false appearances: this time it is a building rather than a woman which is not what it seems. In general, though, Betty Box's interest in moral dubiety and subterfuge was not shared by the mass audience, who preferred villainy to be more directly expressed. Her comedies, however, did well in the *Kineweekly* ratings. *Miranda* (1949) has a marvellous lightness of touch and brittle characterization. It is about a mermaid (Glynis Johns) with a glistening tail and a voracious sexual appetite. She falls in love with a doctor (Griffith Jones) and eventually conceives a mer-baby by him, though it is hard to see how.

Miranda suggests that society finds female desire a disquieting phenomenon. The heroine smells of fish; she talks about her 'tail' with pride, and makes outrageous propositions to all the males she meets. They love it, of course; but the young women connive to remove Miranda from the competition. Only the old nurse (Margaret Rutherford), who is outside the contest, tolerates her. *Miranda* suggests, on a comic level, that convention favours certain kinds of women – complaisant and home-loving – who will fight fiercely for their privileges.

Betty Box's popular Huggett comedies take the same position. *Vote for Huggett* (1948), *Here Come the Huggetts* (1948) and *The Huggetts Abroad* (1949) have a fine eye for the disquiets of the lower-middle class family. The first Huggett film was *Holiday Camp* (1947), whose politics were very different. Scripted by Muriel and Sydney Box, *Holiday Camp* celebrates mass culture. Its project is to suggest that all 'outsiders' – the upper-middle-class spinster, the unmarried mother, the rootless sailor – can be part of one social family. Muriel and Sydney also scripted *Here Come the Huggetts*, which shares political similarities with *Holiday Camp*. But Betty Box's other two Huggett films lack that radical edge. They are more conservative in their sexual politics, probably because Muriel was no longer involved in scripting. *Vote for Huggett*, for example, deals with 'Dad's' (Jack Warner) attempt to gain a seat on the local council, which is complicated by 'Mum's' (Kathleen Harrison) ownership of a piece of disputed land. The whole film rests on the protagonists' joyful acceptance of patriarchal structures. *Vote for Huggett* ends with Dad (in stentorian mode) warning Mum: 'There's two things in the world I can't abide, pretty women and clever women, and you're neither ... if I hear you talking about rates and taxes and all that drivel, I'll take a stick to you.' Mum is overjoyed ('Joe, do you really mean that?') and throws her arms around him.

Betty Box's comedies affirm the comforts of the sexual status quo. They suggest that patriarchy provides a comfortable billet for those women willing to play the game. The melodramatic mode was less suited to Box's talents. She reworked the 'bad girl' motifs so prevalent in the cinema of the period, but with a heavy overlay of ambivalence.

In the 1950s, more women attempted advancement to producer level, but few were successful; those working as production secretaries or production co-ordinators could not get screen credits because they were not in the ACT, and so did not advance up the career ladder. Some, like Dora Wright, made it to production manager, but no further. Other women were advantaged by family connections: Elizabeth Hiscott produced her husband's film *Tons of Trouble* (1956). Anna Neagle was encouraged by Herbert Wilcox to produce *These Dangerous Years* (1957), *Wonderful Things!* (1958) and *The Heart of a Man* (1959). She felt that she had something special to offer:

> At a script conference for example, men often seem to have cardboard ideas about what a girl is and what she is thinking. That's where a woman producer can help, from her own understanding. I think too, it can be of great help to the girls in the cast if one has been an actress oneself. (Neagle, 1974, p. 195)

Other women had producer credits, but they were only for B-features.[5] Otherwise, women only produced children's films, the best of which was Barbara Woodhouse's wonderful *Trouble for Juno* (1957), in which the Great Dane enacts a stellar reprise of *Rescued by Rover*.[6]

Many contemporary critics queried women's competence as producers. *Picturegoer* told its mainly female readers that women could only operate in a 'feminine' way: 'charm, tact, an infallible method of getting their own way, instinct for colour and dress – and patience. WHETHER they can make the budget meet is another point.'[7] *Cinema Studio* brought up the old saw of 'feminine intuition' in describing Betty Box's professionalism: she was also 'happily married . . . soft-spoken and gentle in manner'.[8]

Betty Box was the only woman to work as a major feature producer in the 1950s. As in the 1940s, she had a broad definition of the producer's job, including the choice and nuancing of projects. She made *The Clouded Yellow* (1950) for Rank, and the script she commissioned from Janet Green placed a deviant girl and a vengeful older woman at the guilty centre (S1700). Box's *Doctor* films were all made for Rank and directed by Ralph Thomas. It was her idea to reformulate the Richard Gordon book, and she cast Bogarde as Simon Sparrow, in the teeth of opposition from Earl St John (Bogarde, 1979, p. 172). After initial indifference, John Davis was enthusiastic about the films. Whenever Box wished to produce a less formulaic film, another *Doctor* vehicle was the price she had to pay (MacFarlane, 1997, pp. 88–9). The *Doctor* films present the establishment as robust. Most of the aspiring doctors would rather fornicate than heal; only Simon Sparrow is insecure. In each film, Sparrow flees from a woman with a voracious appetite for food, which is obviously shorthand for other hungers. In *Doctor in the House* (1954), the female swot who has the temerity to be confident is cruelly undermined. In *Doctor at Sea* (1955), Brenda de Banzie is miscast as the devious daughter of the company boss. In *Doctor at Large* (1957), Sparrow's nurse fiancée (Muriel Pavlov) gives up her medical studies because they are too difficult. In each case, Box tickles up the sexual status quo and reinvigorates it.

Betty Box also produced *Campbell's Kingdom* (1957), which fulfilled her new interest in location shooting (MacFarlane, 1997, p. 86). However, it was an ill-conceived attempt at the adventure genre. Check-shirted Dirk Bogarde administers brutal caresses to the heroine, who retorts: 'I did want you to kiss me, but not like that.' *Campbell's Kingdom* differs from the usual Rank representations of masculinity, since the hero is fatally ill, but it is an uneven film with which Box was ill at ease.

With her subsequent films, Box was hamstrung by strong original texts. *A Tale of Two Cities* (1958) was superbly paced, and organized with a marvellous eye for texture. But nothing could be done with Dickens's female characters, who must perforce be either vapid or manic. Box and Thomas refused Technicolor for the film, mistakenly thinking

black and white would give it an art-house cachet. They became dis-
illusioned with Rank's backing, suggesting that the film be retitled *I Love
Lucie* or *Doctor in the Bastille* (Clarke, 1974, p. 199).

Little could be done with the original text of *The Wind Cannot Read*
(1958), since the novelist Richard Mason wrote the script. Box also had
trouble with *The 39 Steps* (1959). The original novel and the Hitchcock
film had set intractable precedents. Minor and unsuccessful adjustments
were made. The crofter's wife, so touchingly played by Peggy Ashcroft in
the 1930s film, was robustly acted by Brenda de Banzie, who gives the
hero a smacking kiss: 'There's plenty more where that came from!' Box's
creativity had operated in a looser way in the postwar period, when more
varied projects were offered to her.

In the 1960s, the Rank empire was in economic and cultural crisis, and
the Americans financing British independents were suspicious of women
producers. As ever, there were a number of women who produced their
husband's films. Virginia Stone produced several low-status films with
her husband, such as *The Password Is Courage* (1962). Adrienne Fancey
produced a nudist film for her husband, *Some Like It Cool* (1961), which
had plenty of wobble but little thrust. Betty Box's career went into a
quality nosedive in the 1960s, as the decline of the Rank Organization
impinged severely on her. She was forced to make three workaday *Doctor*
films, and her other 1960s comedies lacked her customary lightness of
touch. Her contemporary dramas, such as *The Wild and the Willing*
(1962), were morally conservative. The only film in which she showed her
old form was *No Love for Johnnie* (1961), which dealt with a corrupt
Labour MP and was a tightly constructed and cynical film. Box wondered
if the Rank Organization 'liked the character being so corrupt because he
was, after all, left-wing' (MacFarlane, 1997, p. 87).

Some new women producers made a start in the 1960s. Beryl Vertue,
who developed such a remarkable career in the 1970s, began as secretary
to scriptwriters Galton and Simpson, and became manager and then
director of Associated London Scripts. When this was bought out by the
larger Stigwood company, Vertue became an executive producer; her first
production was *Till Death Us Do Part* in 1969.[9] Vertue was an excellent
fixer with an instinct for popular taste, but had little interest in narrative
structure or hands-on filming. Zelda Barron was production assistant on
If . . . (1968) and *Morgan – A Suitable Case for Treatment* (1966), but
found it difficult to rise higher: 'We women are loved dearly in the film

business as long as we're doing our womanly job, in addition, of course, to making the coffee, handing out aspirins and pats on the head' (Muir, 1987, p. 85). Aida Young began her producing career in the 1960s too. She initially sought employment with a major producer, who told her, 'Look, when we start employing blacks on our unit, then we'll start using women.' Despite having no capital or connections – 'a girl in a freelance market, you might as well cut your throat' – her talents caught the attention of Michael Carreras.[10] Hammer initially gave her associate producer jobs on films with overtly 'feminine interest' such as *She* (1965), *One Million Years BC* (1966) and *Slave Girls* (1966). Young was promoted to full producer in 1967, when another producer broke his leg. The problem was that by then the vitality of the Hammer formula was exhausted. Little room for manoeuvre remained, and that was abrogated by powerful in-house directors just reaching their peak. *Dracula Has Risen from the Grave* (1968) was directed by Freddie Francis, who had entrenched ideas about pace and structure. *Taste the Blood of Dracula* (1969) was a marvellous evisceration of the Victorian paterfamilias which owed everything to the Freudian preoccupations of director Peter Sasdy. And *The Scars of Dracula* (1970) was directed by Roy Ward Baker. Judging by his lack of control in other films, the severe continuity errors in *Scars* should be attributed to him.

Young was given remakes with little status. *When Dinosaurs Ruled the Earth* (1969) was a rehash of earlier prehistoric epics. When director Val Guest tired of the project, admitting that 'maybe I'm not very good at working with a woman producer', Young was able to re-edit the picture herself to her own tastes. Guest did not protest, because 'what the hell, it's not as though we're talking about *Citizen Kane*' (Weaver, 1994, p. 122). In *The Vengeance of She* (1968), Young revisited Rider Haggard country. This time she had a real opportunity with the material, since director Cliff Owen was relatively weak, and the hints of feminism in the film should doubtless be attributed to her. Bemused Ayesha-lookalike Carol (Olinka Berova) is told that 'you belong to no man except the one you choose yourself'. This time it is a male who is destroyed by the immortalizing flame. And instead of marching between the legs of the statue of Ayesha, the armies wriggle under the breasts. But it is small beer. Any autonomy Young had was sabotaged by the casting. Hero John Richardson sported a mountainous Bobby Charlton coiffure and an ursine chest-wig, and was seemingly unable to speak in the first person.

Young enjoyed her time at Hammer nonetheless, but was irked by her lack of status: 'When strangers came up and said "tell me where the producer is", they thought I was joking. They thought I was Wardrobe or Continuity.' Since the only other females were editors 'shut away in a room', Young felt increasingly isolated, and when American studios offered her work in the 1970s, she accepted with alacrity.[11]

As we have seen, conditions in the 1970s film industry were parlous, but there were unpredictable effects on the interventions women were able to make. There was a significant increase in the number of women working as producers, many of them shifting between film and television. To be sure, some women such as Dorothy Hindin and Erica Masters were producing children's films, but many were involved in large-scale feature production. As Esther Rantzen put it, fewer women in the industry were now content with submissive roles, and with thinking: 'I'd rather be the blossom with the dew still on my petals. I choose not to brave the fierce heat of the sun and try for a difficult job in a man's world' (Muir, 1987, p. 225). However, a substantial proportion of female newcomers were working as executive producers, which is a lower-status and more hands-on role.

The older practitioners were coming to the end of their careers: Betty Box with the lamentable *Percy* films and Aida Young with *The Likely Lads* (1976). Beryl Vertue continued the work she had begun in the late 1960s, acting as executive producer for a whole tranche of comedies, as well as for *Tommy* (1975).[12] Vertue exhibited a robust and pragmatic style in the 1970s, and founded her own small company, Hartswood Films. She began to get more personally involved in the filming process: 'I have to feel passionate about a subject, because it's a slog and there's no point unless you believe in it ... I am a good editor. I steer writers, make them understand moods, values and boundaries.'[13] However, she claimed that one of her key skills was that she could 'still make a good cup of tea'.[14]

Some women found niches in the burgeoning sex-film market of the 1970s. Olive Negus-Fancey was executive producer of films such as *Not Tonight Darling* (1971) and *White Cargo* (1974).[15] Hazel Adair, who created *Crossroads*, became a scripter/producer under the pseudonym Elton Hawke (McGillivray, 1992, p. 103). She produced sex comedies such as *Keep It Up Downstairs* (1976), and was robustly defensive of popular culture.[16] But many women producers sought more challenging fare. Jean Wadlow, who had built up a large portfolio in television, produced *One Hour to Zero* (1976) and set up Wadlow Grosvenor International, which went into the lucrative corporate video production market.[17] Joyce Herlihy produced the Sex Pistols' *The Great Rock 'n' Roll Swindle* (1980), and Patricia Casey did *And Now for Something Completely Different* (1971).

Some women negotiated the crossover between television and film better than others. Carole J. Smith, for example, had a distinguished television career, and produced the outstanding *Edward Burra* (1973) and the witty children's cycle *Trouble with 2B* (1972). Jo Douglas, on the other hand, although an accomplished TV producer (*6.5 Special* in the 1950s, and solid work throughout the next decade) managed the transition less well. In 1972 she produced *Dracula AD 72* and *Our Miss Fred*, which were both awkward and strained.[18]

Clearly, working conditions in the period were more conducive to some kinds of creativity than others. In the increasingly tacky film culture of the 1970s, women could step into the breeches (as it were) of male producers who had left the business in rage or despair. We should remember, however, that such women could not operate as producer-auteurs in the manner of Korda *et al.*, for the simple reason that they did not represent the investors of the company; nor did they own the capital. They were hired, often on a film-by-film basis, by those who did, and they were appointed for their organizational skills.

In the more entrepreneurial industry of the 1980s, women producers began to make a major impact. The most powerful ones deployed feminine metaphors when discussing their work. Norma Heyman, for example, who cut her teeth in Britain and went on to produce *Empire State* (1987) and *Dangerous Liaisons* (1988), presented herself as 'mother-as-producer', though often 'the mother becomes the headmistress'. Heyman saw the production role as better suited to females, because it required communication and personnel skills, whereas direction was solitary and individualistic:

> My love and sympathy goes to those poor men who want to direct. They're all so different, but when it comes to shooting, they're all alone on that set. That's why they have to have the strongest and the best around them.[19]

Linda Myles, too, thought that women now made a better fist of production: 'I'm very reluctant to plug traditional female virtues, but I think maybe one does care that little bit more'. Myles produced *Defence of the Realm* (1985), and spent fifteen months on the project, working on the script with the writer and director and developing a fierce loyalty to the project. Nonetheless, 'the first day on the set they thought I was the make-up girl. Now they call me Lady Guv.' Myles had a robustly pragmatic attitude: 'First of all you have to give up the vocabulary of film theory. It just gets in the way. No-one on set is going to understand if you start talking about "objects of desire".' But she preferred Gainsborough to Ealing, and wanted 'a cinema that deals with strong emotions and the darker forces. I wish we could make more films that released the repressed' (Muir, 1987, p. 221).

Many women producers specialized in medium-budget features, because low-budget ones were bad box-office in the period and because they were not offered the blockbusters. Susan Richards, for example, who had commissioned the *First Love* series for Channel Four, produced a range of middle-budget films, including *Mr Love* (1985). Richards had a robust dislike of ambiguity, and preferred mainstream cinema.[20] Sarah Radclyffe too preferred middle-budget films, because expensive productions usually encountered artistic interference: 'I'd be very unhappy at having to compromise for financial or commercial reasons when it comes down to it.' Radclyffe produced *My Beautiful Laundrette* (1985), *Caravaggio* (1986), *Sammy and Rosie Get Laid* (1987) and *Wish You Were Here* (1987). She was very committed to the script as a privileged discourse: 'if the script is good enough, people will want to work on it. If you don't believe in the script, it's hard to persuade people to work on it for less than the usual rate.' Radclyffe liked the idea of 'profit participation' for heads of department in order to turn films in on time.[21]

Some major women producers entered films briefly and then returned to television. Verity Lambert, for example, took time off to produce *Clockwise* (1985) and *Dreamchild* (1985). Tara Prem came from *Play for Today*, and produced *Accidental Death of an Anarchist* (1983) and *She'll Be Wearing Pink Pyjamas* (1985). She preferred texts with a realist edge, and returned to television, which was more suited to her tastes.[22] Other producers had different origins. Actress Susan George entered production because she was 'motivated by frustration about the lack of good parts'.[23] Some women specialized as executives. Joyce Herlihy moved from being associate producer on *Merry Christmas Mr Lawrence* (1982) and *Insignificance* (1985) to executive producer on *The Adventures of Baron*

Munchausen (1988). Jill Pack, who produced *On the Black Hill* (1987), developed a distinguished career as production executive on *Caravaggio*, *Distant Voices, Still Lives* (1988) and many others. Some of the women producers tried to impose their signature on the film texts. Patsy Pollock, for example, had a considerable input into the script of *Rita, Sue and Bob Too* (1986), encouraging Andrea Dunbar and helping her to structure it (Kelly, 1998, p. 173). But for the most part, producers such as Penny Clark (*Ascendancy*, 1983) and Elaine Taylor (*The Supergrass*, 1985) concentrated on doing an efficient job. The days of the heroic producer-auteur were over.

It would appear, then, that there were few opportunities for women producers until the 1970s and 1980s. By that time, however, the very nature of the job had changed, and the producer's role had more to do with prompt delivery than inspirational control. With hindsight, the careers of Betty Box and Aida Young appear to be exceptions in their respective periods. Box had more authorial success in the late 1940s, when a degree of creative freedom was possible at Gainsborough under her brother Sydney. Conditions with Rank in the 1950s were more intractable, and Box was progressively squeezed. Young's career flourished in the late 1960s, but by that time Hammer was past its best. The key to a successful production career is when the producer's upward mobility is exactly matched by the fortunes of the company. If either one of them is past their best, little good can ensue. The clue to success in art as well as in life lies in knowing when one's employer, or indeed oneself, is past the creative peak.

Notes

1. Their films (all for British National) were *The Seventh Survivor* (1941), *Sabotage at Sea* (1942), *Lady from Lisbon* (1942) and *Welcome Mr Washington* (1944).
2. *The Independent*, 11 December 1991.
3. Interview on BFI microfiche with Box, undated, but must be 1950s from internal evidence. See also interview in the *Daily Mail*, 6 October 1955.
4. *The Independent*, 11 December 1991. See also *Cinema Studio*, August 1951, and *Picturegoer*, 7 December 1946.
5. Marjorie Deans produced *This Girl Is Mine* (1950), Margot Lovell did *Never Say Die* (1950), Miriam Crowdy did *Dangerous Assignment* (1950), Phyllis Shepherd did *Death Is a Number* (1951) and Barbara Emary did *You're Only Young Twice!* (1952).
6. Mary Borer produced *The Case of the Missing Scene* (1952), Kay Luckwell did *Noddy in Toyland* (1958), Mary Field did *The Lone Climber* and *The Mysterious Poacher* in 1950.

7. *Picturegoer*, 12 May 1956.
8. *The Cinema Studio*, August 1951.
9. For details on Vertue's early career, see *Screen International*, 3 January 1976.
10. Both quotes come from Young's BECTU interview. See also *Little Shoppe of Horrors*, April 1978, and an interview in *Screen International*, 6 December 1975. Young produced television and film features before Hammer. A complete credit list is on the SIFT catalogue in the BFI Library.
11. BECTU interview with Young.
12. Vertue had executive producer credits for: *Cat and Mouse* (1974), *The House in Nightmare Park* (1973), *Steptoe and Son Ride Again* (1973), *Up the Front* (1972), *The Alf Garnett Saga* (1972), *Up the Chastity Belt* (1971), *Steptoe and Son* (1972), *Up Pompei* (1971) and others.
13. *Screen International*, 22 January 1992. See also *Broadcast*, 19 December 1997.
14. *Screen International*, 2 January 1976.
15. She also produced *Games That Lovers Play* (1970). Olive Negus-Fancey was the stepmother of Adrienne Fancey, who distributed a wide range of sex films in the period (McGillivray, 1992, pp. 110–11). Adrienne Fancey was also executive producer of *The World Is Full of Married Men* (1979).
16. See interview with Adair in *Broadcast*, 9 March 1994. Other women producers of sex films were Sheila Miller with *A Touch of the Other* (1970), and Elizabeth Curran and Rosemarie Walter with *Penelope Pulls It Off* (1975).
17. See an interview in *Broadcast*, 3 April 1987. Wadlow also produced children's films such as *The Man from Nowhere* (1976).
18. For Douglas's obituary, see *Film and TV Technician*, February 1989.
19. *Producer*, Summer 1989.
20. Interview in *Screen International*, 22 December 1984.
21. *Producer*, Spring 1988. Radclyffe claimed to have insufficient confidence to direct, and left to produce more films in America.
22. *Radio Times*, 11 July 1981.
23. *Producer*, Summer 1988. George owned a production company with her husband, and used her star status as a figurehead. Other women producers were Sue Baden-Powell (*White of the Eye*, 1986), Felicity Heberdene (*Space Riders*, 1984), Arlene Sellers (*Scandalous*, 1984) and Jackie Stoller (*The Innocent*, 1985).

9

Writers

Novels written by women constituted a substantial minority of the raw material of films in the 1930s. The novels selected were mainly middlebrow and written after 1918.[1] Women also made an important contribution to scriptwriting in the 1930s, but when assessing the extent of their creative input, we must remember that there are different sorts of script – the adaptation of someone else's original text, or the construction of one's own scenario from scratch. We need to establish the degree of script control by different producers.

After the coming of sound, writers were at a premium. Someone had to write the dialogue, but payment depended on the project. According to John Paddy Carstairs, really big films in the 1930s could only get 90 seconds of screen time in the can per day, whereas a low-status film could complete 7 minutes:

> These figures are only possible on a wordy script – a long dialogue scene well played in a close shot way may not need a lot of alternative angles or changes of set-up, and in the cases of the quickies, it was more a question of speed than good technique that caused us to clock up so much complicated picture per day. (Carstairs, 1942, p. 135)

The American production companies in Britain demanded completed shooting scripts at very short notice, so that scriptwriters, secretaries and typists had plenty of work, but it was stressful to deliver.

In effect, scriptwriting was a new profession in Britain. But it was in a state of disarray, and the informal arrangements opened up spaces for female professionals. During the early part of the decade, a writer could shift from being a script collaborator to a dialogue specialist or a sole writer, and he/she might work on several projects at a time, or be moved from one to another. Scriptwriters could change companies with relative ease, and short-term contracts for one or two pictures were common. Of course, women scriptwriters were disadvantaged by the predominantly male culture of the studios. For example, when Alma Reville was working with Beverley Nichols and John Paddy Carstairs on the script of *Nine Till Six*, producer Basil Dean organized a script 'barnstorming' weekend in Brighton, but somehow forgot to invite Reville (Carstairs, 1942, p. 58).

Aspiring women scriptwriters had to enter the trade via more circuitous routes than their male competitors. Evelyn Barrie, for example, had to do crowd and extra work in order to gain entry into the industry: 'I had been blessed with a certain quality of looks and I had some clothes. This was my chance. I would study film technique and be paid a guinea a day for it' (Lee, 1937, p. 182). The difficulties women encountered in Britain during this period replicated those in Hollywood, as Frances Marion, the great MGM scriptwriter, recalled:

> When we carried the scripts on which we were doing re-writes, we made sure they were in unmarked, plain covers. We knew male writers were complaining about the 'tyranny of the women writers' supposedly prevalent at the studios then. (Francke, 1994, p. 29)

Indeed, some women screenwriters were called 'corpse rougers' – those who specialized in plumping life into dead scripts.

Each British studio had different scripting arrangements. BIP did not mind 'from what honest source a story comes', which meant that they liked getting something for nothing (Lee, 1937, p. 86). The studio head Walter Mycroft always intervened at script level, and he encouraged competition between writers: he would give the same story to six different writers, and let the best person win. But woe betide anyone at BIP who had intellectual pretensions. Writers who turned out 'high-brow junk' were summarily dismissed (Ackland and Grant, 1954, p. 44).

BIP's star scriptwriters were a husband-and-wife team, Sydney Courtney and Lola Harvey. Norman Lee ingenuously suggested that this was 'an ideal combination. The husband supplied the male point of view, the wife adds the womanly touches' (Lee, 1937, p. 150), and his apophthegm is an interesting example of the way critical judgements may be affected by sexual stereotypes. Interestingly, Courtney and Harvey described their own craft from a rigorously patriarchal perspective, referring to their target audience as male:

> The costume film intrigues him. He is definitely proud or faintly abashed by his want of knowledge of the period depicted ... the little man enjoys the musicals. Gangster stories appeal to the last remnant of his boyhood days. Show the average cinemagoer the average things he does in an average day, and you're on safe ground. (*ibid.*, pp. 158–9)

Courtney and Harvey's own scripts always defend the male in crisis: a daughter is dissuaded from a posh boyfriend since 'he will teach you to look down on your father because he drops his aitches, and fans 'is tea with 'is 'at'.[2] Their scripts are punitive towards females. *Lost in the Legion* describes dancers in an Eastern nightclub thus:

> Some dancers are flashy and foreign looking. One or two have a definite 'touch of the nigger'. They are pretty but over made-up. Two girls stand out in direct contrast. ... They are palpably British, and, while dancing well, in precise step with the others, we see by their faces that the whole thing is abhorrent to them. (S13855)

These scripts are attuned to currents in popular culture, but they are ill-proportioned, and have prescriptive views about gender and national identity.

Courtney and Harvey were eased out by Mycroft in 1934.[3] He replaced them with Marjorie Deans, and she turned in some competent scripts, but there were few opportunities for creativity.[4] It is interesting to contrast her lacklustre scripting for Mycroft with her work for Korda's *Catherine the Great* (1934). Korda allowed considerable latitude to his script-writers, and Deans's is a very tightly conceived script, which presents the old Empress as a dominatrix: 'there's only one way for a poor defenceless woman to treat a man, and that's to get the upper hand of him in the first five minutes and to rule him'. Deans's script contains a thoroughly gendered analysis of political power. Catherine presents herself to her soldiers as

> a woman like your mothers and your sisters. I know it is a bad wife who leaves her husband because he has been cruel. But it is a good

mother who will fight everyone to save her children. You are my
children, and I come to you as the mother of all Russia.

Gaumont-British and Gainsborough's scripting arrangements were
much less draconian than BIP's. Michael Balcon took a gentlemanly
attitude to his scriptwriters, and he was the only major producer to
provide real freedom for female writers. The most important of these was
Marjorie Gaffney, who had a wide range of screenwriting credits for both
of Balcon's companies. Gaffney's scripts were all superbly crafted, with
some sexual radicalism and a competent range of discourses. Her work
for the Jessie Matthews films was a major contribution to their artistic
success. In *Evergreen* (1934), Gaffney makes the original play more
risqué, and emphasizes the 'family romance' aspect. The hero retorts to
the enraged theatre audience: 'You've been had? What about me? I've
been in love with her for weeks and had to go about London calling her
Mummy.' Gaffney also shows a fine regard for the mechanisms of
cultural exchange: 'this young lady cannot possibly have defrauded the
public, because she delivers the goods' (S4361). Gaffney's script for *First
a Girl* (1935) also intensifies the sexual radicalism of the original. The
heroine (a women pretending to be a man in drag) complains that 'I can't
be a man all my life', whereupon the drag artist retorts, 'you can have
time off, then you can knit and knit to your heart's content'. Later
Gaffney has her exclaim: 'You've changed my clothes, you've altered my
hair, you've messed up my life . . . but you can't mess about with this [she
taps her brain box]. I shall think what I like – when I like' (S4364).
Gaffney's other scripts are remarkable in various ways. *My Old Dutch*
(1934) shows a clear analysis of the effects of film on mass audiences that
is very explicit for the period (S6073). The script of *Me and Marlborough*
(1935) is closely identified with the point of view of the heroine, and it
describes the problems attendant on her male disguise with unusual
acerbity (S4384).

Dorothy Farnum worked for Balcon too, and turned in her most
distinguished script for him, *Jew Süss* (1934). She and her co-writer
A. R. Rawlinson revised the original novel, giving a radical spin to the
analysis of class structure and foregrounding the theme of women as a
means of exchange.[5] Farnum also co-authored *The Constant Nymph*
(1933) with novelist Margaret Kennedy. This is a very ambitious script,
which makes detailed technical suggestions that there be 'a frequent co-

ordination of musical and visual motifs throughout the picture'. It accords music an erotic role in the narrative: 'Tessa is being killed by music, dying of the strains of ecstasy' (S4381).

Like Gaffney, Farnum's work was less competent when she was not working for Balcon. Her script of *Lorna Doone* (1934) for Basil Dean took very few risks with the original novel. Farnum's script for *The Forbidden Territory* (1934) had occasional flashes of wit. The hero recalls that 'I took up stamp collecting to cure myself of a woman. In six months I was using the back of her photograph for a scribbling pad' (S14105). But the script is a pot-boiler nonetheless.

Alma Reville too did excellent work for Balcon. The scripts of *The Passing of the Third Floor Back* (1935) and *The 39 Steps* (1935) are masterpieces of wit, structure and understatement, and more subtle than her non-Balcon work. There are, however, problems in assessing Reville's work. Donald Spoto suggests that Reville's husband Alfred Hitchcock insisted that her name be added to credits in order to swell the family coffers, and that her contributions were merely 'given in the ordinary manner of a helpmate's suggestion' (Spoto, 1994, p. 146). Nonetheless, we should attribute Reville with some autonomy, and accord her the same degree of intentionality as we should to any other professional.[6]

The novelist Margaret Kennedy also worked for Balcon, but not exclusively. Her best work for him was *The Constant Nymph*; her script of *Little Friend* was slack. Indeed, much of Kennedy's 1930s film work was perfunctory, and her screenplay for Basil Dean's Mozart film, *Whom the Gods Love* (1936) was risibly ill-conceived. The workmen exclaim, 'it's our Mozart!', and the hero's wife sagely notes that 'some day, years after we are both dead, they will discover that you are a great man' (S307). The trouble was that Kennedy despised film work. She thought that film audiences were 'a community which never reads', and the film business would 'break the heart' of any real intellectual (Kennedy, 1942, p. 29). Kennedy could not work well in any mass-cultural context.

So Balcon provided sympathetic conditions in which Gaffney and Farnum (and possibly Reville) could flourish. But only in one of his companies; all the opportunities for female scriptwriters were at the more high-minded company, Gaumont. The more low-status and comedy-oriented Gainsborough had very few female scripting credits.[7] There was a clear policy decision to confine women to more serious topics. Alexander Korda's approach to his scriptwriters was different again. He was interested in buying quality from America if he could; otherwise he employed his cosmopolitan friends. Accordingly, he gave R. C. Sherriff a free hand, because he had done good scriptwriting jobs at Universal (Sherriff, 1968, pp. 289–94). He did the same with Frances Marion in *Knight without Armour* (1937). Korda took on a few other women scriptwriters, mainly for one-picture contracts. Clemence Dane, Marjorie Deans and Margaret Kennedy did one each; Dorothy Greenhill scripted three. None of these scripts challenged the urbane representation of women which was normal at London Films. But there was one important exception: *Men Are Not Gods* (1936). The scenario was by the American Iris Wright and it starred the American actress Miriam Hopkins. It was a most untypical film for Korda, and this must be attributed to the script, which was written jointly by Wright and the director Walter Reisch.

Men Are Not Gods deals with a young secretary who becomes obsessed with an actor playing Othello. He returns her obsession, and is on the point of strangling his wife (playing Desdemona) on stage. The secretary, who is in the theatre audience, disrupts the performance/ murder by a hysterical outburst. The script is unique for the intensity of regard which it gives to the chasm between the male and female emotional repertoire. The heroine is naïve, since she is taken aback by the discomfiture of desire. The hero is urbane, since he knows that what he feels has been felt before by others. He loves the secretary because 'you're the representative of the great public. You're the unreserved seat.' He proceeds to reserve the seat: 'I want you where I can find you alone and waiting for me.' The script proceeds to contrast the hero's verbal pyrotechnics with the heroine's emotional literacy. It is an extremely powerful analysis of erotic obsession and sexual difference. Korda's policy of 'buying in' quality had an unpredictable outcome on this occasion.

Otherwise, British companies employed women scriptwriters in different ways. British National's resident female writer was Doreen Montgomery, while ABPC's was Elizabeth Meehan.[8] ATP had a range of fairly senior writers (Farnum, Reville, Kennedy) whom they used regularly. Herbert Wilcox avoided female scripters whenever he could. Twickenham hardly employed any women at all. Its leading scenarist was H. Fowler Mear, whose efforts were occasionally improved by director Bernard Vorhaus. According to Vorhaus, Mear 'regularly provided lethal scripts peppered with stock gags culled from his own personal joke books'.[9] The smaller or poorer the company, the more itinerant the female workforce. Butcher's, for example, often employed inexperienced women for one script, and their names never appeared again. The same happened at Argyle. It may well be attributed to the legal requirement that the quota screenwriter had to be British. There is certainly an enormous tranche of women screenwriters with single credits about whom nothing is known, and who slipped away into anonymity or perhaps family life.

Scriptwriting was mainly a collaborative affair. It was very rare for anyone, let alone a female, to have solo scripting credit. The only examples in the 1930s were in quota quickies. Kathleen Butler had some sole scripting credits, but she worked under such extreme pressure (seven scripts in 1936 for the American quota company George Smith Productions) that the scripts were stereotyped and mainly in one genre. Lydia Haywood and a few others had solo credits too. American companies gave substantial employment to British women scriptwriters, but only for one-picture contracts: Evadne Price at Paramount, Billie Bristow at United Artists, Margaret McDonnell at RKO, Alison Booth at Fox British, Elizabeth Meehan at Warner Bros. So although British women scriptwriters gained employment and sometimes sole scripting credits from American companies, the professional enhancement was often limited.

During World War II, women's novels constituted a smaller proportion of overall film output. Half of the women's novels which were filmed were by Gainsborough. As we have seen, Gainsborough would not employ female scriptwriters in comedy, but some women specialized in the genre elsewhere: Kathleen Butler wrote the Gert and Daisy films, Barbara Emary the Old Mother Rileys. There were fewer women scriptwriters in proportion to the men: only one, Diana Morgan, worked at Ealing, for example (Morgan, 1994, pp. 313–14).

Doreen Montgomery and Aimée Stuart made major scriptwriting contributions to the Gainsborough melodramas, helped by Margaret Kennedy and Kay Strueby. They were a highly politicized group, being founder-members of the Screenwriters' Association and enjoying a privileged relationship with the producers. They adapted the original novels in interesting ways, giving them greater contemporary relevance and raising their emotional temperature. Characters in the scripts are judged by their emotional literacy, but at the same time the female characters are set implacably against each other. The Gainsborough scripts are quite moralistic, but the harsh messages they bear are not endorsed by those embedded in the costumes or the décor. The script of *The Man in Grey* (1943), for example, which was adapted by Margaret Kennedy and Doreen Montgomery, instructs that the Lockwood character be filmed to look 'just like a witch', and that the cautionary words 'never make no friends of women' be inserted into the gypsy's warning (S168). In *The Wicked Lady* (1945) script, which Aimée Stuart co-wrote with director Leslie Arliss, much attention is given to female competition. Barbara has stolen Caroline's fiancé, and Caroline remarks: 'And this wedding dress. You might as well wear *that* while you're at it.' To which Barbara retorts: 'Wear *that*? I wouldn't be buried in it' (S308). On the whole, the Gainsborough scripts show women as greedy and strange. They are presented with no attention to historical register, of course.

There was one major change in World War II scripting practices: women began to write solo adaptations of their own original work. Two good examples are topics which were specifically attuned to wartime conditions for women. The first was Clemence Dane's *Perfect Strangers* (1945). It developed the radical interpretations of marriage which had informed her earlier plays (Dane, 1935a and b). The second was *Great Day* (1945), which was scripted by Lesley Storm from her own play. *Great Day* was written as a tribute to the Women's Institute, and all the theatrical critics stressed that it was made for, and enjoyed by, female audiences.[10] The film script departs very little from the original text. It was produced by the British arm of RKO, and directed by Lance Comfort, who went on to make a number of films on female topics after 1945. *Great Day* deals with the combined labours of a group of women from all classes when Mrs Roosevelt visits their Women's Institute; it also tells the story of wilful landgirl Margaret, who spurns her rich farmer fiancé in favour of a penniless soldier.

Quite simply, *Great Day* is a masterpiece, which combines radical sexual politics with a ravishing visual style; the latter owes much to the cinematography of Erwin Hillier. However, it did badly at the box-office, probably because of a hamfisted publicity campaign. The script makes a strong argument for the vigour, inventiveness and communality of women. They can turn their hands to anything, whereas the males are presented as emotionally incompetent. Class relations are also handled in an interesting way; anything that looks like an attempt at middle-class social control is roundly rebuffed. The final shot is a leftwards pan after the arrival of Mrs Roosevelt. The women are seen from her point of view, and the camera sweeps across them as they prepare to display the products of their labour. It shows them, young and old, barmaid and lady of the manor, to the heart-wrenching strains of 'Jerusalem'. *Great Day* is powerful because it combines an argument about female autonomy with one about the inefficacy of a middle-class explanation of the world.

Other female scriptwriters came to the fore during the war years. Muriel Box began to write for the cinema, and the fact that she was married to Sydney Box doubtless helped her role as co-producer of *The Seventh Veil* (1945). This describes the career and neuroses of concert pianist Francesca (Ann Todd). It focuses on her family romance with her guardian Nicholas (James Mason), who has a Byronic limp and a fondness for knuckle-rapping and emotional strappado. Francesca is cured of her ailments by the psychiatrist (Herbert Lom) and his needle, and she rejects her other suitors in favour of Uncle Nicholas. *The Seventh Veil* was an extraordinary success, quickly earning over £1 million and winning an Oscar for the screenplay.

As Caroline Merz (1994) has noted, Muriel Box had been 'in training' for feature films during the early years of the war, and worked at every level at Verity films – scripting, production, direction and administration. The joint diaries kept by Muriel and Sydney Box during the war years indicate the intensity of their collaboration. They were written alternately by them – 'when I'm too lazy or tired he takes over' – but all the entries about *The Seventh Veil* are in Muriel's handwriting.[11] The diaries provide vital material about the constraints on a woman film-maker's life at that time. After tailoring a script, she spent time turning a sheet sides to middle; she had to deal with her sick daughter, taking her to the studio when she could not attend school. At the same time as she was plotting *The Seventh Veil*, Muriel Box was preoccupied by murky tales about repression, family loathing and retribution. One of her drafts in the 1944 diary proposed:

> A play in which a girl says it is inevitable that she should kill her mother, and shows that whichever course of action she took, the result was the same – this is worked out differently three times but with the same result. An argument for Kharma – the soul has to suffer certain things, and cannot escape them, in order to progress.

Sydney Box first heard about the use of narcosis for the treatment of shell-shock, but Muriel originated the idea of using it to treat a woman artist crippled with psychosis. Like the other scripts they co-authored, labour was unequally divided. Muriel produced the ideas, the plot structure and characterization, and Sydney tidied it up: 'I used to do the overall plot . . . then Sydney would "diddy it up" wherever he could' (MacFarlane, 1997, p. 89).

Muriel's original script for *The Seventh Veil* was extremely radical: 'the girl was the only person who appeared on the screen. The other characters were to be filmed in shadow, voices-off or reflections in the piano or mirrors' (Todd, 1980, p. 57). Ann Todd was unable to tolerate this, so Muriel amended the script. She was also present everywhere on set, since Compton Bennett was an inexperienced director. Besides advising Todd on acting technique, she organized the costumes and the requisite coupons (MacFarlane, 1997, p. 90). The filmed version mounts a powerful argument that patriarchal structures cripple women, until they internalize those structures and learn to love their oppressor.

The Seventh Veil begins with Francesca (Ann Todd) on the very cusp of the menarche. She is playing in a stream, and one of the first things she says is 'my knickers are wet'. The first event of her adolescence is the death of her father. She is sent to her cousin Nicholas (James Mason), who hates women – even the cats are male – and who has an overweening love of control. He trains Francesca in music, and will tolerate no followers. Her first sweetheart is seen off, and the second, a painter, is commissioned to paint her portrait. This picture is of the greatest interest. Francesca's body is off balance: her hips are facing the piano, but her shoulders and knees are twisted round to the viewer, and one knee is folded over the other. She complains that the posture gives her pain 'in places I didn't know I had'. Yet it is this portrait, with the coherence and balance of the woman's body utterly compromised, which cousin Nicholas places where his mother's picture had been.

Box's script evinces the utmost optimism about personal transformation. At the beginning, the psychiatrist discusses the paths to self-knowledge:

> The human mind is like Salome at the beginning of her dance, hidden from the world by seven veils – veils of reserve, shyness, fear. With friends, the average person will drop one veil, then

another, maybe three or four. With a lover, she will take off five, maybe six. But never the seventh veil. You see, the human mind likes to cover its nakedness and keep its private thoughts for itself. Salome dropped the seventh veil of her own free will, but you will never get the human mind to do that. And that is why I use narcosis. Five minutes under narcosis, and down comes the seventh veil.

It is an audacious piece of writing, which compares the truth to a naked body, and self-delusion to a garment. The human psyche is conceived in female terms. By the end of the film, Francesca has acknowledged that her creativity and repression are intimately connected, and there is an intense recognition of a fresh start which is a kind of utopia of the spirit. The psychiatrist (Herbert Lom) says: 'I can promise you a complete cure . . . you see, the past is over for her now, quite over. Her mind is clear, and the clouds have been swept away. She is no longer afraid.'

In the postwar period, more novels by female writers were filmed, and they were more up-market texts. More women screenwriters were in sole command of a scripting project. Kay Strueby had solo credit on *The Shop at Sly Corner* (1947), as did Kathleen Butler on *I'll Turn to You* (1946) and *The Temptress* (1949). Florence Tranter had sole billing for *Piccadilly Incident* (1946) and *The Courtneys of Curzon Street* (1947). There were others, and clearly female scriptwriters were being given more responsibility with a range of projects. Some scripting interventions were more informal: for example, Kay Walsh suggested the transformation of the end of *Great Expectations* (1946) and her ideas were accepted by Cineguild (Brownlow, 1997, p. 208). Elizabeth Montagu was brought in at short notice by Korda for a range of projects, but was rarely credited properly.[12] However, some scriptwriting conditions were inimical to women's creative intervention. Marjorie Deans (1946) was developing as an advanced feminist novelist in the postwar period. She was credited as script editor for *Caesar and Cleopatra* (1946) but was caught in a pincer movement between the colossal egos of George Bernard Shaw and producer/director Gabriel Pascal; as a result, she was only permitted a little light clipping. Her account of what she would have liked to do is poignant:

Even though our work is seldom, if ever, published, though the multigraphed records of our labours, tattered and dog-eared from countless hurried thumbings of script-girls, assistant-directors and technicians in search of executive guidance, pile up dustily on forgotten shelves at Elstree and Denham, we must not be content to clothe our ideas in drab, perfunctory, carelessly chosen words. They must supply the quickening flame which is to kindle the imagination of all the creative workers on the production – the director, the actors, the musical composer, the designers. How can they do that if they themselves are not aglow? (Deans, 1947, p. 48)

Many female screenwriters had to share credits, and we can assess their contribution by making comparisons with their other work. Lesley Storm had come into her scriptwriting prime with *Great Day*, and her postwar film form continued interesting. She had honed her craft with successful stage plays which created powerful roles for women.[13] *The Fallen Idol* (1948) was based on Graham Greene's story, and he collaborated with Storm on the script, which gives more emphasis to the two female roles. The first script of *Adam and Evelyne* (1949) was by Noel Langley, but Storm restructured it in her scenario, and again expanded the heroine's role. Young Evelyne's guardian Adam falls in love with her, although she thinks he is her father ('he's the most wonderful looking father in the whole world'). This muddle leads to some incestuous by-play, which was intensified by the casting of Stewart Granger and Jean Simmons, who were then married to each other. The script of *Adam and Evelyne* also contains some vitriolic remarks about the sex war. Adam advises: 'Never let a woman think she trusts you – you will have to prove that she can't'; while a woman complains that 'men are the most ghastly moral cowards' (S902). These must have been added by Storm, since there is nothing of that tone in any of Langley's other work.

Storm's last script work of the period was on *The Golden Salamander* (1950). The original novel was by Victor Canning, who worked with Storm on the script. Again there are interesting alterations. The symbolic significance of the golden sculpture is written up, while its literal meaning is obscured. The script's structure echoes *Casablanca*'s treatment of expatriate culture and *The Maltese Falcon*'s use of an unfathomable object. Again, a bigger and better part is written for the female protagonist.

Doreen Montgomery's postwar career is also interesting. During the war, her Gainsborough scripts had raised the emotional temperatures of the original novels, locating the action more firmly within a middle-class context. Montgomery could not find a niche at Gainsborough when the Boxes reformed scriptwriting practices. As a result, she went freelance, but found very few projects. However, her script of *While I Live* (1947) is extraordinary. This film, popularly known as *The Dream of Olwen*, was based on the play *This Same Garden* by Robert Bell, who worked with Montgomery on the script. It is about the death of a young pianist Olwen (Audrey Fildes), whose sister Julia (Sonia Dresdel) has an obsessive love for her. Seemingly, Olwen returns from the dead 25 years later in the form of Sally (Carol Raye). On the face of it, it is a preposterous farrago of incest, somnambulism, necrophilia and reincarnation. Yet it is thoroughly coherent, because the script matches its language to the florid mood of the music. The incestuous passions are far more intense in the script than the play, and the film prevaricates much more about whether Sally really is the reincarnation of the dead Olwen. This is doubtless because the theme of reincarnation was close to Montgomery's heart. She was a spiritualist, and her 1971 book *Voices in the Dark* argued passionately for the continuation of the personality and its talents after death.

Muriel Box was the most important woman scriptwriter in the postwar period. Besides her formal screenwriting credits, Muriel made major contributions to Sydney Box's Gainsborough projects, as their joint diaries for the period show. She advised on every level of production with such films as *Broken Journey* (1948), and was the studio's script director. Muriel's workload was increased because they could not afford top-class scriptwriters and so she felt herself 'compelled to rewrite, cut and polish a script in order to meet the minimum standard required' (Box, 1974, p. 187). Muriel Box thought it should confer tempo and rhythm, light and shade, and dominate the direction.[14] All her scripts of the postwar period were written with Sydney Box, and the division of labour was described by one journalist in the following way: 'She provides the story and the characterisation, mapped out on paper, and Sydney sits down and writes the dialogue. When that's done they quarrel. Out of the battle emerges the final draft.'[15] However, Sydney admitted that Muriel's input was greater: one project was 'mostly Muriel, as usual', and in interviews she claimed the lion's share.[16] She was pragmatic (writing one script just to use up some sets), and aggressive, engaging in a vigorous squabble with Balcon in 1946.[17]

So Muriel Box's contribution to the postwar scripts was on the conceptual and structural level. The choice of topic and the nuancing of the characters were hers. The scripts and the resulting films are sometimes uneven – as if emotions *in extremis* necessitated an awkward roughness. Several of them suffered savage censorship. *Daybreak* (1948) deals with public hangman Eddie (Eric Portman) who marries a young waif Frankie (Ann Todd). She becomes involved with sailor Olaf (Maxwell Reed) and shoots herself. The hangman frames the sailor, officiates at his hanging, and then hangs himself. The script transforms the original tale by eroticizing Frankie. The BBFC was outraged by the film, and demanded some swingeing alterations – the cutting of the violent lovemaking, the shifting of the hanging scene from the end to the beginning, the addition of a moralizing prequel about capital punishment.[18] But even the mutilated version is of enormous power in its portrayal of violent revenge.

Good Time Girl (1947) was heavily censored as well. Muriel Box had originally conceived it as a realist drama, and had read relevant Royal Commission reports to get 'copy'. The film describes the downfall of Gwen Rawlings (Jean Kent), whose desire for 'pretty things' is matched by men's desire for her. She is abused at home, cheated at work and betrayed by a lover until she is unjustly sent to an approved school. She escapes, engages in petty crime and is indirectly involved in murder. The original novel by Arthur LaBern is neutral about blame, but the film script carefully locates social deprivation as the source of Gwen's problems: 'Perhaps in the bedraggled, blowsy yet somehow pathetic figure of her mother, we can see the tragedy of her life.' Gwen is also credited with sexual chutzpah, rather than ordinary sluttishness as in the novel. She sleeps with her middle-class lover Red, and next morning 'looks like any other young wife might look. She is happy and humming a little tune.' At the approved school the head girl Roberta, with 'a certain masculine quality about her', has lesbian yearnings: 'There is a definite attraction on the part of Roberta for Gwen ... she runs her fingers through Gwen's hair' (S14300).

The BBFC again insisted upon a moralizing prequel, and accordingly one was furnished so that Gwen could be presented as an Awful Warning. The lesbian motif was downplayed. But what remains in the finished film (and what, to repeat, is largely absent from the book) is Gwen's uncomplicated pleasure in the flesh: in textures, in touch and taste, which are experienced without guilt.

The Brothers (1947) is significant too. The subject chosen by Muriel Box is that of the violent emotion evoked in two Scots brothers Fergus and Hector (Maxwell Reed and Finlay Currie) by their servant Mary (Patricia Roc). Because she inspires so much desire, the male community decrees her death.

A key scene deals with the loss of Fergus's thumb. He and Mary make love by the sea, and then he tries to tickle some sea-trout. As he pokes among the rocks, a conger-eel draws his thumb down into its throat. He cannot withdraw it, and finally he cuts off his own thumb in order to escape the incoming tide. It is a scene packed with sexual symbolism. Mary is a Phallic Woman, whose dangerous sensuality threatens the physical penis. It is the most direct evocation of the fears of *vagina dentata* in British cinema. Of course, the conger scene was in the original novel, and Sydney Box disingenuously averred that it was 'taken straight from the book'.[19] But the film script locates the event more intensely in the narrative, and it takes up proportionately more time than in the novel. The script also does not invite the viewer to see the event, as the novel does; the engulfing is more dreadful because it is imagined. Most of Muriel Box's postwar scripts experimented with female protagonists who aroused fierce emotions but who had neutral ones themselves.

In the 1950s, approximately the same number of novels by women were filmed as in the 1940s, but they were more highbrow. Women had fewer screenwriting credits. They had worked on approximately 150 scripts in the 1940s; this fell to below 80 in the 1950s. But although there were fewer female screenwriters, they worked on more major projects. Muriel Box scripted several films which she also directed, and Joan Henry co-scripted two of her own novels. Some women had solo scripting credits: Janet Green with *The Clouded Yellow* and *Sapphire* (1959), Joan Henry with *Passionate Summer* (1958); Anne Burnaby with *The Yellow Balloon* (1952) and *Operation Bullshine* (1959). Doreen Montgomery wrote three solo scripts.

Muriel Box co-authored several scripts with Sydney Box. Some were more conventional than others. That of *Street Corner* foregrounds the aggravations of parenthood, and it gives space to the opponents of women's work. One man explains why he dislikes policewomen: 'In the first place it's unfeminine, in the second place it's uneconomic and in the third place it's dangerous, because it's a well-known fact that women are flighty, impetuous, undependable, anti-social and easily led' (S13139).

He is proved wrong by the policewomen's actions, but they are given no verbal space to rebut him.

Other Box scripts are more radical. *Too Young to Love* (1960) sticks closely to the play by Elsa Shelley.[20] The two extant screenplays of *The Truth about Women* are unambiguously signed as the solo work of Muriel, although Sydney is credited in the final film. The first screenplay is a lighthearted hotchpotch of feminist ideas, white slavery and unexpected childbirth. The second hinges on the gulf between the sexes. The heroine Ambrosine says:

> Women want to be women all right. They just have a different definition of what the word means. To a man it generally means an unpaid cook-housekeeper-nursemaid-mistress. To a woman it means a person, an equal partner in the business of life, free to do what's right and best for herself.

The hero Humphrey defines marriage rather like the Cold War: 'Peaceful co-existence in a state of emergency, with threats and sanctions and promises and treaties, and endless conferences at which a good time is had by all.'[21] The script argues that relationships between such opposite species can only result in stalemate. The more unhampered Box was, the more uncompromisingly feminist were her scripts: 'Unable to chain myself to the railings, I could at least rattle the film chains' (Box, 1974, p. 222).

Anne Burnaby's scripts for ABPC also had strong feminist undercurrents. They foregrounded the oppressions of family life and the superiority of 'feminine' qualities, and problematize conventional definitions of masculinity. In *No Time for Tears* (1957), she argued that 'Mummyishness' should be a male attribute, and in *The Young Wives' Tale* (1951), the hero revealingly remarks:

> I think any unattainable woman is desirable. The trouble is, so few are. . . . This is the climax, this is the moment that always comes; when the unattainable becomes the attainable, when one knows that one can, but one doesn't. It's then that men feel God-like. (S1500)

Burnaby's plots are multifaceted, with marvellous irony and proportion. According to J. Lee Thompson, she fought very hard to get her way in ABPC's script department.[22]

Joan Henry found ABPC a conducive place to work. Her script of her own novel *Yield to the Night* (1956) was preoccupied with the complexity of women's feelings. *The Weak and the Wicked* (1954), too, was based on another of her novels, *Who Lie in Gaol*, a reformist piece. The script replicates the radicalism of the original, insisting on the gendered nature of the punishment system. Henry also scripted *Passionate Summer* for Rank, a steamy jungle tale. The script has a heavy overlay of popular Freudianism (S6482). All Henry's scripts foregrounded gender issues, but they were badly crafted. Their construction was lumpy, with 'bunching' around key episodes, and the characterization was clumsy. Henry was lucky that her best-selling novelist status guaranteed her a place at ABPC.

Janet Green's work in the 1950s was solid. Rank's henchmen valued her reliability, and her scripts for *Lost* (1956) and *Sapphire* were socially liberal, but conservative on the gender front. Green's scripts all have a quiet moment, a space for retrenchment. There is one in *Sapphire*, when the black doctor recalls being touched by a white racist, who was surprised that his black colour did not rub off: 'The problem is, something came off on me.' *The Clouded Yellow*, which was based on Green's own story, deals with her favourite theme of duplicity. The Secret Service is nasty and brutish, and the real villain (as in her later *Victim*) is the older woman (S1700). Green's forte was the police procedural. Occasionally, she liked to insert little jokes, as in this extract from an overheard conversation in *Eyewitness* (1956):

> I've always thought that a touch of the old whip is much kinder in the long run. When she started snapping at me, I snapped right back and of course she started crying when she realised she wasn't going to get supper. This morning she was right as rain and as loving as you could ask for. (S14059)

After the eavesdropper has been worked up into a lather of indignation, 'she' is revealed as a cocker spaniel bitch.

Lesley Storm continued to work on high-profile projects in the 1950s, and she scripted her own play *Tony Draws a Horse* (1939). Since the film was explicit about the 'obscene' drawing, it caused offence in high quarters. Rank's distributors offered it to the BBC for television transmission, probably because it did badly in the cinemas and they were hoping to recoup their outlay. The BBC was outraged: 'by its very nature it is not satisfactory for the start of a television experiment'.[23] Besides being odiously sophisticated, it dealt with an assertive professional woman, which made it additionally repellent. Anyway, Storm's script was marvellously crafted, as was her *The Spanish Gardener* (1956) and *The Story of Esther Costello* (1957). Both scripts had a fine sense of the raw emotion a film could carry without overbalancing into bathos.

Other women writers turned in scripts which developed their existing skills. Jill Craigie's script for *The Million Pound Note* (1954) made witty, well-balanced play with complex economic ideas. Her script for *Windom's Way* (1957) was radical yet entertaining. It presented a swingeing critique of Empire: Windom (Peter Finch) tells the colonial administrator that the Malays 'want to do something you don't want them to do, so you call them agitators'. And the political radicalism is underpinned by a wry perspective on female roles. Windom's marriage is a wreck, yet the village headman rejoices that he has a woman 'to delight his eye, administer his needs, and comfort his heart' (S15202).

Doreen Montgomery, who had created such wild scripts in the 1940s, continued with *Dance Little Lady* (1954). This was a hyperactive tale which contained a lame ballerina, child abuse and arson. Its register combined melodrama with acerbity. The villain says of the maimed ballerina: 'As great dancers go . . . she went', and the worst thing that can be imagined is 'to grow into a critic' (S6417).

There were radical differences between 1950s and 1960s practices. Women's novels which were filmed were more lowbrow than the 1950s. There was a substantial decline in scripts by women – from 6 per cent of the whole to 4 per cent. More importantly, the overall profile of women's screenwriting careers changed radically. During the 1950s, women had worked on high-status projects and had sole-authored some important films. All that changed in the 1960s. To be sure, some women scripted their own novels and plays; but the days of the female 'career' scriptwriter were over. Doreen Montgomery moved into television scriptwriting, Janet Green and Anne Burnaby did little work, and there were few female writers with multiple credits: Lyn Fairhurst scripted B-features, and Mary Cathcart Borer only wrote children's films. More husband-and-wife teams collaborated: Pip and Jane Baker, Jan and Mark Lowell, Hugh and Margaret Williams, Edward and Valerie Abraham. It was rare for women to have solo credits. Elizabeth Jane Howard scripted *The Very Edge* (1963), and Jan Reed *That Kind of Girl* (1963). The first dealt with miscarriage and frigidity, and the second with illicit pregnancy and venereal disease. The only field in which women now had a free narrative hand was in the area of sexual regulation or crisis.

Nell Dunn was the most uncompromising adapter of her own work. Her screenplay for *Poor Cow* (1967) maintained key aspects of the novel – the disjointed perspectives, the stream-of-consciousness technique and the tender evocation of the sensual pleasures of motherhood. Dunn made feminist insights more explicit, but put them in the mouth of someone unused to theorizing: 'I've always wanted, not power, but I've always wanted to have something that was mine. If I'd have been like an old brass I'd have had power.' The heroine Joy is expressive and sexually explicit: 'He was going so slow and I was coming so much' (S1532). Janni persuaded Anglo-Amalgamated to take the subject because Ken Loach was directing (Walker, 1974, p. 377). Loach had the sense to leave Dunn's script untouched, and the film is a rare combination of avant-garde style and an exclusively feminine perspective. *Poor Cow* is markedly different from *Up the Junction* (1968), because that was scripted by Roger Smith and directed by the less adventurous Peter Collinson. *Up the Junction* had first been directed by Loach for television, but the freshness and radicalism of the book and play were vitiated by the film. Nonetheless, it still presented a lively and optimistic account of women's desires.

Other women adapted their own writing too. I suggested in Part I that Shelagh Delaney radicalized her play *A Taste of Honey* and intensified its feminism. To a lesser extent, she did the same with the script of her story *The White Bus*, which was filmed as a short by Lindsay Anderson in 1967. There is more focus on the female characters, but their handicaps are laid on with a trowel: 'a group of girls suffering from severe conjunctivitis march from the sick bay holding onto each other for guidance'. The attack on sexism is bungling: the heroine 'removes the false bust she habitually wears and which he is specially interested in. She hands it to him' (S1405). The same leaden humour suffuses Delaney's self-indulgent script for *Charley Bubbles* (1967). *Films and Filming* was right when it argued that 'The quality that Miss Delaney possesses in abundance is the gift to write dialogue that is a little larger than life.'[24] Structure and proportion were not her forte.

Margaret Drabble wrote the screenplay for *A Touch of Love* (1969) from her novel *The Millstone*. It was competent and solid, with a good contrast between narrative light and shade (S6160). But it did little business, because the production company Amicus was too careless to fuss about casting or visuals. Edna O'Brien adapted her own *Girl with Green Eyes*. It was tightly constructed, but *I Was Happy Here* (1965), based on her own story, was sloppy, and her script of *Three into Two Won't Go* (1969) sensationalized Andrea Newman's original. To be sure, O'Brien was entrepreneurial. She offered a script to Christopher Lee because he had good vibrations. But as he dryly remarked: 'it was vibrators rather than vibrations that the part called for' (Lee, 1977, p. 256). It takes some perseverance to make sex boring, but O'Brien managed it, because in her texts the act (like the heroine) is always the same.

I suggested in Part I that Ann Jellicoe's feminist play *The Knack* had been transformed by male scriptwriters into a 'masculinist' text. The same happened to Margaret Forster's *Georgy Girl* (1966). Forster became pregnant after accepting the scripting commission, and surrendered it to Peter Nichols: 'Being a novelist fitted in with motherhood, being a script-writer didn't. The film people expected me to put the film first at all times – fools' (Forster, 1995, p. 265). Forster's novel had drawn a careful distinction between those who choose motherhood (Georgy) and those who have it thrust upon them (Meredith). Both kinds have their reasons. Nichols's script destroyed this balance and 'blamed' Meredith, so that Charlotte Rampling was baffled about her character's motivation and had to seek out Forster for guidance (*ibid.*). In addition, Nichols constructed Georgy as a plain, galumphing creature, and Lynn Redgrave was forced to gain a stone in order to ensure her unattractiveness (Kalter, 1979, p. 68). Bruce Carson (1998) has suggested that, in spite of all, Georgy is still an unruly woman whose desires motivate the text. But consider how Georgy ends up: with an elderly husband whom she does not desire, and with her back turned to her own generation and culture.

Clearly, script adaptation was a very tricky business in the 1960s, as Gavin Lambert recognized:

> You can slip and fall both ways; through slavishly literal respect for the original, and through fear of being too slavishly literal. You can seldom be too faithful to the form of the original. You have to break the mould.[25]

This was a difficult lesson to learn, especially when the original text was your own. Many, if not most, women who tried it came unstuck, and the consequences were severe for writers in future decades.

A major transformation for women writers was effected by the 1970s industry. It filmed very few texts by women: at the beginning of the decade there were versions of novels by the Brontës and Iris Murdoch, but by the end, virtually all that was selected for adaptation were the sex sagas of Jackie Collins. Scripting patterns changed radically too. The agenda of the new women directors, such as Christine Edzard and Sally Potter, entailed writing their own scripts. The days of the woman career scriptwriter were now over.[26] Jackie Collins adapted her own novels, but the resulting scripts are a combination of sensationalism and jerky dénouements. Only Ruth Prawer Jhabvala was turning in quality work: her early scripts for Merchant–Ivory, *Autobiography of a Princess* (1975) and *The Europeans* (1979), were subtle and tightly formed, and boded well for her later work.

In the 1980s, film-makers chose to film different types of novels by women. While the perennial Agatha Christie novels were used, more highbrow texts were filmed as well: novels by Doris Lessing, Jean Rhys and Angela Carter were translated into important films.[27] There were changes in female scriptwriting practices too. It was still an integral part of women directors' work to write their own scripts: Lezli-An Barrett, Zelda Barron, Christine Edzard, Sally Potter and Mai Zetterling used scriptwriting as a means of claiming sole authorship of their films.[28] Other women made major interventions without having a substantial scripting portfolio. Nell Dunn, for example, rerouted the script of her play *Steaming* (1981). It was directed by Losey, whose work had become unceasingly unfriendly to the female presence. *Steaming* concentrates exclusively on a group of women in a Turkish bath and shows men only through female fantasies or discourses. As in the original play, the characters were feisty: 'Go for what you want! We must put up a fight. Even if we lose, we go down fighting' (Wandor, 1987, pp. 147–9). Losey's wife instigated the project and wrote the script with Dunn, and they effectively outmanoeuvred Losey (Ciment, 1985, pp. 386–90). So a director for whom women were 'a subject of perplexity', according to his wife, was responsible for a film which celebrates their laughter and intransigence.

Other women scriptwriters made small but significant contributions. Eva Hardy scripted *She'll Be Wearing Pink Pyjamas* (1985), and constructed the narrative so that an Outward Bound course becomes a kind of feminist *rite de passage* for the participants. And Angela Carter scripted her own stories *The Company of Wolves* and *The Magic Toyshop*, which retained the radical mythology of the originals. But otherwise, Ruth Prawer Jhabvala was the only woman career scriptwriter of the decade. She had an almost sculptural approach to the films she scripted for Merchant–Ivory in the 1980s, carefully planning scenes into blocks of action and emotional intensity, and writing always with the editing room in mind.[29] She was interested in learning to operate intuitively with a novel, rather than translating it straightforwardly into linear visual narrative.[30] Jhabvala's 1980s scripts foreground female relationships in a more intense way than in the original novels, and they are all concerned with the interlacing of male with female experience. *Heat and Dust* (1983) was based on Jhabvala's own novel, and the narrative is set in motion by the imaginative drive of Anne (Julie Christie) to reconstruct the life of her relative (Greta Scacchi). In its loose to-and-fro motion, it replicates the swing of her consciousness, and its spasmodic identification with its own creation. Jhabvala's script of *The Bostonians* (1984) attaches more emphasis to the feminist material than James's original novel. In *Room with a View* (1986), the script gives much more narrative space and complexity to all the female leads than Forster's text does. In *Maurice* (1987), the social values espoused by both the Durham and Hall factions are displaced onto the mother and daughters. And Jhabvala radically reworks Bernice Rubens's novel for *Madame Sousatzka* (1988). In the original, the absurdity and creativity of the protagonist are finely balanced; the script weights the scales positively in her favour.

We can conclude that the 1930s and the 1950s represented the golden decades for women scriptwriters. The informality of the 1930s industry opened up a space in which women writers could flourish, while the new distribution arrangements of the 1950s provided career opportunities for women scriptwriters, who were able to specialize. Scripting work in the 1940s, which was a volatile period for women writers, was dominated by the work of Muriel Box. The 1960s and beyond witnessed a steady decline in opportunities for women scriptwriters. The industry became less receptive to the skills of the female wordsmiths and, with a few exceptions, they fell upon hard times.

Notes

1. Such as, for example, Daphne du Maurier's *Jamaica Inn*, which was produced by Mayflower in 1937, or Winifred Holtby's *South Riding*, which was produced by London Films in the same year.

2. From the script of *Tonight's the Night* (S10523), BFI Library. The same pattern obtains in their script of *The Outcast* (S15419), also in BFI Library. See also *Old Soldiers Never Die* (S14571), in which they had a major hand.

3. Before 1934, he also occasionally employed Alma Reville, Helen Simpson and Clemence Dane. See Dane (1964). Mycroft also employed Elizabeth Meehan, Doreen Montgomery, Nina Jarvis and Lesley Storm on a casual, uncredited basis. There is some useful material on Clemence Dane's career in PRO BT 64/108. This contains a draconian contract drawn up with her in 1937 by Motion Picture and Theatrical Industries Ltd, stipulating that she must work either alone or in groups as instructed, must give no press interviews and that her services can be sold on at any time.

4. Some of the films Deans scripted for Mycroft in 1936 were *Someone at the Door*, *Ourselves Alone* and *The Tenth Man*.

5. See shooting script of *Jew Süss* (S4383), Balcon Collection. See also Farnum and Rawlinson (1935).

6. See interview with Reville in *Sight and Sound*, Autumn 1976. She also scripted *The Secret Agent* (1936) and *Young and Innocent* (1937) for Gaumont-British.

7. There are two female scripting credits at Gainsborough: Gaffney in *My Old Dutch* and Reville in *The Lady Vanishes* (1938). At Gaumont-British, on the other hand, there were five each from Alma Reville and Marjorie Gaffney: three each from Marian Dix, Maude Howell and Dorothy Farnum and one each from Margaret Kennedy, Bess Meredyth and Daisy Fisher.

8. Montgomery wrote four scripts for British National, including *Lassie from Lancashire* (1938). Meehan wrote four for ABPC, including *Over She Goes* (1937).

9. Brown (1986).

10. See Storm (1946), p 2. For other material on Storm, see Morgan (1994), pp. 399–402.

11. Muriel and Sydney Box Papers, diaries for 1943–7, Box 7.

12. Interview with Elizabeth Montagu (the Hon. Mrs Varley) by the author and Vincent Porter in 1999. Korda valued Montagu's multilingual skills and gave her work on the script of *Anna Karenina* and a translation of Louis Hémon's *Marie Chapdelaine*, which was eventually made as *The Naked Heart* (1949).

13. See Storm's obituary in the *Daily Telegraph*, 20 October 1975.

14. Muriel and Sydney Box Papers, diary entry for 1 March 1950.

15. *John Bull*, 5 October 1946.

16. Muriel and Sydney Box Papers, diary entry for 29 February 1944; MacFarlane (1997), p. 98.

17. Muriel and Sydney Box Papers, diary entries for 14 March 1944 (on sets), 6 March and 27 March 1946 (on Balcon squabble).

18. See Joan Lester's article in *Reynold's News*, 23 May 1948, and 'Open Letter to the Critics' about the censorship, quoted in Aspinall and Murphy (1983), p. 87.

19. Sydney Box, letter to the editor, *Evening News*, 16 May 1947.

20. Annotated screenplay, Muriel and Sydney Box Papers, Item 8.1.

21. *Ibid.*, Items 5.1 and 5.2.
22. Interview with Lee Thompson by Vincent Porter in 1999.
23. BBC Written Archives, Caversham, T16/76/2, memo from Cecil Madden, 13 June 1950.
24. *Films and Filming*, November 1961.
25. *Ibid.*, May 1960.
26. Patricia Latham only scripted children's films, such as *The Copter Kids* (1977). So did Rosemary Sisson, with films like *Ride a Wild Pony* (1976). Suzanne Mercer had many credits, but only for sex films such as *Groupie Girl* (1970) and *Naughty!* (1971).
27. Lessing's *Memoirs of a Survivor* and Rhys's *Quartet* were both released as films in 1981.
28. Barrett both directed and scripted *Business as Usual* (1987). Barron did the same with *Secret Places* (1987), Potter with *The Gold Diggers* (1983) and Zetterling with *Scrubbers* (1982). Edzard scripted and directed *Biddy* (1983), *Little Dorrit* (1987) and *The Fool* (1990).
29. *Sight and Sound*, Winter 1978/9.
30. *Interview*, November 1990.

10

Directors

In the 1930s, women experienced extreme difficulties breaking into the technical side of production, and also into the union, the ACT.[1] Although the chaos and informality of the industry meant that there were some opportunities for women, few of them were in direction. Culley Forde, Walter Forde's wife, directed by proxy: 'he would never make a move without her say-so. When he had shot a scene, he would turn to her and if she nodded approval he had it printed' (Dryhurst, 1987, p. 225). Miles Mander complained about the studios' unwillingness to allow women to direct on their own. He argued that scriptwriter Marjorie Gaffney (who had co-directed with him) could be as eminent as the American Dorothy Arzner, because she was experienced in a range of film areas and had 'a picture mind'.[2] But no one paid any attention. Mary Field had a distinguished career as a documentary film-maker, but she never worked in features.

During the war, some women gained experience in documentary direction, such as Louise Birt, Dora Nirva, Ruby Grierson and Jill Craigie. However, the Films Division of the MoI had a very odd definition of what films were suitable for women to direct. Muriel Box, for example, was not allowed to direct *Road Safety for Children*, which she had scripted herself (Box, 1974, p. 163). According to Aida Young, most of the male documentarists 'sneered at feature films', and did not encourage their female apprentices to try them. The problem was that documentary inevitably declined in the postwar period, and women film-makers found the transition to features especially difficult. When Young tried her hand at feature directing, the technicians made fun of her: 'When I said "Quiet, please", all the electricians in the gantry mocked me with "Quiet, please!"[falsetto]. I was a joke.'[3] So she turned to producing, in the hope that it would be less humiliating.

In the postwar period, Muriel Box directed retakes if any were needed after editing.[4] Her first major stab at directing came with *The Lost People* (1949). She was drafted in to rescue the project from contract difficulties, but saw it as mere 'picture cobbling', although she had written the script herself with Lesley Storm.[5] It was not until the 1950s that she was able to direct films in earnest.

Jill Craigie had directed the documentary *Out of Chaos* in 1944, but had failed to gain distribution because it was thought uncommercial (MacQuitty, 1991, p. 293). Del Giudice admired her socialist élan ('I was very useful to have around when he had politicians at his table'),[6] and he backed her to direct the documentary *The Way We Live* (1946). However, Rank's deputy John Davis tried to stop production because he disliked documentary and women directors, and it was only by extreme effort that Craigie persuaded them to allow her to continue. In the end Rank appealed to Davis: 'You see, John? We can't stop it, can we?' (Drazin, 1998, p. 46). Craigie set up her own production company with producer Bill MacQuitty to direct the feature *Blue Scar* (1949). This was made with money from MacQuitty himself, John Sutro and the Coal Board, and it dealt with the effects of nationalization on a mining town. Shot on location using local people, it featured a love interest which Craigie and MacQuitty were reluctantly compelled to use. No distributor would touch it – 'You don't even speak our language' – but after an energetic campaign by Craigie, Korda agreed that British Lion give it a limited run as a second feature.[7] Small wonder that Craigie directed so few films.

In the 1950s, women mainly directed children's films: Patricia Latham with *John on the Run* (1953), Olive Negus with *Faithful to the Rescue* (1956), Kay Mander with *The Kid from Canada* (1957). Margaret Thomson directed *Child's Play* (1954) for Group Three, which was a comedy about a child's invention of atomic popcorn.[8] Women were not generally encouraged to direct those second features which Wolf Rilla called 'a marvellous training ground, for a director the equivalent of weekly rep' (ACTT, 1983, p. 94). This was one reason for the paucity of female directors in the 1960s. Mainstream critics felt that 'Directing movies has always been a man's job since the days of Griffith and de Mille. It has always been doubly difficult for a member of the fair sex to crash into the business of megaphone-wielding.'[9]

Jill Craigie became discouraged from directing in this period, raging against the 'unseen, insidious censorship' that was operated by official bodies. She felt that feature films were hamstrung by the national distaste for offence:

> In an age when the colonies are bursting with dramas and conflicts, we are left with Maugham, Conrad and Kipling, romance between white people, the last war, and adventure stories with an undercurrent of praise for the present administration.[10]

Craigie turned to scriptwriting instead, and produced some marvellous work. However, Muriel Box and Wendy Toye did manage major directorial careers in the 1950s, and this can be attributed to the bloody-mindedness of the former and the sublime insouciance of the latter.

Muriel Box had many directing credits, and this made her a role model for *Girl* magazine's Real Life Stories.[11] Mainly, journalists were condescending about her work, which was dismissed as 'an overfull Box of tricks'.[12] No one, of course, made that joke about Sydney. *Nursery World* made a point of reviewing her films, and *Reveille* thought she 'looked like the happy housewife she is'.[13]

Box's diaries give insight into her eclectic reading (Krishnamurti, Jung), her feminism and her unfilmed projects: 'this one is set 2,500 years hence when women will have achieved ascendancy over men in society'.[14] She filled her spare time by making curtains and worrying about domestic arrangements. Her first direction of the decade was *The Happy Family* (1952), scripted by herself and Sydney. The direction was Sydney's job, but he omitted to tell backers that Muriel was doing it; the Boxes said 'we' to journalists to conceal the fact that a woman was directing alone. The film deals with bureaucrats planning the demolition of a family home to make way for the Festival of Britain. *The Happy Family* was blighted by the death of George VI, since newsreel clips of him played a key part in the film and it had to be re-edited.[15] It also had severe finance problems: producer/financier John Woolf found out that a woman was directing, and withdrew funding at a late stage (MacQuitty, 1991, p. 308).

The Happy Family should be compared with *Passport to Pimlico* (1949). Both deal with communities under bureaucratic siege, but Box's film foregrounds women. Indeed, she even organized a special preview for women only.[16] She gave the role of the psychic sister Ada (Dandy Nichols) greater emphasis than in the original play. All her predictions are mocked by male family members: all of them come true. In a prolonged final shot, she achieves enlightenment and levitates, floating free above family turmoil. It is awkwardly managed, with the shot held rather too long, but nonetheless it is an interesting moment. Large, silly Ada reaches nirvana, while the men are gawping below.

Street Corner (1953) had the same scripting and distribution arrangements. The film was conceived by Muriel as a female riposte to *The Blue Lamp* (1950), but there were problems with Scotland Yard, who disliked the film.[17] *Street Corner* envisages a new moral order. Wayward girls are shown that the maternal embrace of society, as articulated by the policewomen, is preferable to a life on the margins. Yet the film is preoccupied by marriage. The widowed Susan (Anne Crawford) would rather be a housewife than a policewoman. One errant woman is advised to return home: 'he's a good man and he'll be waiting for you'.

To Dorothy a Son (1954) was made independently using the Boxes' own money.[18] It is a comedy about an American singer (Shelley Winters) who will inherit her uncle's fortune if her ex-husband (John Gregson) is still childless on a specific date. His pregnant wife Dorothy lies beached upstairs, and no one can be delivered until she is. The whole film hinges on a pregnancy no one sees, and pain no one hears; but they all stand to profit from the outcome. Box's conciliatory tact was necessary during filming. Winters did not wish to be directed by a woman. Moreover, her gestures varied so much that there were serious continuity problems: it was like 'shooting on a female volcano' (Box, 1974, p. 220). Peter Rogers's script expressed ideas which Box hated: 'Men were made to wear the pants and pants were made to carry the dough.' To her great chagrin, there was a roar of male approval from the preview audience, and she snorted: 'Anyone would think men had never had the handling of money in this country – so much for female emancipation!'[19] Distributors would not grant *To Dorothy a Son* a West End première, probably because it was independently financed.[20]

The Beachcomber (1954) dealt with the reform by missionary Martha (Glynis Johns) of drunken beachcomber Ted (Robert Newton). It was distributed by Rank and scripted by Sydney Box from a Somerset Maugham tale. The film celebrates Martha's inventiveness. She performs surgical operations unaided and insists that marriage can reform her undeserving lover. *The Beachcomber* focuses on Martha rather than on the *flâneur* Ted, as in the original. There were problems during production, however. Newton was paralytically drunk every lunchtime, so shooting schedules had to be rearranged, and all Box's charm was required.[21] Money was tight, and there were no doubles. Earl St John demanded radical cuts to the finished film, and it faced serious censorship difficulties.[22]

Box then directed *Simon and Laura* (1955) for Rank. This was a satire about a battling theatrical couple (Kay Kendall and Peter Finch) who star as themselves in a television series. Box directed with a marvellous lightness of touch. It is a self-referential film, with appearances by TV celebrities like Gilbert Harding, Lady Barnet and 'Mr Teasy-Weasy'. *Simon and Laura* makes capital out of media preferences for anodyne family life, and shows the can of worms beneath. Again, there were troubles on set, as neither star wished to be directed by a woman. They asked Earl St John to take Box off the film.[23] He refused, but it was an uncomfortable experience for her.

Eyewitness was made for Rank, and scripted by Janet Green. It combined crime and chase elements with a hospital story. Box skewed Green's script to give more narrative attention to the female characters – the chief nurse (Belinda Lee) and Mrs Hudson (Ada Reeve). The heroine reproves the hero for rampant consumerism: 'nothing we have really belongs to us'. Apart from these touches, *Eyewitness* is just a modest little thriller. Box was irked by John Davis's interference in the stars' clothes: 'Very soon we shall be expected to show every artist in their underwear in case producers and directors lose all sense of judgement in such matters.'[24] Production difficulties were intense, and she came to think that 'Making a film is like having a baby – very nice once it's over.'[25]

Rank turned down *The Truth about Women*, and it was made for Beaconsfield. Based on Box's own play, a *jeu d'esprit* about an author who writes his amorous autobiography, it is an extremely cynical piece. The only 'truth about women' that the author can produce is a collection of blank sheets (Box, 1939). Box was convinced that the combination of feminism and humour was repellent to 'the dark side of Wardour Street', when British Lion tried to prevent a West End showing.[26]

Subway in the Sky (1959) was a thriller based in Berlin, which Box transformed from the original, an unremarkable play about an Army fugitive. The film is set in a flat on top of a skyscraper. Box makes repeated shots of the building from below and afar, and films the flat so that it seems labyrinthine. She sexualizes the *mise en scène*, with the phallic exterior and the vaginal recesses of the interior, and it is embellished by scenes of erotic intensity. These are focused on the heroine (Hildegarde Neff), whose gaze patterns, transformed skin tone and discarded clothing imply everything but show nothing.

Box's last film of the decade was *Too Young to Love*, made for Beaconsfield and distributed by Rank. Muriel and Sydney based their script on Elsa Shelley's play *Pick-up Girl*, which dealt with a promiscuous girl and had been a great theatrical success in London. The play had vanquished censorship objections and had raised public awareness of female delinquency (Cotes, 1949, pp. 47–61). Elsa Shelley collaborated with Muriel on the script, which intensified the coverage of abortion and venereal disease.

Muriel was proud that every single person involved in the film was female, except producer Herbert Smith. She found it fitting that an X-rated film by women should deal with unruly female sexuality, without 'nudes/neurotics/killers/corpses/ghosts/ghouls'.[27] *Too Young to Love* considers the apparatus of social control brought to bear on female unchastity, and discusses the causes and pleasures of promiscuity. It is a very bleak and radical film.

Too Young to Love was overtaken by conservative publicity campaigns. Tommy Steele and Cliff Richard were approached to speak out against female unchastity, and Beverley Nichols and Godfrey Wynn were prompted to write an article blaming the working mother: 'How teenagers can go wrong when both parents go out to work'.[28] Rank organized 'talker' previews, at which the film was prefaced by edifying speeches from local worthies.[29] These hamfisted campaigns scuppered the film.

Muriel Box's career in the 1950s was remarkably varied. She worked with different companies, and none of her films were firmly rooted generically. Box made cross-genre films for small companies, such as *The Passionate Stranger* (1957) and *This Other Eden* (1959). She remained experimental throughout the decade, and met with the utmost intransigence from the industry.

Critics often lumped Wendy Toye with Muriel Box: 'Being women they specially enjoy making men look foolish . . . being women they know well that feminine stars must look wonderful on the screen.'[30] In fact, their work was quite different. All they had in common was their gender, the bad reviews they received and the refusal by some distributors to grant their work West End premières.[31] Toye's background was theatre and ballet, and she came to film-making with a solid reputation as a choreographer and stage director (Merz, 1994, p. 127). In 1992, Toye suggested that this partially accounted for the difference in their work. She argued that her experience of working with actors advantaged her on the studio floor; Box had problems because she was primarily a writer with an axe to grind (Dixon, 1994, p. 149). Toye always refused the label of feminism:

> I think an example of doing something and getting on with it and not being a crashing bore about things is probably better than getting onto a platform and making some speech about it all. By being didactic, you alienate a large part of your audience. (*ibid.*, p. 142)

Toye thought the director's role was to interpret the mood of the script, determine the visual designs, structure the narrative and choose the cast and the music. Indeed, she often played music to prospective actors to judge their suitability.[32] She wanted to make films which were 'distinctly British' with a strong fantasy element, and she aspired to make musicals using her choreographical talents.[33] Her films were mainly comedies, in which the protagonists' body language was tightly organized and the narratives had a fluid yet rigorous structure. Toye's papers show an extraordinary control over detail. She took notes from her visual imagination: under 'things I'd like' for *Raising a Riot*, she saw mental snapshots of 'someone up a tree, dog at bottom', and 'sink full of brown water and peel'.[34] Her notes also contain charming little drawings, which she called 'comic cuts'; these are not storyboards, but surreal *aides-mémoire* to the fit between visual and script discourses.

Toye first worked in films when she assisted Sir Anton Dolin on the choreography of *Invitation to the Waltz* (1935), in which she also danced. It was not until 1948 that she worked in films again, when she choreographed the ballroom scene in *Anna Karenina* (1948). Korda was impressed by her at once, and after seeing her *The Stranger Left No Card* (1952), which won the Cannes prize for best short fiction film, he kept offering her work. She refused *The Man Who Loved Redheads* (1955), which was 'not my sort of film at all'.[35] Eventually she accepted *The Teckman Mystery* (1954) to appease Korda. This was a turgid spy project in which the heroine (Margaret Leighton) turns out to be the villain. Toye shook the script by the scruff of the neck, altered the structure, tightened the characterization and added long speeches by the heroine. Her sketches make it clear that it was a composed film: she choreographed the editing with the music.[36] It is an extremely competent film, smoother and more professional than Muriel Box's thrillers.

Raising a Riot (1955), Toye's next full-length feature, was made for Korda, and dealt comically with Kenneth More's dismal attempts at housekeeping. Toye's notes insist on running visual gags to bind the film together, and repeated shot patterns to jog the audience's memory. Her re-edit is masterly in its control, and also in the tact with which she presented it to her producer: 'Which do *you* prefer of the two versions?' Toye felt that women were the best judges of domestic mayhem, and so she took her housekeeper along to the preview.[37] Of course, the script had its radical moments. The heroine asks: 'Do you know what a woman has to be? A cross between a saint and a dray horse, a diplomat and an automatic washing machine, a psychiatrist and a bulldozer, a sanitary engineer and a mannequin.' But Toye took the sexual politics for granted, and concentrated on narrative drive and wit.

After Korda's death, Toye's contract was taken over by Rank, but 'They'd got me and they didn't know what to do with me much'.[38] She directed *All for Mary* (1955) for producer Paul Soskin, who did not particularly like the film's humour, and wanted her to re-shoot many scenes. The film dealt with the amorous competition of two hapless males who catch chickenpox and are humiliated by Nanny (Kathleen Harrison). Again Toye's papers show her extensive interventions. She set up all the master shots and angles, and inserted sections into the script ('My mother she is Polish, my father she is a Turk, I am raised in Bessarabia.'/ 'Ah, nice girl, Bessarabia.'). She intensified the dominance of Nanny. An Army general bellows: 'Hullo Nanny! This is little Winkle', and a disaffected protagonist complains: 'I think your Nanny did something Freudian to you in the nursery.'[39] *All for Mary* is a skilful debunking of myths about masculinity and romantic love.

Toye's last film for Rank was *True as a Turtle* (1957), which was about a sailing trip in a leaky hulk. The slight material is invested with layers of meaning about social and sexual difference. The hero is forced on the trip during his honeymoon to please his boss, and the sailing community is riven with class division. More importantly, gender divisions are extreme. The men love sailing, the women hate it; men are in the open air, women are cooking down below. Toye's notes insist that even on deck, gender reigns supreme: 'The women are sitting on the hatch covers and skylights and the men are in the Cock Pit [sic].'[40] *True as a Turtle* is tight, fast and marvellously crafted, and its tone is wry. Toye solved the technical problems of filming on a boat by mounting the camera on a specially constructed trolley, which was called 'Wendy's Toy'.[41]

Toye's 1950s films are not essentially subversive. Rather, they are a sophisticated riposte to extremism of all kinds. Her specialism lies in appearing to treat important things as if they were nothing. Such a laconic film-maker was increasingly ill at ease in the frantic, 'committed' cinema of the late 1950s.

In the 1960s, the decline of women directors was catastrophic. Sarah Erulkah directed *The Hunch* in 1967 and Jan Darnley-Smith *A Ghost of a Chance* in 1968, but these were both short children's films. Joan Littlewood directed her own theatrical success, *Sparrows Can't Sing* (1962), and the film had vitality and professionalism. However, Littlewood was caught in the toils of managerial and financial bungling, and she was refused permission to re-shoot key scenes herself (Littlewood, 1994, pp. 644–56). It was the last film she directed for decades. Ariel Levy began her career with a number of apprentice assistant-director credits on films like *Scream and Scream Again* (1969). But it was all small beer.

Both Wendy Toye and Muriel Box's film careers foundered in the 1960s. Toye only made one feature, *We Joined the Navy* (1962). It was a Navy comedy, a genre which suited Toye, and she inserted small grenades into the anodyne script. She wanted the Captain to say: 'As Churchill said, the Navy runs on three things: Rum, Bum and Baccy. Remember that, and you'll all be admirals.' She also wanted to include a song for the stripper, in which she presented herself as 'a great big bundle of beauty paid to please'.[42] However, such salaciousness was regarded as inappropriate in a film directed by a woman, and accordingly was cut from the script. The film sank without trace. Anyway, Toye's informal methods did not suit film production of the period, and she returned to ballet and theatre work. Of her work in this period, she commented that 'Women dare not be less than the best men. Perhaps, later on, when it becomes more accepted, they can be as bad as some of the men.'[43]

Muriel Box's film career failed for different reasons. Her diaries for the 1960s make painful reading, since they map the death of her marriage. They also chart the intensification of her feminism. When Box first read Betty Friedan's 1963 *The Feminine Mystique*, she was 'delighted to find I am not such an eccentric as I feared'. Box was annoyed to find a Day of Circumcision in her diary, and proposed that there should be 'a Day of the Menopause to balance things'.[44] Such views did not endear her to the film establishment, especially when she was no longer backed by her husband's cash or protection. Accordingly, Box's last feature film was *The Rattle of a Simple Man* (1964). Based on Charles Dyer's play, and scripted by him, the film was a lacklustre affair which dealt with the changing emotions of Percy (Harry H. Corbett) towards a prostitute (Diane Cilento). Dully staged and unimaginatively constructed, *The Rattle of a Simple Man* was an uphill task for Box, and she managed to make very little of it. The lumbering naïveties of the hero were matched by the vicious mendaciousness of the heroine, and the best that could be said was that they deserved each other. Box then left filming and set up the successful Femina publishing house (Box, 1974, p. 249).

In general, women directors in the 1970s shunned mainstream cinema, or were excluded from it. Ariel Levy managed some assistant director credits on *Hands of the Ripper* (1971), *Nothing But the Night* (1972) and *No Sex Please – We're British* (1973), but never gained full director status, and left for America in 1980. There was, however, an enormous increase in women directors of avant-garde and feminist films, often with specialist non-theatrical distribution. A number of production, exhibition and distribution networks were built up which privileged or specialized in films directed by women: among them were the London Film-makers' Co-op, Cinema of Women, the Berwick St Collective and The Other Cinema.[45]

The increase in the number of avant-garde feminist directors can be ascribed to two factors: to exasperation with mainstream industrial practice, and to the stylistic cul-de-sac in which British film narrative found itself. In a sense, the venality and corrosive cynicism of the industry fuelled the rage and focused the creativity of women directors. They wished to make an alternative cinema – alternative both in terms of the sexual politics of its conditions of production, and in terms of narrative strategies. Quite simply, the women directors of the 1970s avant-garde felt that mainstream fashioning of talent was unacceptably restrictive, and accordingly they set about a radical redefinition of the role of the director. With an ambitious élan which had been absent from British film culture for many years, women directors claimed authorship of scripting practices and took responsibility for the overall 'look' of their films.

Many of them came from an academic fine art background or from dance, rather than from the traditional film schools. An important contradiction which they had to resolve was that, when working alone and controlling lighting and editing, they were insulated from industrial conflict but could only progress very slowly. When working in a collective or with members of the ACTT union, their interests would inevitably collide with others'.[46]

Mainly working from very slim resources, the new films often had a disarmingly straightforward approach to artistic action. The Berwick St Collective's *The Nightcleaners* (1975), for example, which was a protest about women's wages, was originally conceived as a linear narrative; it was then radically edited so as to discomfort the viewer's sense of space and time. Other women film-makers used more traditional methods. Esther Ronay's marvellous *Women of the Rhondda* (1972) used interviews with women involved in the miners' strikes of the 1920s, and intercut them with domestic and industrial backgrounds.

Sally Potter was undoubtedly the most imaginative of the new directors. She began her directing career with *Thriller* (1979), which was financed by the Arts Council.[47] The film was scripted and edited by Potter, who also did the camerawork and sound. *Thriller* is in effect a radical reworking of *La Bohème*, and it takes issue with the way in which women's death is a key motif in classical narrative, particularly grand opera. *Thriller* describes the opera story and then deconstructs it, insisting by the quotation of the theme music from *Psycho* that all female protagonists are disposable and that the males' artistic display is founded on their suffering. The film splits the heroine into good (Mimi) and bad (Musetta), into young (Mimi) and old (the seamstress in the photograph), and most radically into white (Mimi) and black (Colette Laffont). The latter is the only one to escape patriarchy, by laughter. She searches for answers in the journal *Tel Quel* ('I was searching for a theory that would explain my life'), and when she comes to the names of Marx and Freud, she explodes with raucous mockery. The icons of male theoretical culture are as complicit as its works of art.[48]

Potter's rereading of the opera is a major cinematic innovation. The problem is, of course, that texts like *La Bohème* give pleasure not because they are narratives about women's oppression, but because they display sublime virtuosity. Opera of this type modulates its moods with remarkable subtlety, because its creators are thoroughly *au fait* with the technical requirements of the medium. The fact that *La Bohème* (or *Tosca*, or *Suor Angelica*) are predicated on the death of female protagonists is simply because they are a product of late patriarchy, and they replicate the ideological conditions of their period with unusual and often offensive directness. The sexual politics of earlier operas by Mozart or Handel are much more subtly inscribed. The inevitable mistake made by Potter and other avant-garde feminists of the period is that they based their analyses of culture on a conspiratorial model, which views works of art as complicit in the oppression of the weakest. This leads to a view of high art as an oppressive monolith.

Potter did not like the feminist incorporation of psychoanalytic theory into film-making: *Thriller* 'had come out of my practice in performance [as a dancer] ... Lacan is not my wellspring. Theory as a prescriptive model for film-making is absolutely deadening.'[49] Indeed, Potter's explicit refusal of the Lacanian theory of the Lack has a profound effect on her feminism, which is of an optimistic and combative nature:

> What I'm saying is that it's no good dwelling in the land of the victim. And even though we have to acknowledge our oppression and all the things that have been taken away, including our pleasures, nevertheless there's a point of view which is extremely handy, which is to see the paradoxical advantages of our situation and to see our inner strength.[50]

Laura Mulvey's films, on the other hand, cannot be understood without reference to her theoretical work. Mulvey's influential article 'Visual pleasure and narrative cinema' mounted 'a total negation of the ease and plenitude of the narrative fiction film'. Mulvey viewed the traditional pleasures of cinema (identification and imaginary release) as a matter for censure. She adduced a reading of Freud (on scopophilia) and Lacan (on the Lack) into a theory about mainstream cinema's privileging of the male gaze.[51] Mulvey co-directed two films with Peter Wollen in the 1970s, both of which contained radical redrawings of the cultural map. *Penthesilea, Queen of the Amazons* (1974) focused on the Amazons' challenge to patriarchy, and it broadened that historically specific issue into a more general one about women's role within the symbolic order. *Penthesilea* is about silence and absence – about the world's unwillingness to hear women's discourse, or to see their proper appearance. Mulvey and Wollen wished to inaugurate a new artistic language outside history and the symbolic order, and they bravely confronted the issue of how to make bricks without straw.[52]

Riddles of the Sphinx (1976) suggestively converted the Oedipus myth into an evocation of the power of the Sphinx: 'she is outside the city gates, she challenges the order of the city, with its order of kingship and its order of knowledge'. The film deals with one individual's struggle against social constraints. The female principle (and principal) bears the signs of both exclusion from, and incorporation within, the symbolic order. That which most distinguishes women from men – their ability to bear children – is the most heavily coded activity of all:

> We live in a society ruled by the father, in which the place of the mother is suppressed. Motherhood, and how to live it, or not to live it, lies at the roots of the dilemma. And meanwhile the Sphinx can only speak with a voice apart.[53]

This is a powerful formulation, and the resolution of the battle over the world of signs is made through the projection of images which are thoroughly ambiguous. The sequence of the female acrobats is a case in point. Strong and colourful, they soar through the air and are clearly meant to signal a muscular femininity free from the shackles of patriarchy. Yet as a metaphor for autonomy, the acrobat sequence also implicitly links female creativity to a sinuous and powerful body. The more desirable leap – from acrobats to sinuous *intellectual* inventiveness – is obscured. It is the same with the sequence of the mercury puzzle. It is clearly intended to signify the difficulty of female negotiation through the patriarchal labyrinth. But it also contains a spiritual meaning: the hesitant progress of one isolated drop of mercury to union with the larger mass below can also evoke the tremulous desire of the individual for incorporation within the One. This is inappropriate, since *Riddles* is a profoundly materialist film.

Mulvey stressed that her films were not made for mass consumption, nor should they be shown on television:

> They weren't made with a wide audience in mind but with the intention of changing particular people's attitude to film – on the one hand, women interested in questions of representation and, on the other hand, people involved in film and interested in film and politics.[54]

This restricts the films' appeal to radical academics, a social group whose sense of its own importance scarcely needs bolstering. It is a pity, since the films themselves are suggestive.

Other feminist film-makers of the period took issue with what they saw as the crushing effects of the habits of historical representation. Susan Clayton directed *The Song of the Shirt* (1979), which was based on a Chartist novel and initially conceived as a video project for Women's Aid. It required specialist distribution, since Clayton 'never thought the film would stand up on its own because that's not why we made it. We made it as an intervention in debates that were going on in feminist history.'[55]

Clayton developed the narrative through techniques of distanciation. Seamstresses and historic notables such as Mayhew addressed the camera direct, wearing historical dress but set against modern backgrounds (Cowie, 1980, p. 90). The politics of *The Song of the Shirt* foregrounded psychoanalytic discourse. When combined with an awareness of the complex issue of evidence and 'history from below', it led to an intense self-consciousness:

> Our position was that you can't just write women back into history. You can imagine, you can create all kinds of imaginative reconstructions, but if you are actually looking at the material of history, you can try to explain why women are absent, but I don't think you can actually construct a female voice in a specific historical instance that has the power to explain its absence.[56]

Of course, ordinary characterization had to be eschewed, which made viewing *The Song of the Shirt* a bracing experience. The ideas behind the text were worthy, but the finished film was a testament to the robustness of the old viewing habits. Clayton's historical reconstruction should be contrasted with Bill Douglas's *Comrades* (1986), which dealt with the Tolpuddle Martyrs. *Comrades* lacks the propagandism of Clayton's film, and is altogether more humane because, although mildly experimental, it has made a settlement with the epistemological habits of its audience.[57]

The issue of visual pleasure is an acute one in the case of avant-garde texts. The question to be asked is whose pleasure is being evoked, and what cultural capital is required to decode the films. Clayton's, Mulvey's and Potter's 1970s work deploys a visual style with some rigour and puritanism. For Potter, visual pleasure is predicated on the desire to reform not only the language of mainstream culture but also its emotional undertow:

> What is the pleasure if it's based on female pain? ... There's everything right about wanting to dismantle oppressive stereo-types, there's everything right about fighting oppression, there's everything right about wanting to make pleasure that isn't causing somebody else pain.[58]

In this period, some feminist film-makers construct films with sparse textures, in which the script is the dominant discourse and the intellectual stimulus is extreme. The work of Christine Edzard provides a strong contrast. Edzard scripted and directed *The Little Match Girl* (1977) and *Stories from a Flying Trunk* (1979). With a background in set and production design, her work was visually lush and inventive, with narra-tive lines drawn from traditional sources. In these films, Edzard displayed a fondness for episodic structure and for a *mise en scène* which was a cornucopia of contrasting textures and colours. She was preoccupied by history, which she conceived in a politically radical manner but repre-sented as a series of lush vignettes. One of Edzard's early sidelines was to make and equip doll's houses, and dress the tiny inhabitants. Her cinematic world has the same flavour: she aims to construct a bright and autonomous world.

Other women film-makers used non-realist techniques too. Tina Keane's *Shadow of a Journey* (1980) is an evocative study of Scottish light, shade, sea and birdsong, thematically held together by a soundtrack about the Highland clearances. In *That's Entertainment* (1979), Jeanette Iljohn took 100 feet of film shot at a children's party and subjected it to repetition, slowing down and rearranging it until the incident itself recedes in time. Some women went further down the minimalist path. Annabel Nicholson's *Slides* (1971) discards narrative altogether, and bits of film with fragments of leaves and grass were printed and passed through the viewfinder. Nicholson described how

> 35 mm. slides, light-leaked film, sewn film, cut up 8 mm. and 16 mm. fragments were dragged through the contact printer. The films create their own fluctuating colour and form, defying the passive use of 'film as vehicle'. The appearance of sprocket holes, frameline etc. is less to do with structural concepts and more of a creative, plastic response to whatever is around.[59]

Transformation of traditional forms could go no further than this. Film is floated free from patriarchy and its servant linear narrative, and instead becomes a web of visual textures and sense-impressions.

The 1970s represented a high-water mark in terms of formal innovation by women film-makers. In the 1980s, films directed by women were more varied in their formats, length and genres. Antonia Lant (1993) suggests that this made the films unpredictable commodities, and that the strong regionalism and specialism of women's film during the decade hindered their assimilation in international markets. The point is, though, that by this time many women film-makers were so alienated by mainstream cinema that their exclusion from it was a source of pride.

Avant-garde women directors often constructed short films whose narratives favoured archetypal or fairytale elements. Catherine Elwes's cycle on the seasons, *Spring, Winter* and *Autumn* (1988), fell into this category, as did Tina Keane's *Bed Time Story* (1982), about Bluebeard, and Janni Perton's *In the Lands Where Serpents Speak* (1986), which dealt with the Rapunzel, Snow White and Sleeping Beauty myths. Polly Gladwind's *The Mark of Lilith* (1986) was a rich brew about goddesses and social taboos. Other shorts directed by women were more overtly political and more explicitly feminist: for example, Jo Spence's *Face Value* (1981), Jo Davis's *Ironing to Greenham* (1985) and the Sheffield Film Co-op's *Red Skirts on Clydeside* (1983). To be sure, the 1970s abstract tradition was still extant in such films as Lis Rhodes's *Pictures on Pink Paper* (1982). But for the most part, the most innovative 1980s shorts by women were those which concentrated on the female body: Cheryl Edwards's *To Be Silent Is the Most Painful Part* (1985) and Jayne Parker's *Almost Out* (1984). These films rescued women's bodies from obloquy and humiliation and returned them to their rightful owners.

A number of black women worked with Sankofa, a black London-based film workshop (Diawara, 1993). Maureen Blackwood was the most prominent of the directors. She co-directed *The Passion of Remembrance* (1986) and *Looking for Langston* (1989) with Isaac Julien, and both directed and wrote the screenplay of *Perfect Image* (1988). Blackwood and Martina Attille played a crucial role in the debates about deconstructing conventional images of black women.[60] Maggie's narrative in *The Passion of Remembrance* radically transforms the relationship between gender and racial subordination. Maggie (Antonia Thomas) contains all history, its signs and traces, within her consciousness; out of a collage of repression, rebellion and joy she makes a powerfully coherent argument.

Other women directors had unpredictable relationships with mainstream narrative and distribution networks. Lezli-An Barrett, for example, who made *An Epic Poem* (1982) based on the issues aroused by the suffragette slashing of the Rokeby Venus, thought that mainstream cinema was so hidebound that female creativity could rarely be accommodated:

> No way would a producer send a women director a gangster script, or any other kind of genre, unless it's very much about a woman. But if it's about a prepubescent young girl discovering her sexuality . . . then they'd think well, maybe we should get a woman director for that.[61]

Barrett was rigorous in her methods, favouring 360-degree pans and an exclusive concentration on the point of view of female protagonists. She was understandably irritated when producers 'took me for Lezli Barrett's secretary, expecting a bloke to come walking though the door'.[62] What is significant, though, is that Barrett's next film, *Business as Usual*, made more of a settlement with traditional narrative forms (Hill, 1999, pp. 185–8). Barrett clearly felt that if she wanted to address everyday events, she would have to compromise on style and narrative structure. Laura Mulvey's *Amy!* used a variety of distanciation techniques to encourage the audience to question the normative conventions of biography, but still concentrated powerfully on the charms of identification. Other directors took more straightforward routes. Mai Zetterling's *Scrubbers*, which she also scripted, used an unadorned visual style in which to delineate crime and violence in a girls' borstal. Zelda Barron scripted her own *Secret Places*. She also directed *Shag* (1987) and *The Advancement of Learning* (1989), which were robustly middle-of-the-road vehicles with few pretensions.[63]

So far, it looks as though 1980s women directors continued along avant-garde trajectories laid out before, or else they made an uneasy settlement with mass cinema. But major innovations were made by Christine Edzard and Sally Potter, who broke the frame of established discourses in a subtle yet radical manner. Both directed films which could be contained within the experiential models of mainstream cinema, while covertly questioning them in a profound way. Edzard, for example, constructed a sustained debate with Victorian England in her 1980s films. Sands Films, which she founded with her husband Peter Goodwin, was anachronistic in terms of modern production methods. Financed from capital raised by Goodwin from *Murder on the Orient Express* (1974) and from private bank loans, Sands Films was like a miniature studio of the 1930s. Located in warehouses in Rotherhithe, it had 25 full-time employees including in-house designers, plasterers, dressmakers and a reference library in a fully integrated operation.[64] Sands Films made clothes 'painstakingly handwoven and stitched together without recourse to modern machinery ... using nothing but authentic cotton fabric and materials relevant to the 1840s period'.[65] Such scrupulous purism suffused *Biddy*, which Edzard both directed and scripted. *Biddy* reconstructed the consciousness of a nanny in mid-Victorian England, retrieving her from anonymity and condescension. But Edzard's greatest achievement was her version of Dickens's *Little Dorrit*, which she filmed in two parts as *Nobody's Fault* and *Little Dorrit's Story*. The novel is one of the most densely populated in Dickens's *oeuvre*, as it swoops from the broadest social canvas to the smallest minutiae: his Part the First and Part the Second are Poverty and Riches respectively. Edzard structured her version so as to 'have two looks at the same story', and the second film focused exclusively on Little Dorrit herself, whom Edzard wanted the actress to portray in a 'dry and unexpansive' manner.[66] *Little Dorrit's Story* subjects the original novel to a radical rereading, in which the heroine acts more decisively and inventively. The flatness of delivery alienated some critics, notably Raphael Samuel, who felt that the film presented a sanitized version of the text and that its realism was lacklustre (Samuel, 1994, pp. 114–17). But what critics failed to recognize was that Edzard had excavated a modernist Dickens, in which the certainties about darkness and light, perspective and consistent caricatures could no longer be taken for granted. The canonical text was still there, rather like *Sarrasine* after the ministrations of Barthes's *S/Z*. But Edzard had encouraged the audience to feel that one could take liberties with the text: love it, celebrate it, subject it to a commando raid, reassemble it.

After the Dickens film, Edzard directed and scripted *The Fool* (1990), based on Mayhew's *London Labour and the London Poor*. Again her work displayed a profound historical sense, and a reinvigorated sense of purpose and style. Sally Potter's career too had an upward trajectory. *The Gold Diggers*, which she directed, scripted, edited and choreographed, was a remarkable achievement. It took the form of a female quest, redeployed the musical form, and properly used the talents of Julie Christie. As its unifying metaphor the film deploys gold as a means of conceptualizing the theory of surplus value: it connects the circulation of gold and the circulation of women. On the face of it, the project sounds crushingly dull, but in fact it is rivetingly entertaining, with a quixotic lightness of touch and passages of intense sensual beauty. *The Gold Diggers* is one of the few feminist films of the period able to display the historical resonances of objects and yet to contemplate the world of surfaces with guilt-free pleasure. Potter conceived the structure of the film as a spiral rather than a linear structure: as 'a very strong, sturdy structure, it's familiar in many natural forms and has a history architecturally and spiritually and, of course, biochemically'. The effect of the spiral is to draw the viewer into the vortex of the narrative, and at the same time to prompt them to perceive the gap between sexual stereotypes and glimpse the real person beneath. The Julie Christie character carries with her the memory of star glamour. Potter directs (or frees) her to act so as to assume and then doff that persona: 'in the process of the film she sheds that to an extent, it becomes evidently a form of disguise'.[67]

Potter spent many years preparing for *Orlando*, which was finally released in 1993. *Orlando* was that most *rara avis* of British film culture: a radical, feminist film of breathtaking visual beauty which was a major success at the box-office. Potter managed to get international funding, and of course wrote the script and was heavily involved in the technical aspects of the filming process.[68] *Orlando* is visually sumptuous, with masque-like set pieces (the arrival of the Queen, the dance on the ice). Potter's most visually intense scenes call into question the usual 'truths' about gender ascription and identity:

> I don't think the book [by Virginia Woolf] so much explores sexual identities as dissolves them, and it's that kind of melting and shifting where nothing is ever what it seems for male and female that I think is the strength of the book and what I wanted to reproduce in the film.[69]

And yet one of the most subtle and memorable scenes in the film is that of Orlando's morning awakening with her lover. Shot from above, their bodies are entwined and carefully composed, and it is clear that their very difference from each other is what makes them happy: dark and white, hard and soft, male and female. And indeed, as we discover later, father and mother. It is this very flexibility and lack of doctrinaire narrowness which makes *Orlando* such a remarkable film. It shifts from analyses of empire and property to sexual love and back again, held together in the net of a preoccupation with female creativity.

Overall, then, it is clear that direction by women was not, like some of their other film professions, on a dying fall. From sparse beginnings and false starts, major careers were made – that of Muriel Box, in the teeth of industry intransigence; Wendy Toye, because of her blithe optimism. After a brief lacuna in the 1960s, women's direction took a different tack, and made a full reckoning with avant-garde concepts about artistic form. Women directors gave them a more liberal and humane spin, and throughout the 1980s, they made films of startling originality.

Notes

1. Kay Mander, who later wrote and directed for the Shell Film Unit, was the first woman to join in 1937. She was joined by Muriel Box soon afterwards (ACTT, 1983, p. 69).
2. *Film Weekly*, 4 May 1934, quoted by Tony Aldgate (1998).
3. BECTU interview with Aida Young.
4. BECTU interview with Muriel Box.
5. Box (1974), p. 200. There is a post-production script of *The Lost People* (S364) in BFI Library.
6. Interview with Craigie, in Drazin (1998), p. 24.
7. MacQuitty (1991), pp. 302–3. See also *Picturegoer*, 7 May 1949.
8. See an interesting article on 'Women film directors' in *ABC Film Review*, January 1954.
9. *Weekly Sporting Review*, 3 August 1956.
10. Draft of article on censorship submitted to Balcon, Balcon Collection (H/83).
11. *Girl*, 5 January 1955: 'She is the most famous woman film director in England. She sends all *Girl* readers her very best wishes.'
12. The *Star*, 13 March 1953. There was a nasty article in *The Times*, 16 March 1953: 'Miss Box wants it both ways'. See also the Catholic *Universe*, 15 February 1957: 'Miss Box was presumably not able to be sufficiently detached'.
13. *Nursery World*, 8 December 1955; *Reveille*, 13 May 1957.
14. Muriel Box Diaries, 3 October 1954.
15. *Today's Cinema*, 17 March 1952.
16. *Ibid.*, 28 May 1952.
17. Muriel Box Diaries, 26 July and 12 August 1952.
18. *Ibid.*, 16 June 1954.
19. *Ibid.*, 21 November 1954.
20. *Daily Sketch*, 26 November 1954.
21. Muriel Box Diaries, 17 February and 3 March 1954.
22. *Ibid.*, 26 April and 23 July 1954.

23. *Ibid.*, 1 January 1955.
24. *Ibid.*, 30 January 1956.
25. *Ibid.*, 3 August 1956. She liked the film/baby comparison. She had toothache after finishing every film: 'They say one baby, one tooth. With me, it's one film, one tooth' (25 November 1952).
26. *Ibid.*, 15 January 1958. See also Box (1974), pp. 222–3.
27. Muriel and Sydney Box Papers, Item 8.2.
28. *Ibid.* Considering she was always a working mother herself, this must have inflamed Box.
29. Letter from J. Arthur Rank Association to Sydney Box, 2 March 1960, Muriel and Sydney Box Papers, Box 6.
30. *Evening News*, 14 February 1957.
31. Toye's *The Teckman Mystery* was not given a big première: *Picturegoer*, 1 January 1955. See *ibid.*, 17 March 1956 for a discussion of Toye's critics.
32. BECTU interview with Wendy Toye.
33. *Picturegoer*, 14 April 1956.
34. Wendy Toye Papers, Item 5, BFI Library.
35. BECTU interview with Wendy Toye.
36. Wendy Toye Papers, Item 3.
37. *Ibid.*, Item 5.
38. BECTU interview with Wendy Toye.
39. Wendy Toye Papers, Item 6.
40. *Ibid.*, Item 7.
41. Interview with Miss Toye by the author in 1999.
42. Wendy Toye Papers, Item 8. Miss Toye was at pains to point out at interview that this song was not actually written by her.
43. *Monthly Film Bulletin*, August 1986.
44. Muriel Box Diaries, entry for 31 May 1963; 'menopause' reference appears in 1962 diary.
45. For useful material on specialist distribution and exhibition, see Brunsden (1986), pp. 179–231. For material on feminist distribution networks, see Whitaker (1982). See *Monthly Film Bulletin*, January 1986. For an account of the distribution of *A Question of Silence*, see Root (1985).
46. An interesting discussion of this issue is contained in Dee Dee Glass, Laura Mulvey and Judith Williamson, 'Feminist film practice and pleasure', *Formations of Pleasure* (London: Routledge, 1983), pp. 168–9.
47. See an interview with Potter on *Thriller* in *Framework*, no. 14, 1981.
48. For an alternative interpretation of this sequence, see Jane Weinstock, 'She who laughs first laughs last', *M/F*, 1980, pp. 100–10. For a close, scrupulous reading of the film, see Kaplan (1983), pp. 154–61.
49. Interview with Potter in *Screen*, Autumn 1993.
50. *Framework*, no. 24, Spring 1984.
51. *Screen*, vol. 16, no. 3, Autumn 1975.
52. See interview on *Penthesilea* in *Screen*, vol. 15, no. 3, Autumn 1974.
53. Script of *Riddles*, in *Screen*, vol. 18, no. 2, Summer 1977.
54. Glass *et al.*, 'Feminist film practice', p. 169.
55. Interview with Clayton in *Wide Angle*, vol. 6, no. 1.
56. *Ibid.*, no. 3. See Sylvia Harvey, 'An introduction to *The Song of the Shirt*', *Undercut*, no. 1, March 1981.

57. See an interesting piece on the films in *Monthly Film Bulletin*, September 1987.
58. *Framework*, no. 24, Spring 1984.
59. Annabel Nicholson, quoted in Cinenova catalogue.
60. See an interview in *Framework*, no. 32/3, 1986. See also Attille and Blackwood (1986). See an account of the debates in Pines (1997).
61. *Sight and Sound*, Summer 1989.
62. *Monthly Film Bulletin*, September 1987. See also *Time Out*, 9 September 1987.
63. See *Screen International*, 4 February 1989, and *Time Out*, 10 August 1988.
64. *Sight and Sound*, Spring 1988.
65. *Films and Filming*, December 1987.
66. *Ibid*.
67. Interview with Potter in *Framework*, no. 24, Spring 1984.
68. For material on this aspect of the film, see *Sight and Sound*, March 1993 and *Time Out*, 10 March 1993. For an article on aspects of structure and performance in *Orlando*, see Pidduck (1997).
69. *Screen*, vol. 34, no. 3, Autumn 1993.

Costume Designers

Costume design is a crucial signifying feature of film texts. The clothes characters wear can provide an index to their class, politics and sexuality, and thus access to the intentions of the director/producer. They also provide evidence about the resources available to the company, and about the cultural competence of the costume designer. It goes without saying that there is no 'natural' relationship between women and the needle. It is all a question of status. Most major couturiers were men until recently; the ability to place a dart, turn a hem or design an ensemble is not genetically determined. In the 1930s film industry, for example, all the costume designers were men, except for Doris Zinkeisen. She had specialized in avant-garde stage décor for revues by Cochran, Coward and Playfair, and her *Designing for the Stage* was an influential innovation. Zinkeisen thought that audiences had the unconscious ability to decode complex visual details, and that theatrical and film performances should be led by the *mise en scène*. She valued visual flair and 'fantastic treatment' above all (Zinkeisen, 1938, p. 46). Interestingly, Cochran and others played down the more daring aspects of her designs (Zinkeisen, 1949, p. 2). She designed the costumes for a number of Wilcox/Neagle films: *Bitter Sweet* (1933), *Nell Gwyn* (1934), *The Queen's Affair* (1934) and *Peg of Old Drury* (1935). Her costumes intensify Neagle's sexuality, with little regard for historical verisimilitude. They do not construct a conventional femininity, but a feisty and possibly bisexual persona; Zinkeisen specialized in cross-dressing costumes (Laye, 1958, p. 141). Her designs were witty (the enormous hat in *Nell Gwyn*) and they made a real intervention in the narrative. Indeed, she was rumoured to have taken Neagle's image in hand and to have acted as her 'personality designer' until Herbert Wilcox objected.[1] It is interesting to surmise how the *Victoria* films would have been nuanced had Zinkeisen worked on them, but she left to do costume design in America in 1936.

During the war, more women moved into costume design. At Gainsborough, Elizabeth Haffenden designed all the studio's costume films. She had designed non-realist stage costumes before the war and, at Gainsborough, developed and intensified her style. Haffenden constructed a 'costume narrative' in the films which had its own autonomy and which works on a subliminal level. Characters in love (or about to be) are made to 'match' each other by having similar detailing on the clothes. Haffenden was rarely satisfied with historical verisimilitude; her costumes accentuated sexual difference, and were extraordinarily sumptuous, given the constraints of the war. Haffenden made women's bodies opulent and mysterious, both by the choice of cut and fabric and by the decoration. Margaret Lockwood's costumes in *The Wicked Lady*, for example, construct her as an outrageously sexual being, and the meaning inscribed in the costume goes far beyond that in the script. I have suggested elsewhere that Haffenden's costumes for *The Wicked Lady* deploy a vulval symbolism which is entirely in keeping with the audience and mood of the films. The costumes make repeated use of whorls, vortexes and pleats issuing from a hidden centre, which implicitly evoke the female body (Harper, 1994, pp. 130–1). These ensembles are displayed to the audience but concealed from the male protagonists in the film. In *Madonna of the Seven Moons* (1944), too, the gypsy ensembles, the Pierrot costumes, the fashion show, all carry a great deal of extra information which embellishes the script.

Yvonne Caffin worked as Haffenden's assistant, and she specialized in modern dress. Her designs, too, often led the character who wore them. In *They Were Sisters* (1945), for example, we can form an accurate assessment of the sisters' different characters from their clothes; we can judge Vera by the monstrous peplums which make her body seem open and hungry, as indeed she turns out to be. Similarly, the cut of the suits worn by Charlotte – skimpy, ill-conceived and with misplaced darts – tell us about her state of mind before she opens her mouth.

In the postwar period, women costume designers had varying creative freedoms. Beatrice Dawson worked for a range of companies, and many of her designs were audacious and expressive. Her work in *Trottie True* (1948), for example, took real risks with colour and historical verisimilitude. Other female costume designers remained at Gainsborough.

Elizabeth Haffenden continued her iconoclastic work in *Caravan* (1946). The Spanish and gypsy settings permitted her considerable latitude: the matador costume in particular, with its decorative scrollwork and curlicues framing the crotch of Richard (Stewart Granger) is a celebration of genital sexuality. However, Haffenden found the realist approach of Sydney Box antipathetic to her technique. On *The Bad Lord Byron* (1949) he sent Haffenden contemporary fashion plates to copy, hampering her creative improvisations. She was similarly constrained on *Jassy* (1948). Other women costume designers at Box's Gainsborough produced work which was consonant with the script and unable to challenge it. Caffin's work for *Dear Murderer* and *It's Not Cricket* (1949) was realist, and Joan Ellacott's designs for *Easy Money* (1948) took no risks at all. Only Julie Harris, who had been taken on as a junior to Haffenden during the war, managed to make some creative space in her inventive costume work for *Good Time Girl*, probably because the heroine's transgressive energy had to be signalled in as many non-verbal ways as possible.

In the 1950s, costume design began to be dominated by women. Julie Harris developed a specialism in elegant modern dress, and she was expert at predicting the staying power of new fashions (MacFarlane, 1997, p. 284). She valued tonal coherence, and co-operated closely with art directors.[2] Harris worked on sophisticated films like *Simon and Laura*, and also designed Diana Dors's costumes, including the mink (rabbit) bikini. Glamour wear was Harris's forte, and she devised an 'Alligator' dress for *An Alligator Named Daisy* (1955) with 'a scaly appearance, covered all over with different green-shaded sequins'.[3] Beatrice Dawson continued her flamboyant designs in period films. Her work on *The Importance of Being Earnest* is marvellously inventive. The first dress worn by Lady Bracknell (Edith Evans) gives an index to her character. It has garish colours, a girlish bolero, puffed sleeves and a sprig design – all deeply inappropriate for a dowager. Her costumes for *The Pickwick Papers* (1952) are designed with similar wit.

Other women costume designers were less combative in their style. Joan Ellacott's designs for Rank's *Man of the Moment* (1955) and *Campbell's Kingdom* were workaday. Neither Margaret Furse nor Yvonne Caffin responded creatively to script demands. Anna Duse, Sheila Graham and Doris Lee made forays from theatrical costuming. The most interesting newcomer was Jocelyn Rickards, who was an avant-garde painter and stage designer and created the costumes for *Look Back in Anger* (1959). Unusually, Rickards trusted actresses' instinct for appropriate clothes – Edith Evans was given her sartorial head as Ma Tanner – and she articulated expressionist principles with great flair:

> Designing clothes or costumes for films is not a self-serving device to make the audience stop and wonder at the beauty of your invention; it is rather a means of conveying by a visual signpost the background of each character. If clothes are well designed, they are probably unnoticeable, but should carry within them a number of messages, like what kind of school the character went to, what newspapers he or she reads, what political affiliations he has, what his sexual inclinations are, whether or not his financial position is secure – and if insecure whether or not he cares. All this saves valuable minutes of screen time by getting points across through the eyes rather than verbally. The same rule applies to sets. (Rickards, 1987, p. 58)

By the 1960s, women's dominance of costume design was complete. The old guard was still present: Joan Ellacott continued realist work as before, but could only get films which offered little design opportunity. She left film for television in 1964, where she worked on *The Forsyte Saga*. Yvonne Caffin, who had designed innovative costumes in the 1950s, could only obtain *Doctor* and *Carry On* work, and ceased costume design in 1965. Margaret Furse's designs for *Sons and Lovers* (1960) and *Kidnapped* (1960) were lacklustre. Other experienced designers had better luck. Beatrice Dawson had developed a precise design manner, and continued this in the 1960s. Her work on *The Servant* (1963) was an intelligent interpretation of Losey's definitions of class, and her stylish designs on *Modesty Blaise* (1966) were the only successful aspect of the film. Julie Harris, who had done such inventive colour work in the 1950s, worked best for production designers and directors who were more concerned with mood than action (MacFarlane, 1997, p. 287). Harris always had an excellent sense of how far fashion parody could be pushed, and her work on *A Hard Day's Night* (1964), *Help!* (1965) and *Casino Royale* (1967) was witty. She won an Oscar for the costumes in *Darling* (1965), which exactly catch the heroine's insecurity and eye for style.

Other, younger costume designers were coming into their own, and without exception their work was experimental and anti-realist. Phyllis Dalton designed *Lawrence of Arabia* (1962), *Becket* (1964), *Doctor Zhivago* (1965) and *Oliver!* (1968), and all her period work took small details and amplified them until they dominated the ensemble. Dalton had a brainwave for *Lawrence*: when the Arabs first give Lawrence native robes, they are of ordinary thickness. As he declines into self-obsession, the robes become increasingly flimsy; by the onset of his power mania, the robes are so gossamer-thin that he looks ghostlike (Brownlow, 1997, p. 471). Other younger designers were inventive too. Yvonne Blake, in her work on *Duffy* (1968) and *The Best House in London* (1968), combined flamboyant sexual symbolism with historical authenticity, as did Shirley Russell in *Women in Love* (1969) and *The Music Lovers* (1970). Emma Porteous began an innovatory career with *Entertaining Mr Sloane* (1970). The costumes were humorous: Kath's transparent frock and matching beads, Mr Sloane's tight leather ensemble, Eddy's open-backed driving gloves, even Dadda's rheumy muffler, all spoke volumes.

The most impressive costume portfolio in the 1960s was undoubtedly Jocelyn Rickards's, whose connections with the intellectual avant-garde were very productive. Her credit list included *From Russia With Love* (1963), *The Knack* (1965), *Morgan – A Suitable Case for Treatment*, *The Rattle of a Simple Man*, *Blow-up* (1967) and many others. Rickards instinctively understood artistic innovation, and was happy to work on *The Knack*, in which the style 'was scrupulously visually controlled . . . nothing was used but black, white and a variety of greys' (Rickards, 1987, p. 83). She was primarily an interpreter of the inner actor. On *Morgan*, she dressed and coached Vanessa Redgrave until she had self-confidence:

> To be able to give someone an awareness of their own beauty is like giving them a present . . . I believe too that those who aren't beautiful can be taught to assume beauty at will if they are given enough confidence. (*ibid.*, p. 86)

Rickards's work for *Alfred the Great* (1969) was especially striking. The costumes were imaginatively researched and colour-coded, and Rickards experimented with different dyes and camera filters. The effect was superb, and her work on *Alfred* was the major costume achievement of the decade. Only her work on *Ryan's Daughter* (1970) could challenge it – daring, meticulous, passionate.

The 1970s offered major opportunities for women in mainstream costume design. Some older hands continued into the new decade: Beatrice Dawson did less innovatory work than before in *Zee and Co.* (1971) and *A Doll's House* (1973); Jocelyn Rickards designed the clothes for *Sunday, Bloody Sunday* (1971), although the work was less risk-taking than before; Phyllis Dalton was unable to find challenging projects, and she designed for workaday films such as *Voyage of the Damned* (1976). Designers who had begun in the late 1960s moved into the mature stage of their career: Yvonne Blake began to specialize in historical costume with such films as *Nicholas and Alexandra* (1971), though her work was less exciting than that of Emma Porteous, who worked equally in Britain and America throughout this and the next decade. Porteous's work in the 1970s was both economical and stylish, and her designs for *Swallows and Amazons* (1974) and *The Lady Vanishes* (1979) were marvels of succinctness. However, it is instructive to compare her American with her British designs in this period. *The Island of Dr Moreau* (1977) and *Clash of the Titans* (1981) were made by American majors, and Porteous had both the latitude and the funds to permit daring and ground-breaking designs. Porteous later went on to do remarkable work in America on *Aliens* (1986) and other films: her growing interest in the body as armour could not be accommodated in a British context.[4]

We can conclude that the British industry of the 1970s did not serve female costume designers well if they were disinclined to realism. Shirley Russell was one exception. Her career was intercalated by family matters: 'I couldn't do *Isadora* because I was at the end of a pregnancy, and I didn't do *Rousseau* because the last child was a babe in arms.' She designed the clothes for husband Ken Russell's films, and much of their visual flair should be attributed to her. Shirley Russell developed a liking in the 1970s for what she called 'fantasticated gear'. In *Lisztomania* (1975), for example, she designed Roger Daltrey a jacket with huge lapels featuring keyboard motifs, to be worn over a bare chest. She dressed one of the female protagonists in a Mary Pickford dress with huge matching bloomers.[5] Russell was one of the most imaginative costume designers of the period, as her work for *Savage Messiah* (1972) attests. She always pushed against the limitations of the script.

By the 1980s, there were no male costume designers operating. Some established women continued their costume careers: Emma Porteous divided her time between British and American productions, and developed her flamboyant style in *Octopussy* (1983) and *A View to a Kill* (1985); Phyllis Dalton worked on less ambitious projects, which afforded less space for manoeuvre, such as *The Mirror Crack'd* (1980) and *A Private Function* (1984). In these films, costume facsimiles of the period were required, rather than freewheeling reinterpretation. Shirley Russell chose large projects which did not permit much space for costume innovation, such as *Hope and Glory* (1987) and the American *Reds* (1981).

But more importantly, the 1980s saw the rise of a new school of costume designers, who responded in a dynamic way to contemporary styles. Cathy Cook designed the clothes for *Sid and Nancy* (1986) and *Rita, Sue and Bob Too*, and all her work showed a witty awareness of the minutiae of fashion, and its relationship to class. Monica Howe, with her low-key work for *Britannia Hospital* (1983) and *Distant Voices, Still Lives*, was able to empathize with the script and direction to an unusual extent. Jane Robinson, too, wanted to avoid costumes 'which function in a noisy way'. She had designed *Brideshead Revisited* for television in 1981, and then *Dreamchild, A Handful of Dust* (1987) and *Scandal* (1988). She wanted her clothes to relate closely to the script: 'It's not a matter of whether the costumes are better, it's whether they take their rightful place in the piece as a whole.'[6] Robinson lacked formal training, but worked at making the clothes part of the ensemble: 'I read the piece, talk to the cast, the producer, the director, absorb it all like a computer, combine it with any artistic knowledge I may have, and produce the results with a team of people whose work, again, I know well.'[7]

Sandy Powell had a varied career in costume design, which encompassed stage work for Lindsay Kemp and La Scala. In film, Powell worked best for avant-garde directors who encouraged her flair for visual excess. Her work in *Caravaggio* and other Jarman films concentrated on one detail or feature, which was then expanded to dominate the costume ensemble as a whole. Powell's wonderful work on *Orlando* was more subtle, and combined a scholarly knowledge of period with a slyly satirical take on the gender politics of each one.[8]

Perhaps the most important of the designers for contemporary projects was Lindy Hemming, who did *Wetherby* (1985), *My Beautiful Laundrette* and *High Hopes* (1988). Hemming was primarily interested in the way clothes can signal social mobility and status. *High Hopes* is particularly inventive – the Thatcherites' shooting gear, Valerie's leotard and hats, Wayne's trainers – but Hemming later abandoned this kind of work for the more expressionist designs of *Goldeneye* (1993) and *Tomorrow Never Dies* (1997). Sue Blane was another designer whose clothes showed a sophisticated awareness of fashion resonance. With *The Rocky Horror Show* (1975), Blane had made a crucial input into punk and Gothic fashion. Her work for *The Draughtsman's Contract* (1982) pushed postmodernist stylization to its furthest limits, and in *Absolute Beginners* (1986) and *Dream Demon* (1988) she extended her range into modern and surreal material.

Other women worked mainly in period designs. Judy Moorcroft was responsible for the clothes in *Quartet* and *Passage to India* (1984).[9] Jenny Beaven did *Jane Austen in Manhattan* (1980), *The Bostonians*, *Room with a View* and *Maurice*. Neither of these two designers produced stylized work. The push to costume verisimilitude came strongly from Lean and the Merchant–Ivory team, and the clothes from both designers contributed to the surface interest of the period without intervening in the narrative.

The history of women's costume design is clearly one of gradual progression, moving from a marginal position in the industry to absolute dominance. Costume design in British films was of a quality and inventiveness unparalleled by other national cinemas. With some exceptions, female costume designers made clothes *work* very hard in the films, and they excelled in pushing verisimilitude beyond its limits. From the 1940s, the best costume designs by women deployed the resources of texture and cut to the full, and the most adventurous ones ushered the viewer into a world in which the important emotions – desire, rage, insecurity – could be subliminally expressed. Although I do not wish to take the 'subversive stitch' argument completely on board, it is clear that the female costume designers were often making implicit claims for the autonomy of the discourse encoded in their practice. In their work, more of them took issue with the script, or interpreted it in a loose and creative way, than those who remained constrained by it.

Notes

1. Zinkeisen's obituary in the *Guardian*, 3 January 1991.
2. *Films and Filming*, November 1957.
3. *Picturegoer*, 28 January 1956.

4. See interviews with Porteous in the *Starburst* yearbook for 1995, and *Starburst*, October 1994. Porteous also became interested in tattoos and piercing as part of her costume repertoire.
5. All quotes in this paragraph are from an interview with Shirley Russell, *Films and Filming*, October 1977.
6. *Broadcast*, 2 April 1982.
7. *Ibid*. Other important costume designers of the period were Frances Hoggett, who did *The Strike* (1988), Ann Hollowood, who did *Mr Love* and *Vroom* (1988), and Hilary Buckley, who did *The Magic Toyshop* (1986).
8. For an interview on *Caravaggio* with Powell and production designer Christopher Hobbs, see *City Limits*, 24 April 1986.
9. See *Screen International*, 10 January 1992, for material on Moorcroft.

12

Art Directors

The art director is the person responsible for the overall 'look' of a film. It is his or her responsibility to structure the visual experience of the audience by organizing perspective and proportion, and by dressing sets so as to evoke maximum pleasure or narrative significance. The art director's job is uniquely one which combines intellectual and manual labour: he or she must conceive the whole, and then organize a wide range of technical personnel so as to realize the concept. As a profession, therefore, it relies as much on confidence, assertiveness and bloody-mindedness as it does on creative juice. Of all the careers in the film industry, it is the one which is most difficult to combine with childcare and family life. It calls for long hours, with much set preparation for the next day being undertaken after close of play. Location work and night-time construction are common practice, as are recce expeditions at short notice.

In the 1930s the centre stage in British art direction had been captured by flamboyant, innovative (and mainly foreign) male designers, such as Vincent Korda, Alfred Junge and Erno Metzner. It was almost impossible for women to find a niche. Gladys Calthrop made some forays into film which were largely influenced by her work in theatrical design.[1] Carmen Dillon began her career in 1934 as Ralph Brinton's assistant at the Fox Studios at Wembley. She had met Brinton while training as an architect. When he fell ill she took over the work for *£5 Man* in 1937, and she subsequently had design credits for *The Claydon Treasure Mystery* (1937), *Father O'Nine* (1938), *The Last Barricade* (1938) and others. She made the first of her collaborations with Paul Sherriff in *French without Tears* in 1939.[2]

Dillon worked under some unusual constraints at Wembley. She was not allowed to wear trousers, order anyone around or even go on set.[3]

Not surprisingly, her professional development was hampered. It is difficult to assess Dillon's 1930s work, since most of it was collaborative and some of it belonged to the quota category and is not documented. Interviews with her suggest that she viewed her films in this period as journeyman or apprentice work.[4] Certainly, her sets rarely have a narrative function and they are generally unobtrusive and unenterprising; Dillon had neither the temperament nor the studio resources to challenge the prevailing European influences in British art direction.

During the war, women art directors worked on bigger projects. Olga Lehmann, who was an outstanding painter, worked as a scenic artist, set designer and occasional costume worker.[5] Gladys Calthrop was formally designated 'Art Supervisor' to her friend Noël Coward. At this stage in her career, she was also writing some very sexually 'advanced' novels (Calthrop, 1940). She worked on *In Which We Serve* (1942) (the domestic scenes), *Blithe Spirit* (1945) and *This Happy Breed* (1944), but there were severe tensions between her and the 'official' art directors, and it is impossible to distinguish her work.[6] Carmen Dillon consolidated her position as art director during the war, and had two women assistants, Iris Wills and Colleen Browning. Dillon was contracted to Two Cities, and throughout her time there worked with Paul Sherriff, who had precedence over her. It is difficult to distinguish her work from his. Sherriff appears to have had a more flamboyant personality (Carrick, 1948, pp. 114–15). All Dillon's interviews in the studio's publicity material and the BECTU archive suggest that she, on the other hand, was a reticent and unassuming character. The art work in most of their joint films is not expressive. *The Gentle Sex* (1943) and *The Way to the Stars* (1945) are visually unremarkable: the sets are predictable and the set-dressing is uninspired. *The Demi-Paradise* (1943) misses some excellent design opportunities: both the carnival and the industrial settings are unimaginatively conceived. *Henry V* (1945), on which both Sherriff and Dillon worked, was a different case. Its most innovative scenes from a design point of view are those set in France, which quote *Les Très Riches Heures du Duc de Berri* and duplicate a medieval sense of perspective and colour. Audaciously unrealistic, their design throws into question the relationship between the viewer and three-dimensional space. Attribution of these scenes is fiercely contested. Laurence Olivier claimed in his autobiography that it was his idea to use the manuscripts, but an exchange of letters between him and writer Terence Young suggests that

Roger Furse, *Henry V*'s costume designer, first had the idea (Spoto, 1991, p. 215). However, Dillon, in an unusually assertive interview, also claimed authorship of the scenes: 'In *Henry V*, it was my idea to do it that way, with the French court looking so unrealistic . . . it was very exciting, very bold and daring. I wasn't responsible for the Globe Theatre beginning' (MacFarlane, 1997, p. 178). She makes the same claim in the BECTU interviews.

In the postwar industry, few women were working in art direction. Angela Tremayne and Susan King-Clark did some apprenticeship work, and Olga Lehmann worked briefly for Columbia-British. Betty Pierce, who was a trained architect, worked as assistant to Roger Furse at Two Cities. Pierce is important because, although there is no extant material about her design work, she wrote a series of polemical articles about her craft, in which she insisted on its financial and industrial rigours, and the necessity of a sense of space and proportion. She also provided details about Two Cities design practice which are unavailable elsewhere.[7]

Carmen Dillon was under contract to Two Cities, and was the only women art director with a major portfolio. Dillon detested too structured an environment, and disliked storyboards; the ad hoc arrangements at Two Cities suited her (MacFarlane, 1997, p. 178). For *Hamlet* (1948), Dillon was working in tandem with Roger Furse, who, as production designer, took precedence over her. And in any case, the production was dominated by Laurence Olivier, who permitted little room for artistic manoeuvre (Spoto, 1991, p. 268). The sets of *Hamlet* differ from Dillon's other work, as both Olivier and Furse wanted a stripped and economical look. The challenges Dillon faced were technical rather than artistic: she merely had to make sure that sections interlocked, and that huge cantilevers worked properly.[8] Olivier wanted attention drawn to the emotional dynamics of the play, and he preferred depth of focus in order to force attention onto the faces rather than the sets.

Dillon's other postwar work was uninspired. Her designs for *Vice Versa* (1948) were fussy, and the Indian scenes, in particular, show signs of carelessness. *Cardboard Cavalier* (1949) was an appalling Cromwellian farrago starring Sid Field, but even here Dillon did not let rip: 'I'd have liked to take the opportunity of doing something quite dotty in the sets. Actually we kept them quite authentic.'[9] And indeed the sets are lacklustre. Dillon, like many other women at the sharp end of film production, lacked the clout or the status to break through to a higher level of practice.

In the 1950s, women found it impossible to combine art direction with family life. Hazel Peiser was employed on a casual basis by Rank, but found it difficult to get big projects (Muir, 1987, p. 244). Peggy Gick did not wish to leave two small children to work in the studios, but did some title design and small projects at home.[10] Eileen Diss, although partly trained as an architect, could not leave her children either, and was unable to get freelance film work.[11] Olga Lehmann found it difficult to secure projects, and, apart from her work on *Laughter in Paradise*, did little in Britain and moved to Hollywood.[12] So Carmen Dillon was once again the main woman art director. In her 1950s work, she rarely exploited the full potential of 'getting points across through the eyes', as described by Rickards, and was easily dominated by producers. The sets of *Richard III* (1956) are florid without being interesting, and those of *The Importance of Being Earnest* replicate theatrical space in an unimaginative way. Dillon's work on *Doctor in the House* was blandly realistic: 'a film of contemporary life should take place against familiar backgrounds with realism its most important impact'.[13] *A Tale of Two Cities* is the only film in which she attempted a degree of stylistic autonomy, and it was the only film of which she was ashamed (MacFarlane, 1997, p. 178).

In the 1960s, Dillon was still the only woman doing any significant work. Peggy Gick designed *The Vengeance of Fu Manchu* (1967) and a few others, but left for television. Ken Russell brought in women designers from abroad. Dillon designed two *Carry Ons*, at what she called 'rather a low ebb' in her career.[14] The high point of her work in this period was doubtless on *Accident* (1967) and *The Go-Between* (1970). But Dillon was not Losey's first choice. He had a stormy relationship with his regular production designer Richard MacDonald. Occasionally, they would be temperamentally at odds in their collaborative 'pre-design' work, and would separate temporarily (Ciment, 1985, p. 161). They worked together for all Losey's 1960s films except *Accident* and *The Go-Between*, and Dillon was co-opted to fill the gap. MacDonald's work was always extremely rich visually, while Dillon's was not. Of all Losey's 1960s films, those designed by Dillon are the ones most dependent on the sense of a 'real' place. Stephen's home in *Accident* is inexpressive; it is the bodies and faces which carry information. *The Go-Between* is (for Losey) unusually obsessed with verisimilitude. He seems to have used Dillon primarily as a set-dresser, acquiring the correct objects and period patina (*ibid.*, p. 312). So Losey valued Dillon not for what she could do, but for who she was not.

The 1970s saw the end of the careers of older workers: Peggy Gick with *Kadoyng!* (1972) and Carmen Dillon with such films as *Lady Caroline Lamb* (1972). Dillon ended her career in America with *The Omen* (1976), whose neutral and unimaginative décor was typical of her later work. While the 1970s were a bleak period for women art directors, the 1980s witnessed a marked increase in women designers, many of whom used their skills in both film and television. Anne Tilby, for example, designed *The Lair of the White Worm* (1988) and *Paperhouse* (1988), then moved to television work. Charmian Adams was art director for *Stormy Monday* (1987) and *Queen and Country* (1988), then did remarkable work for television, including *Anglo-Saxon Attitudes* in 1992. Gemma Jackson designed *Doll's Eye* (1982), *Mona Lisa* (1986) and *Friendship's Death* (1987), then migrated to television. Jocelyn James designed *On the Black Hill* and *Distant Voices, Still Lives* and then went to the small screen. Sometimes the move went in reverse. Eileen Diss, who developed a major design career in television, also did film work such as *A Handful of Dust*. Interestingly, all those who designed for both film and television tended to produce sets which were subordinate to the narrative, rather than making claims for visual autonomy. In a sense, Diss spoke for them all when she insisted that the sets should be 'based first on the period ... then on the character of whoever is in them'.[15]

The rest of the women who remained in film art direction in the 1980s tended to specialize in more inventive set design: Marianne Ford, for example, who did *Dreamchild*, which was extraordinarily imaginative, and *White Mischief* (1987). More importantly, most of them were promoted to production designer, which was a job with far higher status and artistic autonomy (male art directors, of course, had been able to progress to production designer since the 1940s). Lucy Morahan had been the scenic artist for Jarman's *Caravaggio*, and she was production designer for his *War Requiem* (1988); her designs were confident and magisterial. Adrienne Atkinson did very refined, inventive work for *Gregory's Girl* (1980) and *Local Hero* (1983); she then operated as production designer for *Comfort and Joy* (1984) and *Killing Dad* (1989), which both deployed a witty sense of play with contemporary styles.

Diana Charnley's career was similarly structured. She designed *Defence of the Realm* and *Clockwise*, and then worked as production designer for *Short and Curlies* (1987) and *High Hopes*. Her work in the latter had a marvellously light touch, and swung between verisimilitude and satire: the sets for Valerie's lounge and Letitia's 'den' were composed with real visual flair.

Undoubtedly, Luciana Arrighi had the highest profile in this field. An Australian who trained in Britain,[16] she was production and costume designer for *Privates on Parade* (1982), *The Ploughman's Lunch* (1983), *Madame Sousatzka* and *The Rainbow* (1988). Arrighi's designs for all these films were a skilled combination of period verisimilitude and audacious stylization. She took great care to match the clothes to the textures and tones of sets, and aimed to achieve a totally composed film. Unfortunately, the projects she was offered were insufficiently challenging. With hindsight *The Ploughman's Lunch* seems a sour film unable to transcend its own period, *Madame Sousatska* seems a quirky prefiguration of *Shine*, and *The Rainbow* was Russell's sad swansong.

Arrighi mainly worked in America after 1988, ostensibly because Britain did not encourage the kind of hands-on work ('picking up a hammer') which she preferred. But her creative work was a significant high-water mark, and is accompanied by some trenchant critical writing which redraws the boundaries of art direction. As early as 1979, she insisted that art direction as a career be superseded by production design, which

> starts at the embryonic stage, when the script is being written; it is then that the visual ideas can be formed before the production begins. During these early stages, a designer also helps with the costing, by suggesting the way people should look; by consulting with the director and the director of photography on the colour schemes to be used ... a production designer will then design for the sets, costumes, hair and make-up, or at least establish the style of these before they are taken over by the individual members of each department ... a production designer is responsible for the whole visual concept, and the art direction is the practical application of design concepts.[17]

In the period, this was the most radical claim to be made for artistic autonomy by a practising designer.

227

In general, women made only a minor input into art direction until the 1980s. Until then, the structure of the industry militated against them, and the job itself was too intractable to combine with traditional feminine roles. Carmen Dillon was the only women to achieve a major career, and her work was artistically dull. The entrepreneurialism of the 1980s was productive for women designers, but one suspects that they were also liberated by the newer, flexible attitudes to family life.

Notes

1. There is a range of material on Calthrop in Hoare (1995).
2. See *Focus on Film*, Spring 1973, p. 20. There is a complete credit list in MacFarlane (1997).
3. Catherine de la Roche, 'The stars behind the camera: Carmen Dillon', *Picturegoer*, 16 July 1949.
4. BECTU interviews with Dillon (1993 and 1994).
5. She worked with Holmes Paul and Wilfred Arnold at British National.
6. L. Ede, 'The Role of the Art Director in British Films 1939–51', PhD thesis, University of Portsmouth, 1999, pp. 47–8.
7. Betty Pierce, 'The art director', *Official Architect*, September 1950; 'The drawing office', *ibid.*, October 1950; 'Construction and materials', *ibid.*, November 1950. There is very useful material in a paper published by the Kinematograph Section of the Royal Photographic Society of Great Britain called *Women Talking: A Symposium on the Part Played by Women Technicians in Film Production* (London: 1947).
8. *Picturegoer*, 16 July 1949.
9. *Ibid.*
10. BECTU interview with Peggy Gick.
11. BECTU interview with Eileen Diss.
12. Lehmann's career in this period and subsequently is fascinating. She worked on sets and costumes for *tom thumb* (1959), *The Guns of Navarone* (1963) and many other Hollywood films. She continued her excellent portraiture work, and did the oil paintings of Charlton Heston and Barbara Stanwyck which played such an important role in *Dallas*. As the *Sunday Times Magazine* noted on 2 March 1986, 'millions of people know her work; hardly anyone knows her name'. From the evidence of an exhibition containing some of her work at the Fry Art Gallery in Saffron Waldon in 1998, her style was extraordinarily vibrant.
13. *Films and Filming*, May 1957.
14. BECTU interview with Carmen Dillon.
15. *TV Times*, 13 April 1991. See also *Broadcast*, 11 August 1975, for her earlier career.
16. Arrighi had worked in theatre in Sydney, and did design training at the BBC, where she met Ken Russell. She subsequently designed his programmes on Rousseau and Rossetti. She later worked with Gillian Armstrong on *My Brilliant Career* (1979).
17. *Cinema Papers*, July/August 1979.

13

Editors

The editor has a crucial input into the flow of the film narrative. A mediocre editor can make a film sluggish; a skilled one can give it rhythm and form. The editor's freedom of creative manoeuvre depends on the director and cameraman – on whether the film has been shot with an eye to controlling the editing process. All a film editor needs is competence with the Moviola and a sense of narrative pace and form. That sounds simple, but in fact the editor can make or break a film, both artistically and at the box-office.

In the 1930s, opportunities for female editors were sparse. Vera Campbell and Thelma Connell had a limited presence, and were beginning their own training. Campbell was treated quite differently from male editorial assistants, and her experience was limited by it (Brownlow, 1997, pp. 86, 103–4). Alma Reville was unique in combining cutting with other film work.[1] The war period offered slim pickings to women editors also, with only Vera Campbell editing her first film, *Yellow Canary* (1943). In the postwar period, women editors had more work, and performed competently rather than creatively. Vera Campbell's editing on *The Courtneys of Curzon Street* and others was unobtrusive and in keeping with director/producer behests. Jean Barker did some very smooth editing on *Quartet* and *The Calendar* (1948), and Monica Kimmick produced some tight cutting sequences in *No Place for Jennifer* (1949). Barker and Kimmick worked together on *Lisbon Story* (1946), in an unusual collaborative arrangement. More women were engaged at a junior level – Helga Cranston, Flora Newton, Marjorie Saunders and others. Indeed, the increase in female editors was the subject of an article in *Good Housekeeping*.[2]

In the 1950s, editing was well populated by women, and the quality of their work improved. Vera Campbell did excellent work in the American-financed *They Were Not Divided* (1950), but her career trailed off into low-status vehicles. Jean Barker too was a skilled worker, and was Muriel Box's favoured editor. Her work on *The Happy Family*, *The Beachcomber* and *Simon and Laura* was creative and slick. Box's other editor was Anne Coates, who had a full curriculum including excellent work on *The Pickwick Papers*.[3] Monica Kimmick did solid editing for ABPC, as did Carmen Belaieff. Thelma Connell edited *The Belles of St Trinian's* (1954) and others, and Joan Warwick worked as assistant editor on the Lee Thompson films at ABPC. Connie Mason worked as a dubbing editor.[4]

Women were unevenly represented in 1960s film editing. Some were lost to television – Joan Warwick, for example – and Monica Kimmick moved into advertising and children's films. Jean Barker only edited two films in the early part of the decade. Noreen Ackland gained her first solo editing credit on *Peeping Tom* (1960) and *The Queen's Guards* (1961), although she had been working as editorial assistant for Powell since 1948. Thelma Connell worked on a range of projects. Early in the decade she specialized in comedies such *The Amorous Prawn* (1962), in which her fast cutting style worked well. She later moved on to bigger projects like *Alfie* (1966) and *You Only Live Twice* (1967). Connell was always a no-nonsense editor with a preference for unproblematical narrative structures.[5] She provided a strong contrast with Anne Coates, an inventive editor who won an Oscar for her work on *Lawrence of Arabia*.

Coates was Rank's niece, and had an impressive career in the 1960s, editing *Becket*, *Hotel Paradiso* (1966) and others. Colleagues were initially suspicious that she was a spy for Uncle. This made her unusually self-effacing, but she soon won professional respect. Initially, Coates wished to direct, but family life inhibited a directorial career: 'It was the children that stopped my directing ... being a woman did curtail my ambitions. My children were more important than movies, and I didn't do location work while they were at school.'[6] Editing was domestically more convenient.

Coates had a rigorous understanding of the editor's craft:

> You need a lot of rhythm and a lot of timing and a dramatic kind of feeling for situations and a lot of emotion, I think, which is a thing that people lack in editing sometimes. They don't cut with enough emotion. (Muir, 1987, p. 106)

Her cutting style was buccaneering: wild, adventurous and unpredictable. She learned a great deal from David Lean, of course, but only seemed to defer to him while following her own narrative head (Brownlow, 1997, pp. 470–1). Women editors had slimmer pickings in the 1970s. The old guard continued – Anne Coates with *Murder on the Orient Express*, *The Eagle Has Landed* (1976) and others, and Thelma Connell with such films as *Endless Night* (1972) and *Call of the Wild* (1973). However, there were few mainstream film editors to replace them. Some worked on children's films – Monica Mead, Ann Chegwidden – but most newcomers worked on films with an avant-garde flavour. The 'invisible mending' practised by mainstream women editors gave way to a more explicit style, in which the rents in the film garment are part of the deconstructive meaning of the texts. The work of Lesley Walker, in *Portrait of the Artist as a Young Man* (1977) and *The Tempest* (1980), is part of that process, as is that of Sarah Ellis in *Winstanley* (1977), in which the editing is explicit and deliberately 'rough'.

Anne Coates achieved even greater status in the 1980s, working on big projects in both Britain and America: *Elephant Man* (1980) and *Greystoke* (1984), for example. Throughout the 1980s, Coates deployed the flamboyant cutting style which had become her trademark. Other, younger editors found it difficult to break into higher-status films, but some managed it: Katherine Wenning with *The Bostonians*, for example. Lesley Walker developed a snappy and fast editing style throughout the decade, with *A Letter to Brezhnev* (1985), *Mona Lisa*, *Cry Freedom* (1987) and *Shirley Valentine* (1989). Some editors, such as Judy Seymour and Nadine Marsh-Edwards, specialized in independent black cinema. But there were increasing obstacles in the path of women editors, one of which was the increasing tendency for women directors to edit their own work.

In general, women's editing careers peaked in the 1950s and 1960s. Anne Coates was a major presence, and her work was more flamboyant than any of the other women editors. Women encountered less outright prejudice in editing than in other technical fields. Muriel Box's BECTU interview is instructive here. Box recalls that she always employed female editors where she could, because otherwise 'you could be absolutely certain that the man will get the job with equal qualifications', whereupon interviewer Sid Cole suggests that women are good editors because they are 'naturally adept at it'. Editing in this light merely requires dextrous fingers, the smaller the better.

But more is at stake. In general, female editors tend to cut on *mood* rather than on action. This makes their films run more slowly, but with greater attention to emotional nuance. The films of Anne Coates and many other female editors are like this, and they are good at respecting expertly timed performances by actors and actresses, rather than truncating them. They are qualitatively different from the styles of male editors, who are more businesslike. The practice of editing is a last and salutary reminder of the gender differences in film work.

Notes

1. Interview with Alma Reville, *Sight and Sound*, Autumn 1976.
2. See an article by Catherine de la Roche in *Good Housekeeping*, June 1947.
3. See *Hollywood Reporter*, 19 March 1996, and *Films Illustrated*, July 1977, for interviews with Coates about this period.
4. For Kimmick, see *Film and TV Technician*, November 1982. For Connell, see *ibid.*, June 1976. For general points on the situation of women editors in this period, see interview with Kitty Wood in the BECTU archive.
5. See *Film and TV Technician*, June 1976.
6. BECTU interview with Ann Coates. Her comments on children are amplified in Muir (1987), p. 107: 'If one of the children was ill, and I went in a couple of hours later, it didn't really matter'.

Conclusion

I had not intended such a radical and enraged book. On reading it over again, it seems to have rather a buccaneering tone – the writings of a female Samson, laying about her enemies with the jawbone of an ass. Perhaps, instead of dedicating it to my mild and oppressed grandmother, I should have dedicated it to the Goddess Kali – the Angry One, Her-Without-Bounds. With her sharp teeth and her laughter, Kali could have exacted her revenge.

But after all, good history must be written with passion. The trick is to balance one's grief for the past with gratitude that parts of it, at least, can be recovered. There is all the difference in the world between settling old scores and redressing the balance. I have tried to do the latter – to restore to film history a sense of the 'dark side of the moon'. This book has so far charted two separate histories. Part I dealt with the way in which women have appeared in film texts, and I hope I have established once and for all the *historically specific* nature of sexual/social fantasy, in British film culture at any rate. Women, like any other group (men, the bourgeoisie, dogs) are a commodity whose image is fashioned according to the requirements of the market. Their function in film is determined by the cultural capital of the person or persons who have won the important battles during production. Sometimes, too, the image of social groups is testament to the misapprehensions or hamfistedness of the 'masters' of the text.

What I hope has emerged is the amazing variety of the forms which women doff and assume. Under certain industrial conditions, they will emerge as a variation of the Monstrous-Feminine; under others, they will be resolute and doughty. Sometimes they are just required to simper and be grateful. It is now clear that, for innovative images of women to emerge, a degree of industrial chaos is necessary. In the 1930s, as a consequence of the 1927 Cinematograph Films Act, the entrepreneurial-ism of the British film industry permitted some film-makers and scriptwriters to take real risks with their female subject matter. It was the same in the 1950s, when the big three distributors (Rank, ABPC, British Lion) were so complex and unwieldy that there were many textual gaps through which iconoclasts could wriggle. But only chaos of a certain type is conducive to new imagery. My analysis of the period from the mid-1960s has shown that when economic crisis is combined with widespread loss of cultural nerve, it is very difficult for film-makers to do anything but take the line of least resistance. Dijkstra suggested that there are specific periods in culture when it is anti-feminine – when there is 'a war largely fought out on the battlefield of words and images' (Dijkstra, 1986, p. vii). It now looks as though mainstream British cinema began its 'anti-feminine' phase with the New Wave, and ended it with Goldcrest Films.

Part II tried to draw the map of female creativity in certain film professions, and to sketch some of the constraints it encountered. I was frankly astonished at what I found. The *unevenness* of development in the different professions, the paucity of some achievements and the heroic nature of others, was remarkable. What has been evident in all the women's work I uncovered was the unquenchable nature of their creativity. To be sure, a few were merely earning a crust between children or parties: some of the 1930s screenwriters, perhaps. But for the most part, what shone through was that if women's creative drive was dammed in some areas, it did not dry up. It simply rerouted itself, and found or made other channels – sometimes a little runnel, sometimes a great river.

But with difficulty. We must not underestimate the problems women experienced in what has always been a male-dominated industry. The only time they found it *relatively* easy was during World War II. This was not due to any goodwill by the producers, but because conscription was decimating the industry of male workers, and producers had to make do with what they could get. Otherwise, women had to struggle to find a foothold on what must sometimes have seemed an impervious rock-face.

Besides being artists, women also bear children. It is clear that certain film professions can be more easily combined with childcare. Editing or scriptwriting fall into this category, while art direction does not. But we must not allow notions of biological determinism (important though they are – try writing a sophisticated scene during a bout of Infant Thunder) to dominate overmuch. We certainly cannot account for the variety of editing or scriptwriting styles in this way. No, women's relationship to film culture in Britain is predicated on their canny recognition of gaps or absences in mainstream practice. Perhaps it is the first time that the notion of the Lack has been really useful.

It would seem that women producers could only flourish under two sets of circumstances: when a flexible studio system was combined with family connections (Betty Box in the 1940s), or when parlous circumstances forced male producers to leave in droves (the 1970s). Apart from the exceptional Wendy Toye and Muriel Box, women only began to flourish as directors in the 1970s, when the mainstream industry was in a cultural pickle. Avant-garde women directors painstakingly unpicked the garment of film culture and fashioned it anew into something radical and exciting, whose consequences are still being worked through. Women writers, on the other hand, flowered during the 1930s and the 1950s, when the informality of the one period and the chaos of the other favoured them. What we must notice is that those two periods are the very ones in which innovative representations of women occurred. It seems very likely that the women writers had a major input into that process.

Other film professions had an improving trajectory, instead of a dying fall. Women art directors became increasingly important, and women costume designers completely dominated the scene by the 1980s. It must fall to someone else to establish whether these improvements continued into the 1990s, or whether British film culture in the last ten years has substantially restructured its representation of women.

One thing is certain: a few women directors in the 1990s have moved into the mainstream. Gurindher Chadha's *Bhaji on the Beach* (1993), Christine Edzard's *As You Like It* (1992) and Sally Potter's *The Tango Lesson* (1997) have all taken major risks, and are films of such artistry that a cautious optimism is possible – always bearing in mind, of course, the lamentable contrast between what women film-makers have been able to achieve in Britain, compared to those in Europe and America.

But perhaps the conclusion should come to come to rest more positively, with the final scene in Potter's *Orlando*. In March 1993 in *Sight and Sound*, she wrote that she wanted to evoke

> a feeling of hope and empowerment about being alive and the possibility of change . . . I want people to feel humanly recognised, that their inner language of hope and desire and longing has found some kind of expression on screen.

Orlando sits in the shade of a great tree while her daughter runs about with a video camera, filming at random. The mother has a utopian vision of an earthly paradise without pain, jealousy or sexual difference, which is hymned by angel Jimmy Somerville. His song brings tears of joy to her eyes, which are filmed in grainy texture by the little girl. She asks, 'Why are you sad?' Whereupon Orlando, transformed by her vision, replies, 'I'm not, I'm happy.'

'I'm happy.'

That seems an appropriate place to stop. We are on a raft floating out into a new millennium: if ever there were a time when change is possible, it is now. John Dryden, when he wrote *A Secular Masque* in 1700, knew all about regret and hope. Let us leave the last word to him:

> All, all of a piece throughout;
> Thy chase had a beast in view;
> Thy wars brought nothing about;
> Thy lovers were all untrue.
> 'Tis well an old age is out,
> And time to begin a new.

Bibliography

Ackland, R. and Grant, E. (1954) *The Celluloid Mistress: Or the Custard Pie of Dr Caligari*. London: Allan Wingate.

ACTT (Association of Cine and Television Technicians) (1983) *ACTION! Fifty Years in the Life of a Union*. London: ACTT.

Aldgate, A. (1995) *Censorship and the Permissive Society: British Cinema and Theatre 1955–65*. Oxford: Clarendon Press.

Aldgate, A. (1998) 'Loose ends, hidden gems and the moment of "melodramatic emotionality" ', in J. Richards (ed.), *The Unknown 1930s: An Alternative History of British Cinema 1929–1939*. London: I. B. Tauris.

Aldgate, A. and Richards, J. (1986) *Britain Can Take It: The British Cinema in the Second World War*. Oxford: Blackwell.

Aspinall, S. and Murphy, R. (eds) (1983) *BFI Dossier 18: Gainsborough Melodrama*. London: BFI Publishing.

Attille, M. and Blackwood, M. (1986) 'Black women and representation', in C. Brunsdon (ed.), *Films for Women*. London: BFI Publishing.

Auty, M. (1985) 'But is it cinema?', in M. Auty and N. Roddick (eds), *British Cinema Now*. London: BFI Publishing.

Balcon, M. (1969) *Michael Balcon Presents . . . A Lifetime of Films*. London: Hutchinson.

Barber, S. T. (1993) 'The films of Stephen Frears', in L. Friedman (ed.), *British Cinema and Thatcherism: Fires Were Started*. London: UCL Press.

Bart, P. (1990) *Fade Out*. New York: Simon and Schuster.

Bartlett, J. (1940) *Political Propaganda*. Cambridge: Cambridge University Press.

Bergfelder, T. (1998) 'Negotiating exoticism: Hollywood, Film Europe and the reception of Anna May Wong', in R. Maltby and A. Higson (eds), *Film Europe and Film America: Cinema, Commerce and Cultural Exchange 1920–39*. Exeter: Exeter University Press.

Bergfelder, T. (1999) 'The Internationalisation of the German Film Industry in the 1960s.' University of East Anglia, unpublished PhD thesis.

Bogarde, D. (1979) *Snakes and Ladders*. London: Triad Grafton.

Bouchier, C. (1995) *Shooting Star: The Last of the Silent Film Stars*. London: Atlantis.

Bourne, S. (1996) *Brief Encounters: Gays and Lesbians in British Cinema*. London: Cassell.

Box, M. (1939) *The Truth about Women*. London: Muller.

Box, M. (1974) *Odd Woman Out*. London: Leslie Frewin.

Britton, A. (1991) *Talking Films*. London: Fourth Estate.

Brown, G. (1986) 'Bernard Vorhaus: a director rediscovered', *Sight and Sound* (Winter).

Brownlow, K. (1997) *David Lean*. London: Faber.

Brunsdon, C. (ed.) (1986) *Films for Women*. London: BFI Publishing.

Burton, A., O'Sullivan, T. and Wells, P. (eds) (1997) *Liberal Directions: Basil Dearden and Postwar British Film Culture*. London: Flicks Books.

Calthrop, G. (1940) *Paper Pattern*. London: Hamilton.

Cardiff, J. (1996) *Magic Hour*. London: Faber.

Carrick, E. (1948) *Art and Design in the British Film*. London: Dennis Dobson.

Carson, B. (1998) 'Comedy, sexuality and "Swinging London" films', *Journal of Popular British Cinema*, no. 1.

Carstairs, J. Paddy (1942) *Honest Injun! A Light-Hearted Autobiography*. London: Hurst and Blackett.

Chadder, V. (1999) 'The higher heel: women and the post-war British crime film', in S. Chibnall and R. Murphy (eds), *British Crime Cinema*. London: Routledge.

Chapman, J. (1999) *License to Thrill: A Cultural History of the James Bond Films*. London: I. B. Tauris.

Chin, T. (1988) *Daughter of Shanghai*. London: Chatto and Windus.

Churchill, S. (1981) *Keep on Dancing*. London: Weidenfeld.

Ciment, M. (1985) *Conversations with Losey*. London: Methuen.

Clarke, T. E. B. (1974) *This Is Where I Came In*. London: Michael Joseph.

Cochran, C. B. (1941) *Cock-A-Doodle-Doo*. London: Dent.

Cochran, C. B. (1945) *A Showman Looks On*. London: Dent.

Connolly, R. (1985) *Stardust Memories*. London: Pavilion.

Cook, P. (ed.) (1997) *Gainsborough Pictures*. London: Cassell.

Cotes, P. (1949) *No Star Nonsense*. London: Theatre Book Club.

Courtneidge, C. (1953) *Cicely*. London: Hutchinson.

Coveney, M. (1997) *The World According to Mike Leigh*. London: HarperCollins.

Cowie, E. (1980) 'The Song of the Shirt', *Camera Obscura*, no. 5.

Dane, C. (1917) *Regiment of Women*. London: Heinemann.

Dane, C. (1935a) *Moonlight Is Silver*. London: Heinemann.

Dane, C. (1935b) *The Moon Is Feminine*. London: Heinemann.

Dane, C. (1964) *Reminiscences: London Has a Garden*. London: Michael Joseph.

Deans, M. (1946) *Men Don't Know*. London: MacDonald.

Deans, M. (1947) *Meeting at the Sphinx*. London: MacDonald.

Delaney, S. (1959) *A Taste of Honey*. London: Theatre Workshop.

Desmond, F. (1953) *Florence Desmond by Herself*. London: Harrap.

Diawara, M. (1993) 'Power and territory: the emergence of Black British film collectives', in L. Friedman (ed.), *British Cinema and Thatcherism: Fires Were Started*. London: UCL Press.

Dickinson, M. and Street, S. (1985) *Cinema and State: The Film Industry and the British Government 1927–84*. London: BFI Publishing.

Dijkstra, B. (1986) *Idols of Perversity: Fantasies of Feminine Evil in Fin-de-Siècle Culture*. Oxford: Oxford University Press.

Dixon, W. W. (1994) 'An interview with Wendy Toye', in W. W. Dixon (ed.), *Reviewing British Cinema, 1900–1992*. Albany, NY: State University of New York.

Drazin, C. (1998) *The Finest Years: British Cinema of the 1940s*. London: Andre Deutsch.

Dryhurst, E. (1987) *Gilt off the Gingerbread*. London: Bachman and Turner.

Dunn, N. (1963) *Up the Junction*. London: MacGibbon and Kee.

Dunn, N. (1967) *Poor Cow*. London: MacGibbon and Kee.

Durgnat, R. (1997) 'Two "social problem" films: *Sapphire* and *Victim*', in A. Burton *et* al. (eds), *Liberal Directions: Basil Dearden and Postwar British Film Culture*. London: Flicks Books.

Eberts, J. and Ilott, T. (1990) *My Indecision Is Final: The Rise and Fall of Goldcrest Films*. London: Faber.

Farnum, D. and Rawlinson, A. (1935) *Jew Süss: Scenario of a Film*. London: Methuen.

Fields, G. (1960) *Sing As We Go*. London: Frederick Muller.

Firestone, S. (1971) *The Dialectic of Sex: The Case for Feminist Revolution*. London: Cape.

Forbes, B. (1977) *Notes for a Life*. London: Collins.

Forster, M. (1995) *Hidden Lives: A Family Memoir*. London: Viking.

Francke, L. (1994) *Women Screenwriters in Hollywood*. London: BFI Publishing.

Friedman, L. (ed.) (1993) *British Cinema and Thatcherism: Fires Were Started*. London: UCL Press.

Fuller, G. (1995) 'Mike Leigh's original features', in M. Leigh, *Naked and Other Screenplays*. London: Faber.

Giles, P. (1993) 'History with holes: Channel Four Television films of the 1980s', in L. Friedman (ed.), *British Cinema and Thatcherism: Fires Were Started*. London: UCL Press.

Gobbi, T. (1979) *My Life*. London: Futura Publications.

Gotfurt, J. (1959) 'Where credit is due', *Films and Filming*, vol. 8, no. 33 (May).

Grant, B. K. (1993) 'The body politic: Ken Russell in the 1980s', in L. Friedman (ed.), *British Cinema and Thatcherism: Fires Were Started*. London: UCL Press.

Grantley, Lord (1954) *Silver Spoon*. London: Hutchinson.

Habichon, C. (1990) *Lilian Harvey*. Berlin: Hande und Spoener.

Haggard, R. (1915) *She*. London: Hodder and Stoughton.

Harper, S. (1994) *Picturing the Past: The Rise and Fall of the British Costume Film*. London: BFI Publishing.

Harper, S. (1997) 'Nothing to beat the Hay diet: comedy at Gaumont-British and Gainsborough', in P. Cook (ed.), *Gainsborough Pictures*. London: Cassell.

Harper, S. (1998) 'Thinking forward and up: the British films of Conrad Veidt', in J. Richards (ed.), *The Unknown 1930s: An Alternative History of British Cinema 1929–1939*. London: I. B. Tauris.

Harper, S. and Porter, V. (1996) 'Moved to tears: weeping in the cinema in post-war Britain', *Screen*, vol. 37, no. 2 (Summer).

Harper, S. and Porter, V. (1999) 'Cinema audience tastes in 1950s Britain', *Journal of Popular British Cinema*, no. 2.

Henry, J. (1952) *Who Lie in Gaol*. London: Gollancz.

Henry, J. (1954) *Yield to the Night*. London: White Lion.

Hibbin, S. and Hibbin, N. (1988) *What a Carry On!* London: Hamlyn.

Higham, C. and Moseley, R. (1983) *Merle: A Biography of Merle Oberon*. Sevenoaks, Kent: New English Library.

Higson, A. (1993) 'Re-presenting the national past: nostalgia and pastiche in the heritage film', in L. Friedman (ed.), *British Cinema and Thatcherism: Fires Were Started*. London: UCL Press.

Higson, A. (1995) *Waving the Flag: Constructing a National Cinema in Britain*. Oxford: Clarendon Press.

Higson, A. (1996) 'The heritage film and British cinema', in A. Higson (ed.), *Dissolving Views: Key Writings on British Cinema*. London: Cassell.

Hill, J. (1999) *British Cinema in the 1980s*. London: Oxford University Press.

Hoare, P. (1995) *Noël Coward: A Biography*. London: Sinclair-Stevenson.

Horn, C. (1985) *Verliebt in die Liebe*. Berlin: Herbig.

Huntley, J. (1993) *Railways on the Screen*. Shepperton, Surrey: Ian Allen.

Hurst, B. D. (n.d., unpublished) *Autobiography*. London: British Film Institute.

Hutchings, C. (1993) *Hammer and Beyond: The British Horror Film*. Manchester: Manchester University Press.

Jarman, D. (1991) *Modern Nature*. London: Vista.

Jellicoe, A. (1958) *The Sport of My Mad Mother*. London: Faber.

Jellicoe, A. (1962) *The Knack*. London: Faber.

Kalter, J. (1979) *Actors on Acting*. New York: Sterling.

Kaplan, E. A. (1983) *Women and Film: Both Sides of the Camera*. London: Methuen.

Kelly, R. (ed.) (1998) *Alan Clarke*. London: Faber.

Kennedy, M. (1935) *Escape Me Never!* London: Heinemann.

Kennedy, M. (1942) *The Mechanical Muse*. London: Allen and Unwin.

Kochberg, S. (1990) 'The London Films of Herbert Wilcox', University of Westminster, unpublished MA thesis.

Kuhn, A. and Radstone, S. (1990) *The Women's Companion to International Film*. London: Virago.

Kulik, K. (1975) *Alexander Korda: The Man Who Could Work Miracles*. London: W. H. Allen.

Kureishi, H. (1987) 'Film diary', *Granta*, no. 22 (Autumn).

Lant, A. (1993) 'Women's independent cinema: the case of Leeds Animation Workshop', in L. Friedman (ed.), *British Cinema and Thatcherism: Fires Were Started*. London: UCL Press.

Lawrence, G. (1954) *A Star Danced*. London: W. H. Allen.

Laye, E. (1958) *Boo, to My Friends*. London: Hurst and Blackett.

Leahy, J. (1967) *The Cinema of Joseph Losey*. London: Zwemmer.

Lee, C. (1977) *Tall, Dark and Gruesome*. London: Vista.

Lee, N. (1937) *Money for Film Stories*. London: Isaac Pitman.

Levy, L. (1948) *Music for the Movies*. Sampson Low.

Littlewood, J. (1994) *Joan's Book*. London: Methuen.

Lockwood, M. (1948) *My Life and Films*. London: World Film Publications.

MacDonald, K. (1994) *Emeric Pressburger: The Life and Death of a Screenwriter*. London: Faber.

MacFarlane, B. (1997) *An Autobiography of British Cinema*. London: Methuen.

Macnab, G. (1993) *J. Arthur Rank and the British Film Industry*. London: Routledge.

MacQuitty, W. (1991) *A Life to Remember*. London: Quartet Books.

Malet, O. (1961) *Marraine: A Portrait of My Godmother*. London: Heinemann.

Matthews, H. and Matthews, M. (1950) *The Britain We Saw: A Family Symposium*. London: Gollancz.

Matthews, J. and Burgess, M. (1974) *Over My Shoulder: An Autobiography*. London: W. H. Allen.

McCallum, J. (1979) *Life with Googie*. London: Heinemann.

McCrindle, J. F. (1971) *Behind the Scenes: Theatre and Film Interviews from the Transatlantic Review*. New York: Pitman.

McGillivray, D. (1992) *Doing Rude Things: The History of the British Sex Film 1957–1981*. London: Sun Tavern Fields.

Merz, C. (1994) 'The tension of genre: Wendy Toye and Muriel Box', in W. W. Dixon (ed.), *Re-viewing British Cinema, 1900–1992*. Albany, NY: State University of New York Press.

Mills, J. (1981) *Up in the Clouds Gentlemen Please*. London: Penguin.

Monk, C. (1995) 'Sexuality and the heritage film', *Sight and Sound* (October).

Monk, C. (1999) 'Heritage films and British audiences in the 1990s', *Journal of Popular British Cinema*, no. 2.

Moore, R. (1943) *Modern Reading*. London: Staples and Staples.

Morgan, M. (1994) *The Years Between: Plays by Women on the London Stage 1900–1950*. London: Virago.

Muir, A. (1987) *A Woman's Guide to Jobs in Film and TV*. London: Pandora.

Murphy, R. (1992) *Sixties British Cinema*. London: BFI Publishing.

Murphy, R. (ed.) (1997) *The British Cinema Book*. London: BFI Publishing.

Napper, L. (1997) 'A despicable tradition? British quota quickies in the 1930s', in R. Murphy (ed.), *The British Cinema Book*. London: BFI Publishing.

Neagle, A. (1974) *There's Always Tomorrow*. London: W. H. Allen.

Nesbitt, C. (1975) *A Little Love and Good Company*. London: Faber.

Niven, D. (1973) *The Moon's a Balloon*. London: Coronet.

Olivier, L. (1982) *Confessions of an Actor*. London: Weidenfeld.

Orton, J. (1998) *Between Us Girls*. London: Nick Hern Books.

Pidduck, J. (1997) 'Travels with Sally Potter's *Orlando*: gender, narrative, movement', *Screen*, vol. 38, no. 2 (Summer).

Pines, J. (1997) 'British cinema and black representation', in R. Murphy (ed.), *The British Cinema Book*. London: BFI Publishing.

Popple, S. (1996) 'Group Three – a lesson in state intervention?', *Film History*, vol. 8, no. 2.

Porter, V. (1997) 'Methodism versus the marketplace: the Rank Organisation and British cinema', in R. Murphy (ed.), *The British Cinema Book*. London: BFI Publishing.

Porter, V. and Harper, S. (1998) 'Throbbing hearts and smart repartee: the reception of American films in 1950s Britain', *Media History*, vol. 4, no. 2.

Porter, V. and Litewski, C. (1981) '*The Way Ahead*: case history of a propaganda film', *Sight and Sound* (Spring).

Powell, M. (1986) *A Life in Movies: An Autobiography*. London: Heinemann.

Powell, M. (1992) *Million Dollar Movie*. London: Heinemann.

Quart, L. (1993) 'The religion of the market: Thatcherite politics and the British film of the 1980s', in L. Friedman (ed.), *British Cinema and Thatcherism: Fires Were Started*. London: UCL Press.

Richards, J. (1997) *Films and British National Identity: From Dickens to Dad's Army*. Manchester: Manchester University Press.

Richards, J. (ed.) (1998) *The Unknown 1930s: An Alternative History of British Cinema 1929–1939*. London: I. B. Tauris.

Rickards, J. (1987) *The Painted Banquet: My Life and Loves*. London: Weidenfeld.

Robertson, J. (1989) *The Hidden Cinema: British Film Censorship in Action, 1913–1972*. London: Routledge.

Robinson, M. (1937) *Continuity Girl*. London: Robert Hale.

Root, J. (1985) 'Distributing *A Question of Silence*: a cautionary tale', *Screen*, vol. 26, no. 6 (November).

Roye (1955) *Nude Ego*. London: Hutchinson.

Samuel, R. (1994) *Theatres of Memory*. London: Verso.

Sherriff, R. C. (1968) *No Leading Lady*. London: Gollancz.

Sherrin, C. B. and Sherrin, N. (1986) *Too Dirty for the Windmill*. London: Constable.

Signoret, S. (1978) *Nostalgia Isn't What It Used to Be*. London: Weidenfeld.

Spoto, D. (1991) *Laurence Olivier: A Biography*. London: Fontana.

Spoto, D. (1994) *The Dark Side of Genius: The Life of Alfred Hitchcock*. London: Plexus.

Storm, L. (1933) *Just As I Am*. London: Cassell.

Storm, L. (1939) *Tony Draws a Horse*. London: French's.

Storm, L. (1946) *Great Day*. London: English Theatre Guild.

Svela, S. (1991) *Bitches, Bimbos and Virgins*. New York: Midnight Marquee Press.

Tabori, P. (1959) *Alexander Korda*. London: Oldbourne.

Tarr, C. (1985) 'Sapphire, Darling and the permitted boundaries of pleasure', *Screen*, vol. 26, no. 1 (January).

Taylor, J. Russell (1962) *Anger and After*. London: Penguin.

Thornton, M. (1975) *Jessie Matthews*. London: Mayflower.

Thorpe, F. and Pronay, N. (1980) *British Official Films in the Second World War*. Oxford: Clio Press.

Timms, H. (1989) *Once a Wicked Lady: A Biography of Margaret Lockwood*. London: Virgin.

Todd, A. (1980) *The Eighth Veil*. London: Kimber and Co.

Towers, H. A. (1949) *Show Business*. London: Sampson Low.

Viertel, S. (1969) *The Kindness of Strangers*. New York: Holt, Rinehart and Winston.

Walker, A. (1974) *Hollywood, England*. London: Michael Joseph.

Walker, A. (1985) *National Heroes*. London: Harrap.

Walsh, M. (1993) 'Allegories of Thatcherism: the films of Peter Greenaway', in L. Friedman (ed.), *British Cinema and Thatcherism: Fires Were Started*. London: UCL Press.

Wandor, M. (1987) *Look Back in Gender: Sexuality and the Family in Post-War British Drama*. London: Methuen.

Waterhouse, K. (1995) *Streets Ahead*. London: Sceptre.

Weaver, M. (1994) *Attack of the Movie Monsters: Interviews with 20 Genre Directors*. Jefferson, NC: McFarland.

Whitaker, S. (1982) 'Feminism and distribution', *Screen*, vol. 23, no. 4 (Autumn).

Wilcox, H. (1967) *25,000 Sunsets*. London: Bodley Head.

Willis, T. (1991) *Evening All: Fifty Years over a Hot Typewriter*. London: Macmillan.

Wolfenstein, M. and Leites, N. (1950) *Movies: A Psychological Study*. Illinois: Free Press.

Wollen, P. (1993) 'The last new wave: modernism in the British films of the Thatcher era', in L. Friedman (ed.), *British Cinema and Thatcherism: Fires Were Started*. London: UCL Press.

Wood, L. (1987) *The Commercial Imperative in the British Film Industry: Maurice Elvey, a Case Study*. London: BFI Publishing.

Young, F. and Petzold, P. (1972) *The Work of the Motion Picture Cameraman*. London: Focal Press.

Yule, A. (1988) *David Puttnam: The Story So Far*. London: Sphere.

Zetterling, M. (1985) *All Those Tomorrows*. London: Cape.

Zinkeisen, D. (1938) *Designing for the Stage*. London: Studio Publications.

Zinkeisen, D. (1949) *Theatre and Other Paintings*. London: Fine Art Society.

Index of Film Titles

Index of Names

Dalton, Phyllis 217–19
Daltrey, Roger 218
Dane, Clemence 12, 18, 24, 40, 56–7, 62, 172, 174, 189
Darnley-Smith, Jan 199
Davis, Jo 206
Davis, John 74–9, 89, 92, 103–5, 159, 192, 195
Davis, Judy 145, 152
Davis, Philip 151
Dawson, Beatrice 214–16, 218
Dean, Basil 18, 168, 171
Deans, Marjorie 24, 165, 169, 172, 177–8, 189
Dearden, Basil 78, 108–9, 119–20
de Banzie, Brenda 105, 159–60
de Grunwald, Anatole 34, 67
de la Roche, Catherine 6
de Moulpied, Helen 32
Del Giudice, Filippo 33, 53, 63–4, 192
Delaney, Shelagh 112, 185
Demongeot, Mylène 104
Dench, Judi 122–3
Denison, Michael 67
Desmond, Florence 23
Desni, Tamara 21
Dickens, Charles 208
Dickens, Monica 34
Dickinson, M. 128
Dietrich, Marlene 22
Dijkstra, B. 234
Dillon, Carmen 222–6, 228
Diss, Eileen 225–6
Dix, Marian 189
Dodds, Olive 4
Dolin, Anton 197
Donat, Robert 22, 40
Donlevy, Brian 93
Donohoe, Amanda 146
Dors, Diana 75–8, 81, 89, 94, 98, 137–8, 215; see also plate
Douglas, Bill 204
Douglas, Jo 163
Drabble, Margaret 185
Drake, Charlie 103
Dresdel, Sonia 179
Driver, Betty 18
Dryden, John 236
Dudley Ward, Penelope 34, 49
Dunbar, Andrea 150, 165
Dunn, Nell 185, 187
Duprez, June 39
Durgnat, Raymond 109
Duse, Anna 215

Dyall, Valentine 47
Dyer, Charles 200
Eaton, Shirley 117, 119
Eberts, Jake 140–1
Edgar, Marriott 14
Edwards, Cheryl 206
Edwin, Grace 27
Edzard, Christine 187, 190, 205, 207–8, 235
Ekland, Britt 129–30, 137; see also plate
Ellacott, Joan 215–16
Ellis, Sarah 231
Elsaesser, Thomas 143
Elvey, Maurice 33–4, 97
Elwes, Catherine 206
Emary, Barbara 165, 173
Emerald, Nell 155
Erulkah, Sarah 199
Evans, Edith 215–16
Evans, Peggy 90
Eyre, Richard 143
Fairhurst, Lyn 184
Faithfull, June 81
Fancey, Adrienne 160, 166
Farnum, Dorothy 170–2, 189
Farr, Derek 84
Farrar, David 60
Field, Mary 155, 165, 191
Field, Shirley Ann 109
Field, Sid 224
Fielding, Fenella 117
Fields, Gracie 18, 20, 25–6, 81
Fildes, Audrey 179
Finch, Peter 111, 113, 184, 195
Finneran, Siobhan 150
Finney, Albert 112
Firbank, Ann 121
Firestone, Shulamith 1
Fisher, Daisy 189
Fleming, Ian 118
Flynn, Errol 93
Fonda, Bridget 145
Fonda, Jane 135
Forbes, Bryan 108, 124, 128
Ford, Marianne 226
Forde, Walter and Culley 191
Forster, E. M. 145
Forster, Margaret 186
Forsyth, Bill 149
Fowles, John 142
Foxwell, Ivan 97
Francis, Freddie 96, 161
Fraser, Liz 98